Reading Diagnosis Kit

Reading Diagnosis Kit

WILMA H. MILLER, (Ed.D)

Professor of Education
Illinois State University
Normal, Illinois

The Center for Applied Research in Education, Inc.
521 Fifth Avenue, New York, N.Y. 10017

© 1974

The Center for Applied
Research in Education, Inc.
New York

ALL RIGHTS RESERVED.

Library of Congress Cataloging in Publication Data

Miller, Wilma H
  Reading diagnosis kit.

  Bibliography: p.
  1. Reading--Ability testing. I. Title.
LB1050.M55   428'.4'2   74-7206
ISBN 0-87628-707-0

Printed in the United States of America

To the memory of my father, WILLIAM ALEXANDER MILLER

ABOUT THE AUTHOR

A former classroom teacher, Wilma H. Miller, Ed.D. has been teaching at the college level for the past nine years. She completed her doctorate in reading at The University of Arizona under the direction of the late Dr. Ruth Strang, a nationally known reading authority. Dr. Miller is a frequent contributor to professional journals and the author of a number of other works in the field, including two corrective reading aids for in-service teachers, *Identifying and Correcting Reading Difficulties in Children* (1972) and *Diagnosis and Correction of Reading Difficulties in Secondary School Students* (1973), both published by The Center for Applied Research in Education. She is also the author of a textbook for developmental reading, *The First R: Elementary Reading Today,* with an accompanying book of readings, *Elementary Reading Today: Selected Readings* (Holt, Rinehart & Winston, 1972), and a guide to secondary reading instruction, *Teaching Reading in the Secondary School* (Charles C Thomas, 1974). Dr. Miller is presently Professor of Education at Illinois State University, Normal, Illinois.

Preface

Often at least 50 percent of the students in a typical inner-city school are disabled in reading. Approximately 25 percent of the students in the typical middle-class suburban school are disabled in reading. These sobering statistics should prove the point that teachers of reading need many diagnostic devices to locate each student's exact reading difficulties effectively before they become so complex that they are very difficult to correct. Today reading instruction at all levels should be based upon diagnostic-prescriptive teaching so that each student's unique reading needs can be met effectively.

The *Reading Diagnosis Kit* is designed to fulfill the extremely important function of helping teachers to diagnose the specific reading problems of a student or a group of students while these problems are still simple enough to be corrected easily. The early diagnosis of reading difficulties not only will enable the teacher to correct reading problems before they become complex, but also will avoid the severe emotional maladjustment which reading disability invariably brings about.

This aid will be useful to several different groups of educators, elementary classroom teachers, secondary content-area teachers, reading specialists at all levels, and elementary and secondary school administrators. It gives the elementary teacher many practical diagnostic devices which he can use with an individual student or group of students in his classroom who have mild or moderate reading problems. It provides the secondary school teacher tools for determining how effectively the students enrolled in his classes can read the selected textbooks. It gives elementary and secondary reading specialists many important, practical diagnostic devices which they can use to determine the specific reading difficulties and their probable causes, of both the moderately and severely disabled readers who are enrolled in a remedial reading program. It also gives elementary and secondary school administrators an overview of the diagnostic devices which are used in reading.

Section 1 of the *Reading Diagnosis Kit* gives the reader specific directions on how to best use this aid. Each of the succeeding 13 sections of the kit first explains a useful diagnostic device in detail, and then provides specific directions for using the device. In each case, several examples of the diagnostic device are included for use at both the elementary and secondary levels. Many of the samples of various diagnostic devices can be reproduced in their present form by the teacher or modified by him in the light of the needs of his own students. Those devices which can be freely duplicated are identified in the text; those which cannot be duplicated are also identified in the text. In the latter case, the device may be obtained from the publisher of the materials, and a convenient address list of Test Publishers is presented in Appendix V, p. 279.

Section 2 describes how to use observation of reading as a diagnostic technique. Several checklists which can aid observation at both the elementary and secondary school levels are included in this section. The next section illustrates how to use oral reading and oral reading tests as a diagnostic device.

Sections 4 and 5 describe the uses and limitations of standardized survey reading tests and standardized diagnostic reading tests. Each section contains a description of some useful tests at the elementary and secondary levels. In addition, Appendices I and II (pp. 271-274) contain a list and description of many other useful standardized survey reading and diagnostic reading tests. Section 6 describes how to use listening comprehension tests as a diagnostic device.

The very useful Individual Reading Inventory is explained in Section 7. This section also includes several complete Individual Reading Inventories which can be freely duplicated and used at both the elementary and secondary levels. Section 8 contains a description of how informal inventories can be used to assess difficulties in the word recognition skills of sight word knowledge, phonetic analysis, structural analysis, context clue usage, and dictionary usage. Sample inventories in each of these word recognition skills, which can be given to students at several different reading levels, are included in this section.

Section 9 presents a description of how to adapt the Individual Reading Inventory for use in content areas such as social studies and science. This section, therefore, is especially useful for intermediate-grade and secondary school teachers. The section contains sample inventories in social studies and science at the elementary and secondary school levels. Section 10 discusses group reading inventories in the content areas at the intermediate-grade and secondary school levels. It also includes sample group reading inventories in social studies and science at both levels.

Section 11 presents the very useful cloze procedure. The cloze procedure can be used to assess comprehension, context clue usage, and textbook readability. The section gives specific directions for constructing a cloze exercise at both the elementary and secondary school levels.

Section 12 explains how an interest inventory can be used to improve reading ability, and includes sample interest inventories for elementary and secondary school students. Various projective techniques are presented in Sections 13 and 14. A projective technique can be used in determining how a student feels about himself and his reading ability. Sample incomplete sentences tests, open-ended stories, reading autobiographies, sociometric techniques, story assignments, and the Wish Test at both the elementary and secondary school levels are included in these two sections.

The reader will find the following to be some of the unique features of the *Reading Diagnosis Kit* which make it especially useful:

- it is the *only* aid for teachers which includes all of the major diagnostic devices for locating reading difficulties.
- it presents devices for diagnosing reading difficulties at both the elementary and secondary school levels.
- it includes samples of each device as well as a detailed description of the device.
- it provides many diagnostic devices which can be freely duplicated for immediate use in the classroom.
- it possesses an especially useful format. The spiral binding allows the teacher to fold back pages flat while using it, and the Table of Contents allows quick location of materials in each section.
- it includes both standardized and informal diagnostic devices.
- it gives on-the-spot help to both elementary and secondary teachers in diagnosing reading difficulties effectively so that they subsequently can provide corrective or remedial instruction.

Wilma H. Miller

Table of Contents

Preface—9

13

8   *Inventories in the Word Recognition Techniques – 163*

9   *Adapting the Individual Reading Inventory to Content Areas – 193*

Appendices

How to Use
This Diagnostic Aid

I f you will read these guidelines for using the *Reading Diagnosis Kit* before you begin using it, you may find that they will save you considerable time. This section is designed to help you learn how to use this aid to the best advantage.

Each of the following 13 sections presents a description of a specific diagnostic technique which you should read first. This description tells you the purposes for using the technique at either the elementary-school or the secondary-school level. After reading the description, you may read the detailed directions for using and evaluating the diagnostic tool. You will note that in most instances the diagnostic tools are easy to administer and score. With the directions, you will also find ways to evaluate the test results to identify specific reading problems so that they can be corrected later. In addition, you will be referred to several good sources which give detailed suggestions on how to correct the reading weaknesses that you have identified by using the diagnostic device. In many cases you already may know how to apply the proper corrective reading instruction.

Last in each section you will find concrete examples of the diagnostic tool which was explained in detail in that section. Many of these samples or models can be copied in their present form or modified in any way that you wish in the light of your own needs. In each case, the models should prove to be especially useful.

Before you utilize a specific device, perhaps you first should consider the grade level and reading level of the students or group of students to whom you are going to give the diagnostic tool. Most of the elementary diagnostic devices can be used with students who are attending the elementary school regardless of their reading ability. Usually there is enough range within each diagnostic tool to make it usable with above average, average, or disabled readers in the elementary school.

Sometimes it is somewhat more difficult to determine what level of diagnostic aid to use with secondary students. Obviously, if a secondary school student has an above average or average reading achievement, you will want to use a diagnostic device which is designed for the secondary school. On the other hand, if a secondary school student is moderately deficient or disabled in reading, you may want to have him complete an elemetary-level diagnostic device if it tests basic word recognition or comprehension skills. However, if the device evaluates a student's interests or adjustment, you may want to have him complete a diagnostic device for the secondary school.

In most cases there is a great deal of overlap between the elementary-level diagnostic tools and the secondary-level diagnostic tools. If one of the devices does not seem to be on the appropriate level, you should try the alternative device. You will soon learn which level of each device is the most appropriate with one student or a group of students.

When you have determined the level of the diagnostic technique that you wish to use, you then can select the type of technique. If you are not familiar with the majority of the diagnostic tools included in the *Kit,* it will be of value to you to read a description of each of the techniques at the outset. Then you will have enough familiarity with all of the diagnostic tools to enable you to choose those which are the most appropriate.

Although the preceding guidelines for choosing diagnostic tools are somewhat general, it is hoped that they will give you ample help in selecting the appropriate diagnostic techniques. Since teacher observation is one of the most basic of the diagnostic techniques, it is obvious that you should use it at the outset with most students to gain a measure of their reading strengths and weaknesses in such areas as word recognition techniques and comprehension skills. The checklists which are designed for the elementary-school level and the secondary-school level will help you to apply observation more precisely. In most cases, you next may want to administer an appropriate standardized survey reading test to gain a measure of a student's general reading ability in such areas as word meaning (vocabulary), paragraph comprehension, and rate of reading. If a student recently has been given a standardized survey reading test, you can obtain his score on this test from his cumulative folder and do not need to administer this type of test to him.

A student's score on a standardized survey reading test will point out those students who need a more detailed diagnosis by the use of the devices found in other sections of this kit. These mainly are disabled readers. All disabled readers should be given an individual reading inventory and/or a standardized diagnostic reading test at the appropriate level. Some disabled readers also may need a listening comprehension test and inventories in the various word recognition techniques. To ascertain their special interests, such disabled readers can be given an interest inventory. They also may need to be given an Incomplete Sentences Test or another projective technique to learn about their emotional adjustment and how they feel about reading.

There are certain diagnostic techniques which can be used with above average, average, and mildly disabled readers who are attending content classes in the intermediate grades or in the secondary school. Such students first can be given a standardized survey reading test to determine their overall reading ability. Then these students can be given an individual reading inventory in a content area, a group reading inventory, the cloze procedure, and an interest inventory.

Perhaps the sequence in which these diagnostic tools can be used can be clarified by considering several student case examples.

Mark is a fourth-grade student who is reading at the second-grade level. Since he has an intelligence quotient of about 100, he should be reading at the fourth-grade level. He is from an upper-lower class home environment. Mark is attending Mrs. Johnson's fourth-grade class. As soon as he entered fourth grade, Mrs. Johnson observed his reading strengths and weaknesses by having him read orally and noting them on an elementary-school checklist which is included in Section 2. By the use of this structured checklist, Mrs. Johnson was able to determine his word recognition and comprehension strengths and weaknesses in general terms. She next gave him one of the standardized survey reading tests listed in Section 4 to ascertain his general reading ability in the areas of word meaning and paragraph comprehension. Since this test found him to be reading on the second-grade level, Mrs. Johnson decided to give him an individual reading inventory to determine exactly his independent, instructional, and frustration reading levels. She also gave him inventories in the word recognition techniques in which he had seemed to be weak by the use of teacher observation—phonetic analysis and structural analysis. Instead, she could have given him a standardized diagnostic reading test as is described in Section 5 to determine his exact difficulties in word recognition skills and comprehension skills. This test could have been supplemented by a listening comprehension test as is described in Section 6. Since Mrs. Johnson should use Mark's interests in planning the corrective reading program, she may want to give him an interest inventory as is illustrated in Section 12 to determine his special interests. If Mark seems to be emotionally maladjusted as a result of his reading disability, Mrs. Johnson may want to give him an Incomplete Sentences Test as is described in Section 13. She also may want to give him one or more of the projective techniques which are described in Section 14.

Thus you see one sequence in which diagnostic tools can be used by an elementary teacher to determine the specific reading strengths and weaknesses of a disabled reader. When Mrs. Johnson has determined Mark's reading skills, reading levels, and emotional adjustment, she should act upon these findings by providing him with a corrective reading program which is specifically prescribed for him in the light of his own skill needs, interests, and self-concept. For specific suggestions on how to do this, Mrs. Johnson can consult one of the professional guides to corrective and remedial reading instruction presented in Appendix III (p. 275). There is little value in diagnosing a student's reading strengths and weaknesses unless his teacher acts upon these findings by providing him with a prescriptive reading program.

Jack is an average tenth-grade student who is enrolled in the secondary school developmental reading program because he wants to improve his study skills in such academic subjects as social studies and science. He is from the upper-lower social class. Jack's basic word recognition and literal comprehension skills are adequate. However, he mainly needs to improve his interpretive comprehension ability, his critical reading ability, his creative reading ability, and especially his ability in the special reading skills which are needed for effective comprehension and study in social studies and science. Therefore, Mr. Hanson, his developmental reading teacher, first will examine Jack's cumulative folder to notice the results of any recent standardized survey reading tests which he has taken. This gives him a view of Jack's overall reading ability, including his vocabulary knowledge, paragraph comprehension, and his rate of reading. Next Mr. Hanson can give Jack a group reading inventory to determine his ability to use the special reading skills which are required for effective comprehension and study in social studies and science. Such group reading inventories are described in Section 10. Mr. Hanson next may give Jack an individual reading inventory which was constructed from a series of social studies textbooks or science textbooks. Such an individual reading inventory is described in Section 9. Mr. Hanson can give Jack a cloze test as is described in Section 11 to determine his ability to read the required social studies textbook and science textbook. Mr. Hanson also can give Jack an interest inventory as is illustrated in Section 12 so that he can recommend supplementary reading material from social studies and science.

This is only one sequence in which diagnostic tools can be used with a secondary school student. The tools which are selected depend upon whether the student is a good, average, or disabled reader. They also depend upon whether a reading specialist or a content teacher is to use them.

Of course, when the secondary school reading specialist or content teacher has determined a student's reading skills and interests, he should act upon these findings to improve either reading instruction or content instruction. Sources to which the secondary school reading specialist can turn for detailed suggestions on how to conduct a developmental or remedial reading program are listed in Appendix III (p. 275). This appendix also gives the content area teacher a number of sources for suggestions on presenting reading instruction and providing for individual reading differences in his content area.

The Reading Diagnosis Kit has been designed to be of the utmost usefulness to you. It is hoped that you will get acquainted with it and find it to be an invaluable tool in helping you to individualize reading instruction by allowing you to prescribe the proper corrective or remedial reading instruction. If it can do this, it will have served its purpose well.

SELECTED REFERENCES

Bond, Guy L., and Miles A. Tinker. *Reading Difficulties: Their Diagnosis and Correction.* New York: Appleton-Century-Crofts, 1967.

Dechant, Emerald. *Reading Improvement in the Secondary School.* Englewood Cliffs: Prentice-Hall, 1973.

Fry, Edward B. *Reading Instruction for Classroom and Clinic.* New York: McGraw-Hill, 1972.

Harris, Albert J. *How to Increase Reading Ability.* New York: David McKay Company, 1970.

Kennedy, Eddie D. *Classroom Approaches to Remedial Reading.* Itasca, Illinois: F.E. Peacock Publishers, 1971.

Miller, Wilma H. *Teaching Reading in the Secondary School.* Springfield, Illinois: Charles C Thomas, Publishers, 1974.

Miller, Wilma H. *Diagnosis and Correction of Reading Difficulties in Secondary School Students.* New York: The Center for Applied Research in Education, 1973.

Miller, Wilma H. *Identifying and Correcting Reading Difficulties in Children.* New York: The Center for Applied Research in Education, 1971.

Strang, Ruth. *Diagnostic Teaching of Reading.* New York: McGraw-Hill, 1969.

Thomas, Ellen Lamar, and H. Alan Robinson. *Improving Reading in Every Class.* Boston: Allyn and Bacon, 1972.

Zintz, Miles V. *Corrective Reading.* Dubuque: William C. Brown, Publishers, 1972.

SECTION 2

Observation as
a Diagnostic Technique

Why should observation be the first diagnostic tool that you should use in determining a student's reading strengths and weaknesses? Since you can observe a student's reading behavior nearly every school day, teacher observation becomes one of the most useful diagnostic techniques.

This section then is devoted to the use of teacher observation for diagnosing reading difficulties at both the elementary-school level and the secondary-school level. The section opens with a description of using teacher observation as a diagnostic tool. Next it describes how you can use teacher observation to diagnose reading problems. The section includes several checklists which you can use at the elementary-school level to make reading diagnosis more precise, and also presents one checklist which can be used to aid teacher observation at the secondary-school level. It is hoped that this section will help you learn how to use teacher observation for the effective initial diagnosis of reading strengths and weaknesses.

Description of Observation as a Diagnostic Technique

The first step in diagnosing a student's specific reading skill strengths and weaknesses usually is by teacher observation. Usually, the teacher should do some type of structured observation before using any other diagnostic procedure which is included in this kit.

Teacher observation is so useful because the teacher often can use this method of diagnosing reading difficulties as part of her ongoing program. She can observe a student's reading behavior many times during the school day—not just during a reading achievement group session. Teacher observation can take place whenever a student is reading either silently or orally. It also can take place whenever a student is learning any of the word recognition or comprehension skills. Teacher observation should be a continuous process which determines each student's specific reading strengths and weaknesses and therefore points the way for further diagnosis or proper corrective reading instruction.

Diagnosing reading difficulties by the use of teacher observation can begin by the teacher's examination of a student's cumulative records. The use of cumulative records can identify a student or a group of students who are weak in one particular reading skill. The teacher then can provide appropriate corrective reading instruction in this particular area. By using a student's cumulative records, the teacher can make assumptions about his reading progress which can be either verified or rejected by using another technique of observation.

Most teachers need the preciseness of observation which the use of a structured reading checklist can give them. Otherwise, they find it difficult to exactly pinpoint a student's specific reading skill strengths and weaknesses. The use of a structured checklist enables them to determine a student's difficulties in the word recognition and comprehension skills exactly, so that these difficulties can be corrected later. Each student's reading skills should be observed on an individual basis, and the teacher should report the results of the observation. A checklist can give the teacher a list of the significant reading behaviors, specific reading difficulties, and a convenient form for recording the results of teacher observation.

There are many checklists available which a teacher can use to guide her observation of reading behavior. This kit includes several checklists which can be used with students reading on the elementary-school level and one checklist which can be used with students reading on the secondary-school level. Some of the checklists which are not included here are mentioned so that you can examine them if you would like to do so.

Checklists to aid teacher observation of reading readiness can be found in the reading readiness workbooks or in the preprimers of most basal reader series. Another checklist to aid observation of reading readiness skills is found in the book entitled *The First R: Elementary Reading Today*.[1] Walter Barbe also has formulated a very good checklist for the assessment of reading readiness.[2]

Barbe in addition has formulated a series of checklists which can be used in aiding observation of reading skills.[3] As was stated, these checklists begin at the reading readiness level and continue through the sixth-grade reading level. They cover such reading skills as sight word recognition, word analysis skills, comprehension, oral reading, silent reading, and rate of reading. They are extremely useful if you are going to use the individualized reading plan since they guide you in determining what reading skills should be stressed at each of these reading levels.

Another checklist for aiding observation of elementary-school reading recently was developed by George and Evelyn Spache.[4] Part of this checklist can help a teacher

---

[1]Wilma H. Miller, *The First R: Elementary Reading Today* (New York: Holt, Rinehart and Winston, 1972), pp. 27-29.

[2]Walter B. Barbe, *Educator's Guide to Personalized Reading Instruction* (Englewood Cliffs: Prentice-Hall, 1961), pp. 142-143.

[3]*Ibid.*, pp. 152-153, 160-161, 168-169, 182-183, 192-193, and 204-205.

[4]George D. Spache, and Evelyn B. Spache, *Reading in the Elementary School* (Boston, Allyn and Bacon, 1973), pp. 380-383.

to observe a child's oral reading behavioral subskills under the main skill headings of Fluency, Word Attack, and Posture.

Another very useful checklist in aiding teacher observation of elementary reading skills is *The Reading Troubleshooter's Checklist.*[5] This checklist is the most useful with disabled readers who are reading at the elementary-school level. The *Troubleshooter's Checklist* includes behavioral characteristics to evaluate these word recognition techniques: phonetic analysis skills, structural analysis skills, and context clue usage. It also has a part to evaluate a student's behavioral characteristics in the comprehension skills. The chart for recording a student's performance in each of these reading skills, which is included as part of this checklist, is extremely valuable.

You also can formulate your own checklist to guide teacher observation at the elementary-school reading level or the secondary-school reading level. You can follow any of the checklists mentioned in this section or the checklists presented in this kit for models.

Directions for Using Observation as a Diagnostic Technique

As was stated earlier, you should try to observe a student's reading behavior on an individual basis. Therefore, you should have a copy of the selected checklist for each student whom you wish to observe. This checklist can be easily duplicated from this kit on a copy machine. However, you also can have the selected checklist typed on a stencil or ditto and then duplicated. In any case, you should have a copy of the chosen checklist for each student you are going to observe so that you will have a permanent record of his reading performance to look at when you are planning his corrective reading program. Later, it may be helpful for you to place this checklist in his cumulative folder.

Then you must select a time when you can observe the student's reading skills in terms of this structured checklist. Often this can be during the regular reading time such as a reading achievement group which you use in the basal reader approach. It also can be during an individual reading conference such as is used in the individualized reading plan, or during a large-group or small-group lesson in a word recognition skill such as that of phonetic analysis, structural analysis, context clue usage, or dictionary usage. You often do not need to plan a special reading lesson to use a checklist.

However, there may be a few times when a special lesson is necessary. As an example, you may need to structure a situation in which a student can read silently while you observe him. You may need to have a teacher aide or a student read a story orally while you observe the reactions of a particular student. However, most teacher observation can occur during regular school activities.

When you are looking for one kind of reading behavior, you should look for a pattern of responses. For example, let us suppose that you are trying to determine if a student can locate the main idea in a story. You probably should have him tell you the main idea of several stories before checking the blank opposite this behavior. You can

---

[5] *Reading Troubleshooter's Checklist* (St. Louis: Webster Publishing Company, 1959.)

ask him to make up another title for the story, to tell you what the story was about in one sentence, or to write an expression of the main idea in his own words. Only when he has demonstrated competency in this reading skill on several occasions can you assume that he really is competent in it.

Let us take another example in this area. If you are to determine a student's ability to use context clues effectively, you should notice his ability to determine the meaning of the unknown words in his oral reading on several different occasions. When you are observing his oral reading, you then should focus on this one word recognition technique. When you have determined from observation that he can use context clues effectively on several occasions, you should check this as being a reading skill in which he is competent. Thus you can see that it may take you quite a while to observe all of the items on a checklist. However, you can begin to provide the appropriate corrective reading instruction in which a student is weak immediately. You do not have to wait until you have observed all of the items on a checklist.

Obviously, there is no formal evaluation of a student's checklist as there is in some of the diagnostic devices which are included in this kit. You do not obtain a standardized score from a reading checklist. Instead, you use the individual reading strengths which you have discovered to build upon while you try to help a student overcome the skill weaknesses which you have located. Corrective reading instruction can take place either individually or in a short-term needs group. A needs group is composed of several students who have the same specific skill weaknesses. There is little benefit for a teacher to diagnose a student's reading difficulties by teacher observation if she does not provide the systematic corrective reading instruction to overcome these specific difficulties. With the proper corrective action, a student will not be so likely to have his minor reading difficulties snowball into a serious reading problem.

For example, if you have discovered by the use of a checklist that a student cannot read orally in phrases but rather is a word-by-word reader, he needs additional practice in this reading skill individually or in a needs group. To improve phrasing, the teacher can give the student much easy, highly interesting material which he will want to read as quickly as possible and therefore is likely to read in phrases. A student also can learn to read in phrases by using a tachistoscope, a hand tachistoscope, or flash cards. Reading in phrases also should be emphasized when the student reads orally. The oral reading often should be done from easy material, and the teacher can show the student how reading in phrases can improve oral reading. A student also can read aloud from easy, interesting material in an audience situation.

As another example, let us suppose that a student is found by teacher observation to be weak in critical reading ability. The teacher then must stress this reading skill. Since critical reading ability often can be presented best in a small-group setting, the teacher can form a group composed of students who are weak in critical reading ability. This reading skill then can be stressed in several different ways. The students in the group can read a story from a basal reader or a content textbook if they are all reading on about the same instructional level. The teacher then can pose questions which call for critical or evaluative responses in which the students must judge the accuracy or truthfulness of what they read. If students are not asked questions which call for critical responses, they usually will not give critical responses. The teacher also can select a topic which each student in the group can research from a reference book, a tradebook, a magazine, or a newspaper on his own instructional or independent reading level. Each student later can share his findings about the topic to determine the areas of disagreement. Students also can learn to analyze propaganda techniques by the use of teacher-formulated worksheets. The teacher's attitude toward promoting a spirit of inquiry in his classroom is another important element in developing critical reading ability. Many more suggestions for developing this very important reading skill are found in the books *Identifying and Correcting Reading Difficulties in Children*[6] and *Diagnosis and Correction of Reading Difficulties in Secondary School Students.*[7]

From the preceding examples you can see how a teacher can use the results of observation to provide corrective reading instruction for a student, a group of students, or an entire class. The professional sourcebooks which are included in Appendix III wili give you detailed suggestions about how to correct any of the reading problems you have diagnosed by teacher observation. You can read the appropriate section in the aid.

Checklists for Using Observation as a Diagnostic Tool

Following are five different checklists for using observation as a diagnostic technique. Several of these have been developed especially for this kit.

The first checklist presented has been specially formulated for the *Reading Diagnosis Kit* to aid teacher observation of reading progress at the primary-grade level. Much of the checklist can be used with students who are reading at the primary-grade level. You can copy and use this checklist, on pages 30-33, directly from these pages.

---

[6]Wilma H. Miller, *Identifying and Correcting Reading Difficulties in Children* (New York: The Center for Applied Research in Education, 1971), pp. 146-149.

[7]Wilma H. Miller, *Diagnosis and Correction of Reading Difficulties in Secondary School Students* (New York: The Center for Applied Research in Education, 1973), pp. 185-188, 197-199.

PRIMARY-GRADE CHECKLIST OF TEACHER OBSERVATION
ON PUPIL'S READING

Name _____ Grade _____ Teacher _____

I. Word Recognition Techniques

    A. Sight Word Recognition
        1. Is able to recognize the words found on the Dolch Basic Sight
           Word List   _____
        2. Is able to recognize Fry's Instant Words   _____
        3. Is able to recognize the words found on the Kucera-Francis
           Corpus   _____

    B. Phonetic Analysis
        1. Is able to identify the lower-case letter names   _____
        2. Is able to identify the upper-case letters   _____
        3. Can recognize the following single consonants and name a
           word containing each one of them
           b, c, d, f, g, h, j, k, l, m, n, p, q, r, s, t, v, w, x, y, and z   _____
        4. Is able to recognize a consonant blend (consonant cluster)
           and give a word containing one of them
           Examples—brown, flag, and sprain   _____
        5. Is able to recognize a consonant digraph (consonant cluster)
           and give a word containing one of them
           Examples—ship, chain, and those   _____
        6. Can recognize each single vowel and give a word which
           contains the long sound of the vowel
           a, e, i, o, u, and y   _____
        7. Can recognize each single vowel and give a word which
           contains the short sound of the vowel
           a, e, i, o, u, and y   _____
        8. Can recognize a diphthong and give a word containing it
           Examples—boy, out, and soil   _____
        9. Is able to understand how *r* after a vowel affects the sound
           of the vowel
           Examples—her, skirt, and fur   _____
      10. Is able to understand how *w* affects the sound of the vowel
           Examples—wall, worm, and world   _____

11. Is able to understand how a vowel is influenced when it is followed by *l*

    Examples—ball, call, and tall   _____

12. Can understand and apply these rules of phonetic analysis:

    a. When two vowels are found together, the first often is long and the second is silent

       Examples—tail, meat, and goat   _____

    b. A single vowel in a word or syllable usually is short

       Examples—can, pot, and nut   _____

    c. A single *e* at the end of a word is silent and makes the preceding vowel long

       Examples—bake, cake, and came   _____

C. Structural Analysis

1. Is able to recognize a base or root word

   Examples—walks, walked, and walking   _____

2. Is able to understand the function of suffixes

   Examples—s, ed, ing, y, en, and es   _____

3. Can understand the function of the following prefixes

   Examples—a, un, in, and be   _____

4. Can recognize the number of syllables in a two- or three-syllable word when hearing it pronounced aloud   _____

5. Can understand and apply these rules of syllabication:

   a. A word usually contains as many vowels as there are syllables in the word   _____

   b. When two consonants come between vowels, one consonant goes with each vowel

      Example—let/ter   _____

   c. When one consonant comes between two vowels, the first syllable usually ends with the vowel, and the second syllable begins with the second consonant

      Example—ta/ble   _____

   d. When the first of two vowels separated by a single consonant has a short sound, the single intervening consonant ends the first syllable

      Example—cam/el   _____

6. Is able to divide a compound word correctly

   Example—play/ground   _____

       7. Can understand and apply the principle of dropping the final
          e and adding *ing*
          Example—baking   _____

       8. Can understand and apply the principle of doubling the final
          consonant before adding *ing*
          Example—running   _____

       9. Can understand and apply the principle of changing *y* to *i*
          before adding *es*
          Example—babies   _____

     10. Can understand the function of a contraction
          Example—doesn't   _____

D. Picture Clue Usage

    1. Is able to interpret a picture literally which is found in a
       reader or a tradebook   _____

    2. Is able to interpret a picture inferentially which is found in a
       reader or tradebook   _____

    3. Is able to use a picture in a reader or tradebook to determine
       the meaning of an unknown word on the same or a nearby
       page   _____

E. Context Clue Usage

    1. Is able to apply context clue usage effectively in determining
       the meaning of an unknown word in a reader or a tradebook_____

    2. Is able to complete a context clue exercise such as the
       following correctly:
       Exercise—Bob hopes to go for a _____ on a train.   _____
                                        red
                                      ride
                                      rake

F. Dictionary Usage

    1. Can use a picture dictionary to locate the meaning of
       unknown words which are met in reading   _____

    2. Can use a simplified dictionary to locate the pronunciation
       and meaning of unknown words which are met in reading   _____

II. Comprehension Skills

A. Literal Comprehension

    1. Is able to answer literal or factual questions which have been
       posed from stories in readers or from tradebooks
       Example—What color was Mrs. Jackson's house?   _____

B. Interpretive Comprehension
  1. Is able to answer interpretive questions which are posed from stories in readers or in tradebooks. These questions call for inferring, drawing conclusions, drawing generalizations, summarizing, and reading between the lines
  Example—Why did Jack like living on a farm better than living in a large city?   _____

C. Critical Reading
  1. Is able to answer questions which call for critical or evaluative responses about stories from readers or from tradebooks.
  Example—Do you think that this story is real or make believe? Why?   _____

D. Creative Reading
  1. Is able to follow up his reading in a problem-solving situation such as by creative writing, construction activities, role playing, or creative dramatics   _____

III. Silent Reading

A. Enjoys silent reading as determined from reactions during silent reading   _____
B. Is interested in reading silently   _____
C. Has proper posture and book position while reading   _____
D. Does not use lip movement or whispering while reading silently ____
E. Does not use head movements while reading silently   _____

IV. Oral Reading

A. Enjoys oral reading   _____
B. Has good expression in oral reading   _____
C. Observes punctuation marks while reading orally   _____
D. Can read in phrases or groups of words   _____
E. Makes few errors on the addition or omission of words   _____
F. Does not repeat words or phrases   _____

Here is a checklist which can be used with students who are reading at the intermediate-grade level. It was formulated especially for the *Reading Diagnosis Kit*. You can copy and use this checklist, on pages 34-37, directly from these pages.

INTERMEDIATE-GRADE CHECKLIST OF TEACHER OBSERVATION
ON PUPIL'S READING

Name _____ Grade _____ Teacher _____

I. Word Recognition Techniques

  A. Sight Word Recognition
    1. Is able to recognize most of the general vocabulary words at sight which are found in general reading and content reading_____

  B. Phonetic Analysis
    1. Is able to use phonetic analysis to determine the pronunciation and meaning of an unknown general vocabulary term _____
    2. Is able to use phonetic analysis to determine the pronunciation and meaning of specialized vocabulary terms from content area textbooks or reference books _____

  C. Structural Analysis
    1. Can recognize a base or root word
      Examples—invents, invented, and inventing _____
    2. Knows the meaning of the following prefixes and can use them in determining the pronunciation and meaning of unknown general vocabulary terms found in readers and tradebooks and specialized vocabulary terms found in content textbooks
      Examples—a, in, un, bi, pro, and re _____
    3. Can understand the function of the following suffixes
      Examples—ly, ful, les, ness, er, and en _____
    4. Can correctly divide polysyllabic words into syllables _____
    5. Is able to understand and apply the principles of accent

      a. In a word of two syllables, the first syllable usually is accented _____
      b. Words of three syllables usually are accented on the first or second syllable _____

    6. Is able to understand the function of primary and secondary accent _____

  D. Picture Clue Usage
    1. Is able to use a picture in a reader, a tradebook, or a content textbook to determine the meaning of an unknown word on the same or nearby page _____

E. Context Clue Usage

1. Can apply context clue usage effectively in determining the meaning of an unknown word in a reader, tradebook, or a content textbook   _____

F. Dictionary and Glossary Usage

1. Can use the dictionary or the glossary in a textbook effectively in locating the pronunciation and meaning of unknown words which are met in a reader, tradebook, or content textbook   _____

2. Is able to understand alphabetical sequence   _____

3. Is able to use guide words   _____

4. Is able to use the pronunciation key   _____

5. Can choose the correct dictionary definition for use in the context of the unknown word   _____

II. Comprehension Skills

A. Literal Comprehension

1. Is able to answer literal and factual questions which have been posed from reading done in readers, tradebooks, or content textbooks

   Example—What was the first word which Helen Keller learned to say?   _____

B. Interpretive Comprehension

1. Is able to answer interpretive questions (inferring, drawing conclusions, drawing generalizations, summarizing, and reading between the lines) which are posed from reading in readers, tradebooks, and content textbooks

   Example—Why does Helen Keller believe that her mother helped her so very much when she was young?   _____

C. Critical Reading

1. Is able to answer questions which call for critical or evaluative responses done from readers, tradebooks, or content textbooks

   Example—Do you believe that Helen Keller's mother should have allowed her to be independent? Why or why not?   _____

2. Is able to evaluate propaganda techniques   _____

D. Creative Reading

1. Is able to follow up his reading from readers, tradebooks, or content textbooks in a problem-solving situation such as by

creative writing, an oral book report, a written book report, role playing, or creative dramatics _____

III. Study Skills

    A. Finding the Main Idea
        1. Can locate a topic sentence in a paragraph _____
        2. Can state a directly stated main idea in a paragraph in his own words _____
        3. Can state the implied main idea in a paragraph in his own words _____
        4. Can give another title for a story or a book which was read _____

    B. Locating Details
        1. Is able to locate the significant details in a paragraph _____
        2. Is able to locate the irrelevant details in a paragraph _____

    C. Following Directions
        1. Is able to follow a one-step direction _____
        2. Is able to follow a two- or three-step direction in proper sequence. _____

    D. Organizational Skills
        1. Can outline a chapter using main headings and subordinate headings _____
        2. Can take acceptable notes from a content textbook _____
        3. Can summarize a paragraph in his own words _____
        4. Can summarize an entire selection in his own words _____

    E. Location of Information
        1. Can use textbook aids such as table of contents, index, and glossary _____
        2. Can locate information in content textbooks and reference books _____

    F. Graphic Aids
        1. Can interpret maps, charts, tables, and diagrams _____

IV. Silent Reading

    A. Enjoys silent reading as determined from reactions during silent reading _____

    B. Is interested in reading reader stories, tradebooks, and content textbooks silently _____

      C. Has proper posture and book position while reading silently   _____

      D. Does not use lip movement or whispering while reading silently ____

      E. Does not use head movement while reading silently   _____

      F. Is able to read silently in thought units   _____

  V. Oral Reading

      A. Enjoys oral reading before an audience   _____

      B. Has good expression in oral reading   _____

      C. Observes punctuation marks while reading orally   _____

      D. Can read orally in phrases or thought units   _____

CHECKLIST FROM THE DURRELL ANALYSIS OF READING DIFFICULTY

Here is the checklist from the Durrell Analysis of Reading Difficulty. The appropriate parts of this checklist can be used at the non-reader level, the primary-grade reading level, and the intermediate-grade reading level. (See next page.)

CHECKLIST OF INSTRUCTIONAL NEEDS*

NON-READER OR PREPRIMER LEVEL

Needs help in:

1. Listening comprehension and speech
   ___ Understanding of material heard
   ___ Speech and spoken vocabulary
2. Visual perception of word elements
   ___ Visual memory of words
   ___ Giving names of letters
   ___ Identifying letters named
   ___ Matching letters
   ___ Copying letters
3. Auditory perception of word elements
   ___ Initial or final blends
   ___ Initial or final single sounds
   ___ Learning sounds taught
4. Phonic abilities
   ___ Solving words
   ___ Sounding words
   ___ Sounds of blends—phonograms
   ___ Sounds of individual letters
5. Learning rate
   ___ Remembering words taught
   ___ Use of context clues

PRIMARY GRADE READING LEVEL

Needs help in:

1. Listening comprehension and speech
   ___ Understanding of material heard
   ___ Speech and spoken vocabulary
2. Word analysis abilities
   ___ Visual memory of words
   ___ Auditory analysis of words
   ___ Solving words by sounding
   ___ Sounds of blends, phonograms
   ___ Use of context clues
   ___ Remembering new words taught
3. Oral reading abilities
   ___ Oral reading practice
   ___ Comprehension in oral reading
   ___ Phrasing (Eye-voice span)
   ___ Errors on easy words
   ___ Addition or omission of words
   ___ Repetition of words or phrases
   ___ Ignoring punctuation
   ___ Ignoring word errors
   ___ Attack on unfamiliar words
   ___ Expression in reading
   ___ Speech, voice, enunciation

INTERMEDIATE GRADE READING LEVEL

Needs help in:

1. Listening comprehension and speech
   ___ Understanding of material heard
   ___ Speech and oral expression
2. Word analysis abilities and spelling
   ___ Visual analysis of words
   ___ Auditory analysis of words
   ___ Solving words by sounding syllables
   ___ Sounding syllables, word parts
   ___ Meaning from context
   ___ Attack on unfamiliar words
   ___ Spelling ability
   ___ Accuracy of copy Speed of writing
   ___ Dictionary skills: Location, pronunciation, meaning
3. Oral reading abilities
   ___ Oral reading practice
   ___ Comprehension in oral reading
   ___ Phrasing (Eye-voice span)
   ___ Expression in reading Speech skills
   ___ Speed of oral reading

—Security in oral reading
—Word and phrase meaning
—
—

4. Silent reading and recall
—Level of silent reading
—Comprehension in silent reading
—Unaided oral recall
—Unaided written recall
—Recall on questions
—Attention and persistence
—Word and phrase meaning difficulties
—Sentence complexity difficulties
—Imagery in silent reading

5. Speeded reading abilities
—Speed of reading (Eye movements)
—Speed of work in content subjects
—Skimming and locating information

6. Study abilities
—Reading details, directions, arithmetic
—Organization and subordination of ideas
—Elaborative thinking in reading
—Critical reading
—Use of table of contents References

7. Reading interest and effort
—Voluntary reading
—Variety of reading
—Self-directed work

6. Reading interest and effort
—Attention and persistence
—Self-directed work
7. Other
—
—
—
—

4. Silent reading and recall
—Level of silent reading
—Comprehension in silent reading
—Attention and persistence
—Unaided oral recall
—Recall on questions
—Speed of silent reading
—Phrasing (Eye movements)
—Lip movements and whispering
—Head movements Frowning
—Imagery in silent reading
—Position of book Posture
—
—
—

5. Reading interest and effort
—Attention and persistence
—Voluntary reading
—Self-directed work Workbooks

CHECKLIST FROM THE BOOK DIAGNOSTIC TEACHING OF READING

Here is a checklist record which can be used at either the primary-grade or the intermediate-grade reading level. It was formulated by Ruth Strang and appears in the book *Diagnostic Teaching of Reading*. (See next page.)

CHECKLIST RECORD OF CLASSROOM OBSERVATIONS
ON PUPIL'S READING*

Name_____Grade_____Teacher_____

Directions: Tally significant observations day by day. Space at bottom of each situation can be used for noting specific errors, interpretations, general impressions, evidence of progress, and recommendations.

I. When Giving Oral Reports

Vocabulary
___Rich
___Words mispronounced
___Meager
___Meaningful

Speech
___Distinct, clear
  enunciation
___Inaudible
___Stuttering
___Incorrect sounds
___Monotonous
___Expressive

Language Patterns
___Complete sentences
___Simple sentences
___Complex sentences
___Good organization
___Repetition of ideas
___Interpretation of ideas
___Imaginative insights

Interests
___Reads at home
___Uses library
___Has own library
___Special collections
___Sports
___Trips with parents
___Science
___Art
___Music
___Shop

Reactions of Peers
___Interested
___Uninterested
___Sympathetic
___Friendly
___Critical
___Hostile

Emotional Factors
___Poised
___Relaxed and happy
___Tense and anxious
___Self-confident
___Shy and embarrassed
___Antagonistic
___Unhappy

II. Oral Reading and Group Instruction Periods

Word Recognition Skills
___Basic sight vocabulary
___Tries to sound words
___Tries to pronounce by syllables
___Tries to analyze structure
___Substitutes another word
___Makes wild guesses

Comprehension
___Answers factual questions correctly
___Gives main ideas
___Tells whole story accurately
___Draws conclusions
___Makes generalizations
___Follows directions

---

*Reproduced from Ruth Strang, *Diagnostic Teaching of Reading* (New York: McGraw-Hill Book Company, 1969), pp. 198-199. Reproduced by permission of the McGraw-Hill Book Company.

——Reverses letters
——Reverses words
——Reverses phrases
——Uses context clues

——Gives sensible reasons on thought questions
——Gives fantastic, irrevelant reasons on thought questions
——Relates reading to experiences
——Unable to relate reading and experiences
——Expression in reading

Peer Relationships
——Gets along well with girls
——Gets along well with boys
——Respects others
——Disturbs others
——Works alone only
——Works well with one other child

Location of Information
——Uses index
——Uses table of contents
——Uses dictionary
——Uses maps
——Uses diagrams
——Uses encyclopedia

III. Dramatization of Stories

Reading Skills
——Reads with expression
——Interprets behavior of character accurately
——Shows little understanding of character
——Interprets sequence accurately
——Reads too slowly
——Reads too rapidly

Personal Development
——Poised
——Relates characters and story to own experience
——Interest evident
——No interest
——Shy, ill at ease

Insight _____

IV. Silent Reading Situation
(Free-Choice Reading or Library Time)

Location of Material
——Finds suitable book quickly
——Follows suggestion of other children
——Has teacher help
——Uses library classification
——Uses table of contents

Attitude Toward Reading
——Engrossed in book
——Enjoyment evident
——Independent
——Dependent upon others
——Uninterested, resists or avoids reading

Reading Level
——Primer
——First
——Second
——Third
——Fourth
——Fifth
——Sixth

Physical Factors
___Holds book up
___Holds book close to face
___Lip movement
___Squints
___Blinks eyes
___Eyes red or watery
___Complaints of headache
___Complaints of dizziness
___Bends over book
___Fatigue posture

Interest
___Animals
___People
___Science
___History
___Adventure
___Fairy tales
___Sports
___Art
___Music
___Cars, planes, trucks, boats
___Rockets
___Armed services

Location of Material
___Takes useful notes
___Selects too advanced
   books
___Unable to find any books
   of interest to him

Attitude Toward Reading
___Easily distracted
___Others

Reading Level
___Seventh
___Others

Insight _____

V. Listening to Story Read Aloud

Interest
___Listens attentively
___Listens part time
___Easily distracted
___Restless and preoccupied

Comprehension
___Evident appreciation of story—talks about it
___Asks related questions
___Responds to humor and excitement
___Answers factual questions
___Tells main ideas
___Tells whole story accurately
___Relates ideas to own experiences

Here is a checklist formulated for this kit which can be used with students at the secondary-school level. This checklist, on pages 44-47, can be copied and used directly from these pages.

SECONDARY CHECKLIST OF TEACHER OBSERVATION
ON STUDENT'S READING

Name _____ Class _____ Teacher _____

I. Word Recognition Techniques

  A. Sight Word Recognition
    1. Has a good stock of general vocabulary terms which can be recognized at sight   _____
    2. Has a good stock of specialized vocabulary terms in a content area which can be recognized at sight   _____

  B. Phonetic Analysis
    1. Is able to use phonetic analysis to determine the pronunciation and meaning of unknown general vocabulary terms   _____
    2. Is able to use phonetic analysis to determine the pronunciation and meaning of specialized vocabulary terms in a content area   _____

  C. Structural Analysis
    1. Is able to use a base or root word to determine the pronunciation and meaning of an unknown general or specialized vocabulary term   _____
    2. Knows the meaning of the following prefixes and can use them in determining the pronunciation and meaning of unknown general or specialized vocabulary terms
       Examples—a, ante, anti, bi, circum, con, de, dis, ex, in, non, post, pre, pro, re, sub, trans, and un   _____
    3. Knows the meaning of the following suffixes and can use them in determining the pronunciation and meaning of unknown general or specialized vocabulary terms
       Examples—able, en, hood, less, ness, er, ment, and ward   _____
    4. Can correctly divide general and specialized vocabulary terms into syllables   _____
    5. Can understand and apply accent in general and specialized vocabulary terms   _____

  D. Picture Clue Usage
    1. Is able to use a picture in a tradebook or a content textbook to determine the meaning of an unknown word on the same or a nearby page   _____

E. Context Clue Usage
1. Is able to apply context clue usage effectively in determining the meaning of an unknown word in a tradebook or a content textbook _____

F. Dictionary and Glossary Usage
1. Can use the dictionary or the glossary in a textbook effectively in locating the pronunciation and meaning of unknown words which are met in a content textbook or a tradebook _____
2. Is able to apply alphabetical sequence _____
3. Is able to use guide words _____
4. Is able to use the pronunciation key _____
5. Is able to choose the correct dictionary definition for use in the context of the unknown word _____

II. Comprehension Skills

A. Literal Comprehension
1. Is able to answer literal or factual questions which have been posed from content textbooks
Example—What is the duodenum? _____

B. Interpretive Comprehension
1. Is able to answer interpretive questions which are posed from content textbooks. These questions call for inferring, drawing conclusions, drawing generalizations, summarizing, and reading between the lines.
Example—Why do you think that deciduous teeth sometimes are called "milk teeth"? _____

C. Critical Reading
1. Is able to answer critical or evaluative questions which have been posed from content textbooks
Example—Do you believe that a teen-ager who has crooked teeth should see an orthodontist? Why or why not? _____
2. Is able to evaluate such propaganda techniques as the halo effect, the bandwagon effect, glittering generalities, testimonials, and emotionally toned words _____

D. Creative Reading
1. Is able to follow up content reading in a problem-solving situation such as an oral book report, a written book report, an experiment, creative dramatics, role playing, or creative writing _____

III. Study Skills

    A. Finding the Main Idea
        1. Is able to locate a topic sentence in a paragraph _____
        2. Is able to state a directly stated main idea in a paragraph in his own words _____
        3. Is able to state an implied main idea of a paragraph in his own words _____
        4. Is able to locate the main idea of a longer passage _____

    B. Significant Details
        1. Is able to locate the significant details in a paragraph _____
        2. Is able to locate the irrelevant details in a paragraph _____

    C. Organizational Skills
        1. Is able to outline a single paragraph of a content textbook using main headings and subheadings _____
        2. Is able to outline a section or a chapter of a content textbook using main headings and subheadings _____
        3. Is able to take notes from a content textbook _____
        4. Is able to summarize a paragraph from a content textbook in his own words _____
        5. Is able to summarize an entire selection from a content textbook in his own words _____

    D. Following Directions
        1. Is able to follow directions in sequence _____

    E. Location of Information
        1. Can use textbook aids effectively such as the table of contents, index, and glossary _____
        2. Can locate information using reference material _____

    F. Graphic Aids
        1. Can interpret maps, charts, tables, and diagrams _____

IV. Silent Reading

    A. Is interested in reading content materials _____

    B. Enjoys reading content materials silently as determined from facial expression _____

    C. Is able to read silently in thought units _____

    D. Has proper posture and book position while reading silently _____

E. Does not use lip movements or whispering in silent reading _____

F. Does not use head movement in silent reading _____

V. Oral Reading

A. Enjoys reading orally in front of an audience _____

B. Is able to read orally in phrases or thought units _____

C. Has good expression in oral reading _____

D. Observes punctuation marks in oral reading _____

Oral Reading
and Oral Reading Tests

I n the early twentieth century, all classroom reading was done orally. When the importance of silent reading was later understood, oral reading lost much of its significance. However, oral reading still has many uses in the diagnosis of reading problems. Usually you can use oral reading as one of the first ways of diagnosing reading problems.

This section is devoted to the use of oral reading as a method of diagnosing reading difficulties. Next, it briefly discusses how to use oral reading in the diagnosis of reading problems. Last, the section presents several sample paragraphs which can be used to diagnose reading difficulties and describes several well-known oral reading tests in detail.

Description of Using Oral Reading to Diagnose Reading Problems

All reading in school was done orally until after 1910. Before that time, silent reading was never taught in American elementary schools. It is obvious that silent reading is much more important for the average adult than is oral reading. How often do you think the average adult reads orally? Most adults rarely use oral reading. Therefore, oral reading should not be emphasized in American elementary schools as much as is silent reading.

Oral reading may no longer be fashionable in American elementary schools because many teachers overemphasized it in a round-robin or barbershop fashion. When oral reading was used in this way, the pupils generally were members of a reading achievement group. Usually all of the children had read the basal reader stories silently. The teacher then called on each pupil in turn in the reading circle to read the next text paragraph aloud. Since the rest of the children usually did not pay attention to the child who was reading orally, this procedure essentially was meaningless. Usually the students only paid attention when they were reading aloud themselves. Even then some students read aloud with little comprehension of what they were reading. There is a well-known story which tells about a boy named Johnny. His teacher asked Johnny to read a paragraph aloud. When he finished reading it, his teacher asked him, "What was that paragraph about," Johnny replied: "I don't know. I wasn't listening."

However, currently oral reading certainly has an important place in the elementary-school classroom. It also has important uses in the secondary school with disabled readers. Oral reading can be used very effectively to diagnose reading difficulties. When it is used for this purpose, a student's oral reading usually is evaluated in terms of its unique characteristics. Some of these characteristics are the following: insertions, omissions, substitutions, mispronunciations, repetitions, and hesitations. A student's comprehension of the material which he read orally can be evaluated. A student's oral reading errors then should be corrected.

Oral reading also is very useful with moderately and severely disabled readers and with slow-learning students. If a student is reading on the primary-grade level, oral reading is especially useful. It adds another sense avenue for such students and should be used quite often with them. With such students, oral reading often need not be preceded by silent reading.

Today oral reading also frequently takes place in an audience situation. When it is used in this way, a student chooses a portion of a story or a tradebook which he wants to read aloud. He then prepares this portion carefully by silent reading and by practice oral reading. The student then reads this portion aloud in front of a group or the entire class while they listen carefully to him. This is very different from round-robin reading.

Today oral reading often is done for a particular purpose. When it is used in this way, the teacher can ask the students in a reading group to find the paragraph or line which answers a particular question and then to read that line out loud. For example, the teacher can say: "Who can read the paragraph which tells how Jim felt when he lost his dog?" When oral reading is employed in this manner, it is being used in a purposeful way rather than in the meaningless manner of round-robin reading.

Thus you can see that oral reading can be done for several important reasons by most students in the elementary school and mainly by disabled readers in the secondary school. Audience oral reading may take place occasionally, even in the secondary school. However, the major purpose of oral reading is the diagnosis of reading difficulties.

Oral reading for diagnosing reading problems can be done in several ways. You can use round-robin reading during which a student reads a paragraph orally on the occasions when you want to evaluate a student's oral reading. Although you can make this evaluation without using a checklist if you know what the common oral reading errors are, often it may be helpful for you to use the part of a structured reading checklist which deals with oral reading. You can find examples of the characteristics of good oral reading in the checklists included later in this section or in Section 2. However, good oral reading is composed of such factors as reading in phrases, using good expression, and observing punctuation marks. The use of a structured checklist often will help you to evaluate the characteristics of a student's oral reading more effectively than is possible without the use of a checklist.

You also can evaluate a student's oral reading during the oral reading of the paragraphs which are included as part of an Individual Reading Inventory. Several examples of such paragraphs at different reading levels are included later in this section and in Section 7 of this kit. When graded reading paragraphs are used, a student reads orally from his copy of each paragraph while you mark his oral reading errors, using a prescribed key on your copy of each paragraph. You mark his oral reading errors in terms of insertions, omissions, substitutions, mispronunciations, repetitions, and hesitations. You then ask him several literal, interpretive, or critical questions about the paragraph and report his answers on your copy of each paragraph.

Later you can determine his independent, instructional, and frustration reading levels. Although this procedure is described in detail in Section 7, here briefly are the characteristics of each of these reading levels:

> independent reading level—the point at which a student is 99% accurate in word recognition and has 95% or better comprehension
>
> instructional reading level—the point at which a student is 90% or better accurate in word recognition and has 75% or better comprehension
>
> frustration reading level—the point at which a student is less than 90% accurate in word recognition and has less than 50% accuracy in comprehension.[1]

You also can use an oral reading test to evaluate a student's oral reading ability. The two most widely used oral reading tests are the Gray Oral Reading Tests and the Gilmore Oral Reading Test. For each test, there are a series of graded paragraphs which the student is to read orally. Usually the copies of the graded reading paragraphs which the student is to read aloud are found in a separate booklet. The teacher also has a copy of the paragraphs in the test booklet on which to record the student's oral reading errors. The teacher marks the errors as the student reads each graded paragraph aloud. Although the marking system for each oral reading test is somewhat different, usually the oral reading errors take the form of insertions, omissions, mispronunciations, substitutions, repetitions, and hesitations.

In most oral reading tests, the teacher has a student begin reading aloud a paragraph which is two or more years below his grade level. He then continues reading each paragraph aloud until he reaches the frustration or ceiling level established for that oral reading test. After he has finished reading a paragraph, the teacher asks him the comprehension questions which are included in the teacher's copy of the test booklet. Oral reading tests mainly evaluate literal or factual comprehension and do not evaluate interpretive comprehension. The teacher records the student's answers on his copy of the test booklet. Later the teacher scores the test and is able to establish a reading grade level.

What type of student should be given an oral reading test? Usually a student can be given an oral reading test if the teacher wishes to confirm his evaluation of a student's oral reading ability as ascertained from observation using a structured checklist. A student may be given an oral reading test if he has recently been given a standardized survey reading test. Since a standardized survey reading test is a silent

---

[1] Emmett A. Betts, *Foundations of Reading Instruction* (New York: American Book Company, 1957).

test, obviously it does not evaluate oral reading ability. The oral reading test may be especially useful with a student who has achieved slightly below average on a survey reading test. If you decide from significantly below average achievement on a survey reading test that a student may benefit from taking a diagnostic reading test, you would not give him an oral reading test. Most standardized diagnostic reading tests also include an oral reading test. If you have decided that you want to give a student an Individual Reading Inventory, you usually would not give him an oral reading test since the Individual Reading Inventory contains a series of graded oral reading paragraphs. Thus you see that an oral reading test usually would be given to supplement the results of a survey reading test.

The Gray Oral Reading Tests can be given from the preprimer through the adult level. On the other hand, the Gilmore Oral Reading Test can be given from the first-grade through the eighth-grade reading levels.

Thus you now understand the purpose for using oral reading and oral reading tests to diagnose reading difficulties so that they subsequently can be overcome in a corrective reading program.

General Directions for Using Oral Reading and Oral Reading Tests

It is quite easy to use oral reading as a diagnostic technique. As was explained in Section 2, you can observe a student's oral reading whenever he is reading aloud. Thus, you can observe his oral reading in a reading achievement group, when he is reading prose or poetry in an audience situation, when he is reading a content textbook, while he is reading an oral book report, or while he is reading some type of directions. The use of a reading checklist devoted to oral reading will help direct your observation. Several brief checklists devoted only to oral reading are included in the following part of this section. You will notice that they guide your observation in such areas as reading in phrases, eliminating oral reading errors, using good expression, and observing punctuation marks.

As was explained earlier, you also can use graded reading paragraphs to diagnose oral reading errors. The next section and Section 7 of this kit provide sample graded reading paragraphs at various levels. As a student reads a paragraph aloud, you mark his oral reading errors. Since this takes a good deal of practice to do efficiently, it is recommended that you tape-record the student's oral reading and mark the errors on your copy of the graded paragraphs when the tape is being played back later. Although you can use any marking system which you are familiar with and which is consistent, this is a good system to use in marking oral reading errors:

Omissions   Circle the entire word or letter sound (mother)

Insertions   Insert with a caret running

Underline and write in all mispronunciations ban band

Draw a line through a substitution and write it in stop spot

Use a wavy line to indicate a repetition *happy*

Put a check mark above a hesitation of more than 5 seconds[2] ✓ *friend*

When you have marked all the oral reading errors, you then can determine the student's independent, instructional, and frustration reading levels using the criteria described in detail in Section 7.

Although these paragraphs detail procedures for giving an oral reading test in general, it is obvious that you should study the next part of this section and the manual of the selected oral reading test very carefully before administering it. You also should administer the test several times on a practice basis before giving it to a student for the actual diagnosis of reading difficulties. However, all oral reading tests are quite easy to give and to score.

In giving an oral reading test, you first should establish rapport with the student. You can tell him that this test is going to evaluate his oral reading and comprehension so that you will know what areas of reading to help him with. You should have the student begin reading a paragraph orally which is at least two grades below his present grade level. If he is a severely disabled reader, you should have him begin reading a paragraph which you suspect is on his independent reading level. He then continues reading orally until he reaches the frustration or ceiling level established by that oral reading test. As the student reads each paragraph orally, the teacher marks his oral reading errors in terms of the prescribed key found in the manual of the selected test.

Although the scoring procedures for each oral reading test vary somewhat, in general you count the number of oral reading errors and the number of correct responses to the comprehension questions. Then you use these raw scores to refer to the appropriate tables in the manual. In most cases you arrive at a grade equivalent score and perhaps a percentile or stanine score. You also may be able to categorize a student's oral reading errors on the record booklet. The record booklet also may contain a checklist of oral reading errors which you can use.

When you have diagnosed a student's specific oral reading difficulties, you should attempt to help him correct these difficulties in an individually prescribed program. Let us consider several examples of oral reading errors to show you several ways in which these errors can be corrected.

As an example, when a student has a great number of substitutions in his oral reading, he often may be overemphasizing context clue usage. Substitutions are not very serious when the word substituted makes sense in the context of the sentence. Substitutions of this type are substituting *house* for *home,* *big* for *large,* or *fast* for *quickly.* On the other hand, substitutions are more serious when they do not make sense in the sentence. Examples of this kind of substitution are substituting *quick* for *quiet,* *goat* for *got,* or *hide* for *hid.*

To correct this difficulty, you first can tape-record a sample of the student's oral reading and ask him to follow along in his book while you play back the tape recording. You can encourage him to find his own oral reading errors and help him to

---

[2]Ruth Strang, *Diagnostic Teaching of Reading* (New York: McGraw-Hill Book Company, 1969), p. 68. Reproduced by permission of the McGraw-Hill Book Company.

notice that these words do not make sense in the sentence. You should encourage him to look carefully while he is reading and to read a little more slowly. A flashed presentation of particularly troublesome words using a tachistoscope, a hand tachistoscope, or flashcards may help him to notice the characteristics of each word more carefully. He also should be given the opportunity to read much highly interesting, easy material in which word recognition is not much of a problem. You can show him his progress concretely by tape recording his oral reading at intervals.

As another example, let us consider how you can help a student overcome repetitions in oral reading. Repetitions should be eliminated as much as possible since they interfere with reading comprehension, prevent smoothness in reading, and slow down rate of reading. A repetition may result from several different causes. Perhaps one of the more common causes of repetition is inadequate word recognition techniques. Since a student does not have a good stock of sight words, he repeats a word or phrase while taking time to see if he can analyze it by using another method of word recognition such as context clue usage, structural analysis, or phonetic analysis. You may want to give him one of the sight word tests which are described in Section 8 of this kit. The three most commonly used sight word tests are the Dolch Basic Sight Word Test, Fry's Instant Words, and the Kucera-Francis Corpus.

When you have determined that a limited stock of sight words is the cause of repetitions, this difficulty can be corrected in several ways. You can choose the words from one of these lists and present them by using a tachistoscope, a hand tachistoscope, flashcards, games which have been designed for this purpose, or exercises which use the sight words in context. The reading of much easy, very interesting material also can be of value in developing reading fluency and therefore eliminating repetitions.

Repetitions also can be caused by poor comprehension of the material. In this case, one of the better ways of eliminating repetition is by the provision of a great variety of very easy interesting material in which comprehension is no problem. Sometimes repetition can be caused by a student's poor self-concept. Since a student is self-conscious when reading orally, he repeats words or phrases while trying to gain confidence. Reading of easy, self-selected, interesting material can build his confidence in reading orally. Allowing the student to self-select and prepare material to read aloud in front of a small group also can build his self-confidence and therefore reduce repetitions. The use of the tape recorder can be valuable in showing a student concretely that his oral reading is improving.

There are many valuable sources which can help you find out how to correct any specific difficulties in oral reading (see Appendix III, p. 275).

Oral Reading Checklists and Sample Tests

The remainder of this section presents oral reading checklists and sample oral reading paragraphs at both the elementary and secondary levels. These materials can be copied and used as they are with your own pupils. Also included are detailed descriptions and directions for using two well-known standardized oral reading tests.

ELEMENTARY-LEVEL CHECKLIST FOR ORAL READING

Name _____ Grade _____ Teacher _____

1. Enjoys reading orally in an audience situation _____

2. Is able to read orally in phrases or thought units _____

3. Has good expression while reading orally _____

4. Observes punctuation marks in oral reading _____

5. Usually does not add words while reading orally _____

6. Usually does not omit words while reading orally _____

7. Usually does not repeat words or phrases while reading orally _____

8. Usually does not point to individual words while reading orally _____

9. Usually does not move the head while reading orally _____

SECONDARY-LEVEL CHECKLIST FOR ORAL READING

Name _____ Grade _____ Teacher _____

1. Enjoys reading orally in an audience situation   _____

2. Is able to read orally in phrases or thought units   _____

3. Has good expression while reading orally   _____

4. Observes punctuation marks in oral reading   _____

SAMPLE ORAL READING PARAGRAPHS AT THE ELEMENTARY LEVEL

Name _____ Grade _____ Teacher _____

A SPACE TRIP* (Third Reader)†

Do you think that you might take a trip into space some day? In the future man may travel to a space station and then go on to visit other planets. When you begin your trip, you can climb into the elevator of the gantry. The gantry or frame which supports a space ship has three stages or parts. When all is ready, your space ship rises slowly at first. Later it moves faster and faster. How do you think you are feeling now? After a while you are comfortable again. By the time the third stage of the rocket is burning, you are 65 miles above the surface of the earth. Since there is no gravity, you can float around the cabin. You feel very strange in your cabin. You can see the Earth. It looks like a blue ball in the sky. The sky looks black to you. You like your space trip very much. When it is over, you may not like to come back home to Earth again.

Comprehension Questions:

1. What is the gantry?
2. Why can you float around the cabin of a space ship?
3. Would you like to take a trip into space when you are older? Why or why not?
4. Why would you feel strange in the cabin of your space ship?
5. Give me a sentence using the word *gravity*.

Number of words <u>172</u>

Number of words correct _____

Accuracy:

90% <u>155</u>
99% <u>170</u>

Comprehension:

95% *Five questions*
75% *Four questions*

---

*Used by permission of McGraw-Hill Book Company, from *Off into Space* by Margaret O. Hyde. Rev. Ed. Copyright © 1966 by Margaret O. Hyde and Bernice Myers.

†See Sheldon, William D. and Mary C. Austin, *Story Caravan, Third Reader.* (Boston: Allyn and Bacon, 1968), pp. 183-190.

Name _____ Grade _____ Teacher _____

FRANK LLOYD WRIGHT (Sixth Reader)*

Frank Lloyd Wright was one of the world's most famous architects. He designed many very important buildings in the United States. He also designed the Imperial Hotel in Tokyo, Japan. This story is about Wright's work in Tokyo. Wright knew that his hotel must fit in with the style of architecture in Japanese buildings but also must be designed so that foreign visitors would feel comfortable in it. The building site for the Imperial Hotel was soft mud, and there had been many earthquakes in that part of Japan. Wright thought that he could float the Imperial Hotel on mud by using concrete piers. Then the hotel could not be damaged during an earthquake since it would be like a ship floating on the ocean. He was going to support the hotel by flexible steel so that it wouldn't break apart during an earthquake. Most architects and engineers were sure that this building would be a failure because it was so different. It also was extremely expensive to build. Wright also designed the furnishings of the Imperial Hotel. When an earthquake struck in 1922, not one bit of damage was done to the new Imperial Hotel. The Imperial Hotel may well have been Wright's outstanding achievement.

Comprehension Questions:

1. Where was the Imperial Hotel built?
2. Why couldn't the Imperial Hotel be damaged during an earthquake?
3. Why was this hotel so expensive to build?
4. Why did the architects and engineers believe that this building would be a failure?
5. Tell me a sentence using the word *architect*.

Number of words <u>187</u>

Number of words correct _____

Accuracy:

　90% <u>187</u>
　99% <u>206</u>

Comprehension:

　95% *Five questions*
　75% *Four questions*

_____

*Abridged and adapted from pp. 294-302, "Frank Lloyd Wright" from *Seven Seas* by Eldonna L. Evertts and Byron H. VanRoekel. Copyright ©1966, Harper & Row, Publishers, Inc., Evanston, Illinois.

SAMPLE ORAL READING PARAGRAPH AT THE SECONDARY LEVEL

Name _____ Class _____ Teacher _____

ABOUT THE SKI PATROL*
(Junior High School Level: Average or Disabled Readers)†

The men in the National Ski Patrol work in the Colorado mountains and are called the "Good Samaritans of the Snows." They wear rust-colored parkas and patrol the Colorado ski slopes in a dedicated way. When they find a skier who has been hurt, they usually unhook his ski bindings, remove his skis, put a plywood splint on the broken limb, and put him on a rescue toboggan. The National Ski Patrol System takes care of more than 20,000 accidents a year, and the ski patrol are a very dedicated group of men. Ski patrolmen have to pass difficult ski-handling and toboggan-handling tests and must take a first aid indoctrination course. Members of the ski patrol have all kinds of occupations such as engineers, architects, lumbermen, and housewives. Once the National Ski Patrol received a call about two planes colliding over the Grand Canyon in Arizona. Three ski patrolmen scaled the vertical crumbly cliff using ropes and pitons. Sometimes the National Ski Patrol rescues skiers who have been caught in an avalanche. They use ski tips and ski poles instead of shovels to dig the skiers out of the mountains of snow which have descended on them in the avalanche. Since these Good Samaritans are so busy with their exploits, they don't have time to boast about them. Instead, they just do them.

Comprehension Questions:

1. What is the nickname of the National Ski Patrol?
2. How many accidents a year does the National Ski Patrol take care of?
3. Why do you think volunteers join the National Ski Patrol?
4. Why do members of the National Ski Patrol have to take a first aid indoctrination course?
5. Give me a sentence using the word *avalanche.*

Number of words 227

Number of words correct _____

_____

*Used by permission of the *Public Employees News.*
†See Woolf, Leonard, and L. Earl Wellemeyer, *Journeys in Reading, Book Two.* (New York: Globe Book Company, 1967), pp. 218-225.

Accuracy:

90% 204

99% 225

Comprehension:

95% *Five questions*

75% *Four questions*

As was explained earlier in this chapter, here is a good system to use in marking the oral reading errors in any of the three preceding paragraphs:

Omissions	Circle the entire word or letter sound (three)
Insertions	Insert with a caret much
Underline and write in all mispronunciations	trap trip
Draw a line through a substitution and write it in	~~every~~ very
Use a wavy line to indicate a repetition	float
Put a check mark above a hesitation of more than 5 seconds[3]	elevator

_____

[3]See Ruth Strang, *Diagnostic Teaching of Reading* (New York: McGraw-Hill Book Company, 1969), p. 68.

GRAY ORAL READING TESTS

by William S. Gray, and Helen M. Robinson (Editor)
Bobbs-Merrill Publishing Company
4300 West 62nd Street
Indianapolis, Indiana 46206

Published in 1963 and 1967

Description of the Tests

The Gray Oral Reading Tests were first constructed and revised by the late William S. Gray while he was Professor and Director of Research in Reading at the University of Chicago. Later Helen M. Robinson with the help of other reading specialists analyzed and revised the tests. The Gray Oral Reading Tests are available in Forms A, B, C, and D. Each paragraph in the tests is self-contained. The first three paragraphs of the tests are appropriate for first grade and the next five are appropriate for grades two through six. The last five passages are equated to alternate grades up to the adult level. There are 13 passages in the entire test.

The difficulty of each passage is increased by vocabulary, sentence structure, and difficulty of concepts. Since the tests are designed to evaluate oral reading ability and not comprehension ability, the passages are followed only by literal, not interpretive, comprehension questions. The manual describes the standardization procedures on pages 25 and 26. The tests were standardized in 1959 and 1960 in elementary and secondary schools and also with selected college students and adults. In general, the students were selected by random sampling. Each subject was given all four forms of the Gray Oral Reading Tests. The standard error of measurement for the tests is given in Table 17 on page 29. Different standard error of measurement is given for boys, girls, and boys and girls combined. The validity of the tests was established by their content and the steps used in their construction. Unfortunately, information about reliability is given only in terms of the standard errors of measurement.

Directions for Giving the Tests

Before giving the Gray Oral Reading Tests, the manual suggests that you study the manual and the test itself very carefully. To administer the test, you need a set of the reading passages for the correct form, a copy of the *Examiner's Record Booklet,* and a stop watch or a watch with a second hand. You should first establish rapport with the student who is to take the test. Then you have the student begin reading the passage which is about two years below his grade level. He continues reading orally until he makes seven or more errors on each of two successive passages. If he makes any errors on the beginning passage, he should return to the preceding passage until he reads a passage without any errors.

As the student reads each passage orally, you mark his oral reading errors in terms of the eight categories listed on pages 5 and 6 of the manual: aid given, gross mispronunciation of a word, partial mispronunciation of a word, omission of a word or group of words, insertion of a word or group of words, substitution of one meaningful word, repetition of one or more words, and inverting or changing word order. The manual shows you how to mark each of these oral reading errors. After a student has finished reading a passage orally, you first record the time in seconds it took him to read the passage. Then you ask him the four literal comprehension questions which accompany the passage. You record his answer to each comprehension question on your copy of the *Examiner's Record Booklet.*

Directions for Scoring the Tests

Pages 6 and 7 of the manual give you detailed directions for scoring the Gray Oral Reading Tests. You are told to first record the time required for reading each passage. Then you count the number of errors made in each passage and recorded on the front page of the *Examiner's Record Booklet.* You also score the comprehension questions in terms of full credit, half-credit, or no credit. Pages 6 and 7 of the manual show you how to do this in detail. You then determine the passage score from the number of errors and time in seconds for each passage. You must consult Table 1 on page 7 to do this. You then select the correct table of norms for boys or girls to determine the grade equivalent. You then enter the grade equivalent in the proper space on the front page of the record booklet. In addition you can use the checklist, which is included in the record booklet to help you determine other characteristics of oral reading such as word-by-word reading, lack of expression, disregard of punctuation, head movement, or finger pointing.

On page 64 following, you will find the *Examiner's Record Booklet* for Form A of the Gray Oral Reading Test reprinted. You can notice how the front page of this booklet was completed using a fourth-grade student's performance. This should help you learn how to score this oral reading test.

Evaluation of the Gray Oral Reading Tests

It is helpful to notice what several reading specialists have stated about the Gray Oral Reading Tests. These tests were reviewed by three reading specialists for *Reading Tests and Reviews.*[4] In this source, Emery P. Bliesmer of the University of Virginia stated that he believed the Gray Oral Reading Tests were carefully developed and can give a good estimate of oral reading ability. Albert J. Harris, Professor Emeritus from the City University of New York, also reviewed this oral reading test. He believed that the weakest feature of the test was the tentative norms which were used. He considered another weakness to be the difficulty of the standards for beginning readers. However, Harris recommended

---

[4]Oscar Krisen Buros, ed., *Reading Tests and Reviews.* (Highland Park, N.J.: The Gryphon Press, 1968), p. 6:842.

this test quite highly for an oral reading test. Last, Paul R. Lohnes of the State University at Buffalo, New York, stated that the Gray Oral Reading Tests were excellently prepared and would be useful in educational research.

In the opinion of this author, the Gray Oral Reading Tests are a very useful instrument for the diagnosing of difficulties in oral reading. The tests are easily administered and scored. Therefore, they can be recommended highly if you wish to give an oral reading test.

EXAMINER'S RECORD BOOKLET

for the

GRAY ORAL READING TEST *

FORM A

Name _Jim B._____ Grade _4-8_ Age _10.0_
School _James Madison_____ Teacher _J. Hanson_ Sex _M_
City _Bloomington_____ State _Illinois_
Examiner _D. Schaeffer_____ Date _May 5, 1974_

SUMMARY

Passage Number	No. of Errors	Time (in Seconds)	Passage Scores	Comprehension
1.	—	—	9	—
2.	—	—	9	—
3.	0	17	9	4
4.	0	31	6	4
5.	1	32	5	4
6.	3	35	2	3
7.	4	40	1	2
8.	7	45	0	1
9.	9/24	—	0	0
10.				
11.				
12.				
13.				
Total Passage Scores			41	
Grade Equivalent			4.8	

TYPES OF ERRORS

1.	Aid	2
2.	Gross Mispronunciation	3
3.	Partial Mispronunciation	2
4.	Omission	4
5.	Insertion	4
6.	Substitution	3
7.	Repetition	6
8.	Inversion	0 / 24

OBSERVATIONS
(Check statement and circle each part)

_____ Word-by-word reading
_____ Poor phrasing
__✓__ Lack of expression
__✓__ Monotonous tone
_____ Pitch too high or low; voice too loud, too soft, or strained
_____ Poor enunciation
_____ Disregard of punctuation
_____ Overuse of phonics
_____ Little or no method of word analysis
_____ Unawareness of errors
_____ Head movement
_____ Finger pointing
_____ Loss of place

COMMENTS: _Jim reads at grade level. However, his expression while reading orally is quite poor._

THE **BOBBS-MERRILL** COMPANY, INC.
A SUBSIDIARY OF HOWARD W. SAMS & CO., INC.
Publishers · INDIANAPOLIS · NEW YORK

Copyright © 1963, The Bobbs-Merrill Co., Inc. Indianapolis 6, Indiana

*Reproduced by permission of the Bobbs-Merrill Publishing Company.

GILMORE ORAL READING TEST

by John V. Gilmore and Eunice C. Gilmore
Harcourt, Brace, and Jovanovich
757 Third Avenue
New York, New York 10017

Published in 1968

Description of the Test

This test was developed by John V. Gilmore and Eunice C. Gilmore. It now is available in Forms C and D. Each form consists of ten passages which are of increasing difficulty and which form a coherent story. The paragraphs become increasingly more difficult in terms of vocabulary, sentence structure, and interest. This test can be used to analyze the individual oral reading performance of students in grades one through eight. The Gilmore Oral Reading Test evaluated oral reading in terms of accuracy, comprehension, and rate of reading. Each of the ten oral reading paragraphs contains five literal comprehension questions. For most students 15 to 20 minutes are required for giving the test.

Pages 25 and 26 of the manual indicate how the Gilmore Oral Reading Test was standardized. It was standardized in 1967 in six school systems. Both Forms C and D were administered in a random fashion in each grade and scored by 15 examiners. Pages 26 and 27 of the manual indicate that the validity of this test was established by computing correlations between the Gilmore Oral Reading Test and two other oral reading tests. According to these correlations, the Gilmore Oral Reading Test apparently is quite valid. Pages 27 and 28 present the reliability data for the Gilmore Oral Reading Test. It appears that the test is the most reliable in terms of accuracy and the least reliable in terms of comprehension.

Directions for Giving the Test

As stated above, the Gilmore Oral Reading Test is now available in Forms C and D. You need to have a spiral-bound booklet from which the pupil will read and an individual record blank on which to record his oral reading errors and determine his scores. When you give the Gilmore Oral Reading Test, you first must establish rapport with the student. You are advised in the manual to have the student begin reading a paragraph orally which is two paragraphs below his actual grade level. If he then makes more than two errors on the selected paragraph, he should go back one paragraph. However, if he makes one or two errors, he can go on to the next higher paragraph. You should go back one paragraph at a time until a paragraph is reached at which the student makes no more than two errors. This is called the *basal* level. The student then can continue reading the paragraphs in sequence until he reaches a paragraph on which he makes ten or more errors. This is called his *ceiling* level. The testing always should stop on this paragraph.

As the student reads each paragraph orally, you record his errors on your copy of the record blank in terms of substitutions, mispronunciations, words pronounced by examiner, disregard of punctuation, insertions, hesitations, repetitions, and omissions. Pages 6 and 7 of the manual show you how to mark these eight kinds of oral reading errors. The manual states that multiple errors are counted as only one error. This means that there can be no more than one error per word.

You also record the time required for the student to read each of the paragraphs orally. Each reading paragraph is followed by five literal comprehension questions. You are to write the number which were answered correctly on the record blank beside each paragraph.

The test summary is found on the back cover and evaluates each paragraph in terms of accuracy, comprehension, and rate.

Directions for Scoring the Test

When you have determined the number of oral reading errors and the number of comprehension questions answered correctly, you should record these scores on the back of the record blank. You should also mark the basal and ceiling levels on this sheet. In the accuracy score, you give full credit (ten points) for each unread paragraph below the student's basal level. In the remaining paragraphs up to the paragraph in which the ceiling level was determined, you count the reading errors and record ten minus the number of errors in the accuracy column.

In computing the comprehension score, you give one point for each question which was answered correctly. In the paragraph below the basal level, you give credit for answering one more question than in the preceding paragraph and so on. In the paragraph immediately above the student's ceiling level, you give credit for answering one less question than was answered at the ceiling level and so on.

In computing the rate of reading score, you record the time needed for reading each paragraph on the back cover of the record blank. You then total the number of words in all of the paragraphs read, except the ceiling paragraph and those below the basal paragraph. You then total the time required for all of the paragraphs read. According to the manual, you then divide the number of words read by the time in seconds and multiply the rate in words per second by 60.

Perhaps all of this will be more clear if you now refer to the sample record blank found on page 68. This student was in fifth grade when he was tested. Since he was given the Gilmore Oral Reading Test in May, he is considered to be in grade 5.8. You can see that his basal level is on the fourth paragraph. Since full credit is given in the accuracy score for paragraphs below the basal level, he was given a score of ten on each of the first three paragraphs. Since he made 11 oral reading errors on paragraph eight, this is his ceiling level. In determining his accuracy score, Table 1 on page 15 of the manual was entered at grade 5.8 (his actual grade level). Therefore, his accuracy score was in stanine 7, and his rating was *above average* in accuracy. To determine his grade equivalent in accuracy, you use Table 4 on page 18 of the manual.

In computing the comprehension score, you see that paragraph four is this student's basal level. Since he answered four comprehension questions right on this paragraph, you give him credit for five comprehension questions correct on the first three paragraphs. Since his ceiling level is paragraph eight and he answered two comprehension questions correctly on this paragraph, he is given credit for one comprehension question on the ninth paragraph. According to Table 2 on page 16 in the manual, he is on the seventh stanine and has an *above average* rating. You notice that you enter this table at 5.8, his actual grade level. According to Table 5, his grade equivalent is 7.5.

To determine his rate of reading score, you add the number of words in the four paragraphs below the basal level and above the ceiling level. You also add the time in seconds required for reading these four paragraphs. You then divide the number of words read by the time in seconds and multiply 2.4 x 60. The rate score of 144 words per minute corresponds to a *fast* rate according to Table 3 on page 17 of the manual. You also enter this table at grade 5.8, the student's actual grade level.

Evaluation of the Gilmore Oral Reading Test

The Gilmore Oral Test was evaluated by two reading specialists in the book *Reading Tests and Reviews.*[5] According to Lydia A. Duggins of the University of Bridgeport, one of the outstanding advantages of this oral reading test is that a teacher does not require any special training to administer it. Duggins stated that the manual contains clear and specific instructions for both administration and scoring. She also stated that another advantage of this test is the use of the spiral-bound booklet which contains the paragraphs for both Form C and D. Duggins further stated that the record blank was very well constructed. Maynard C. Reynolds of the University of Minnesota also reviewed the Gilmore Oral Reading Test. He stated that teachers and reading specialists may well prefer to use this test over any other oral reading test since it is easy to administer and score.

This author also would recommend the Gilmore Oral Reading Test highly. The spiral-bound booklet containing the paragraphs for both forms indeed is very useful. The continuity of the paragraphs makes them quite interesting to use. The record blank also seems to be well designed. The Gilmore Oral Reading Test does not take a great deal of time to administer.

---

[5]Buros, ed., *Reading Tests and Reviews,* p. 5:671.

Student is fifth-grade student tested in May. (5.8)

NAME _____*Bill P.*_____

TEST SUMMARY*   Form C

PARA-GRAPH	ACCURACY		COMPREHENSION	RATE	
	ERRORS	10 MINUS NO. ERRORS	NO. RIGHT (OR CREDITED)	WORDS IN ¶	TIME IN SEC.
1		10	5	24	
2		10	5	45	
3		10	5	50	
4	2	8	4	73	25
5	4	6	4	103	44
6	7	3	3	117	48
7	9	1	2	127	55
8	11	0	2	161	
9			1	181	
10				253	

Basal Level (noted beside rows 1–3)
Ceiling Level (noted beside rows 6–7)

	ACC. SCORE (TOT. "10 MINUS NO. ERRORS" COLUMN)	COMP. SCORE (TOT. NO. RIGHT OR CREDITED)	(1) NO. WORDS READ* / (2) TIME IN SEC.*
	48	31	420 / 172
STANINE	7	7	(1) ÷ (2) × 60 2.4
GRADE EQUIV.	7.2	7.5	RATE SCORE (WPM) 144
RATING	Above av.	Above av.	Fast

*Do **not** count "ceiling" paragraph or paragraphs below "basal."

COMMENTS:

Standardized
Survey Reading Tests

What kind of standardized tests do you think are given today in nearly every American elementary and secondary school? Virtually every elementary and secondary school student in the United States is given a number of standardized survey reading tests during his stay in school. Often the survey reading test is given as part of an achievement test battery. Almost no student in the United States can escape being given such a test. What then are the uses of standardized survey reading tests in the diagnosis of reading difficulties?

This section is designed to help you better understand the function and uses of standardized survey reading tests in the diagnosis of reading difficulties. The section first describes the nature and function of standardized survey reading tests. Next, it presents general directions for administering these kinds of tests. The section closes with a detailed description of two well-known survey reading tests designed for the elementary-school level and one well-known survey reading test which can be used at the secondary-school level. It is hoped that this section will enable you to use standardized survey reading tests more effectively in the diagnosis of a student's reading problems.

Description of Standardized Survey Reading Tests in the Diagnosis of Reading Difficulties

Virtually every elementary teacher and many secondary teachers have given standardized survey reading tests. Sometimes a standardized survey reading test is given as part of an entire achievement test battery which evaluates other content areas such as arithmetic, language usage, social studies, and science in addition to reading. However, both a standardized survey reading test and the reading portion of an achievement test battery are very similar and serve the same purposes. Both a standardized survey reading test and the reading subtests of an achievement test evaluate general or overall reading ability in word meaning (vocabulary), sentence or paragraph comprehension, rate of reading, and comprehension in a specific content area such as social studies or science. Such a test is given to all students at a selected grade level to determine their general reading ability. When it is used in this way, you should be sure that the disabled readers in a class are given a level of the test which they can read with some degree of success. Usually those students who do poorly on a survey reading test then are given a diagnostic reading test or an Individual Reading Inventory to determine their exact reading strengths and weaknesses and reading levels.

What do you think are the major advantages of giving a standardized survey reading test or the reading subtests of an achievement test? One of the major advantages is that either test is norm-referenced. This means that you can compare a student's performance on the test with the performance of students who have similar characteristics such as grade level, age, sex, or geographic location. You then have a concrete basis for comparing the reading performance of one of your students with the reading performance of many students who have similar characteristics.

Another advantage of a standardized survey reading test is that all such tests were formulated by experts in test construction. Theoretically, they therefore are both reliable and valid. When a test is reliable, it evaluates those skills which it is supposed to evaluate consistently. On the other hand, if a test is valid, it measures the skills which it is designed to measure accurately. Although most survey reading tests are reliable, they are not all valid.

You can use standardized survey reading tests as a screening test to determine which students need additional testing and subsequent corrective reading instruction. However, the results then should be used for this purpose. Most standardized survey reading tests and the reading subtests of an achievement test are easy to administer and score. On the average they take about 45 minutes to give. However, far too often the scores on survey reading tests merely are filed in a student's cumulative folder and are not used for the purpose of suggesting additional testing and subsequent corrective reading instruction. When the scores from such a test are merely filed away, a school system cannot justify the time and expense of giving it.

Survey reading tests and achievement tests have several limitations which should be considered. A few of these limitations can apply equally well to any type of standardized test. As an example, you should realize that a student's score on any standardized test can be influenced to a great extent by his attitude toward the test, his interest in taking it, and how he felt on the day when he took it. This limitation usually applies more to a group-administered test such as a survey reading test than to a test which is individually administered. In any group-administered test, the student does not have as much rapport with the examiner as he does in an individual test.

Perhaps one of the most important limitations of a survey reading test or the subtests of an achievement test which relate to reading is that such a test tends to overestimate a student's actual instructional reading grade level by more than one grade. For example, a student who earned a grade equivalent score of 5.4 on a survey reading test actually may have an instructional reading level of approximately 4.0, as determined by an Individual Reading Inventory as is explained in Section 7 of this kit. Indeed, the grade equivalent score on a survey reading test may be a representation of a student's frustration reading level rather than of his instructional reading level. This probably may be due somewhat to the guessing factor found on a survey reading test.

To illustrate this very important point, Edward Fry of Rutgers University cautioned in his book against the "orangoutang" score, which can result from pure-chance guessing on a survey reading test. Fry discussed the "orangoutang" score which is the result of pure-chance guessing in this manner:

> Suppose we took an orangoutang and taught him to put a pawprint in one of four squares. He could choose any square he wished. Next we place a typical multiple-choice item in front of him with four choices. After he has read the item, he chooses one of the squares in which to place his pawprint. On the average, out of 100 items he will get 25 correct by pure chance; this raw score of 25 correct can then be translated into a grade-level score.[1]

Fry computed the "orangoutang" score for the California Reading Test, Junior High Level at 5.2. This means that a nonreader can score at the fifth-grade reading level on this survey reading test due to pure-chance guessing. The author once had a nonreader in second grade to whom she gave the Stanford Achievement Test, Primary II Battery. On this test, the student scored 2.5 at the end of second grade although he actually could recognize less than five words. This should indicate that you should consider the scores on a survey reading test to be only an indicator of a student's actual reading ability.

Another limitation of such a test is that it may measure a student's knowledge rather than his reading ability. Sometimes the questions on the paragraph comprehension subtest can be answered as the result of experiential background. In this case, a student could answer some of the comprehension questions without even having read the paragraph. Then, too, on some survey reading tests literal comprehension is emphasized at the expense of higher-type comprehension such as interpretive comprehension and critical reading. Survey reading tests also have been criticized because the vocabulary subtest often presents terms in isolation rather than in context. Since any word often has more than one meaning, a student may not know the meaning of a word which is required on the test. However, he actually may know another meaning for this word.

Another significant limitation of most standardized tests is that they do not recognize a student's unique cultural and experiential background. Most survey reading tests do evaluate a student's background of experiences to some extent. Therefore, a socially different student may perform less well on such a test than he would on a test which more nearly reflected his experiential background.

However, standardized survey reading tests or the subtest on an achievement test, which relate to reading, most certainly have a unique place in the diagnosis of reading difficulties at both the elementary- and secondary-school levels. As one of the beginning stages of reading diagnosis, you should administer a good, standardized survey reading test or the reading subtests of an achievement test to each student in

---

[1]Edward Fry, *Reading Instruction for Classroom and Clinic.* (New York: McGraw-Hill Book Company, 1972), p. 18.

your elementary classroom. At the secondary-school level, the guidance department often gives all of the students in eleventh grade a survey reading test. In this instance, you merely can obtain the scores on this test from the guidance department and proceed with additional diagnosis if necessary.

In reading diagnosis, a survey reading test probably should be preceded only by teacher observation using a structured checklist as was described in Section 2 of this kit. Since a survey reading test is quite easy to administer and score, you can well give it early in the school year. Then you can determine from the results of this test which students in a class need additional diagnosis by the use of a diagnostic reading test, an Individual Reading Inventory, or an oral reading test. In general, these are students who score one or more years below their grade level. However, in making this judgment, you also should consider their intellectual level. To do this, you can compare a student's percentile rank on an intelligence test with his percentile rank or stanine score on a survey reading test. If a student receives a considerably higher percentile rank or stanine score on the intelligence test, he may not be reading up to his potential level. However, if possible, you should use an individual intelligence test rather than a group intelligence test to evaluate intellectual ability. Since a group intelligence test often measures reading ability as well as intellectual ability, it tends to underestimate a student's actual intelligence if he is a disabled reader.

A number of standardized survey reading tests and achievement tests are found in Appendix I of this kit, page 271. You also can obtain a list of most of the standardized survey reading tests and achievement tests currently in print by consulting the book *Reading Tests and Reviews.*[2] In addition to listing the tests, this book contains an evaluation of many of the tests.

General Directions for Using Standardized Survey Reading Tests

In general, standardized survey reading tests and the reading subtests of achievement tests are fairly easy to administer and score. They do not require a trained examiner. At the elementary-school level, much of the time the classroom teacher gives all of his students a survey reading test or an achievement test. If the teacher wants to appraise the students' general or overall reading ability so that he can plan their program and pinpoint the students who need further testing, he usually gives the survey reading test near the beginning of the school year. On the other hand, a teacher sometimes gives a survey reading test near the end of the school year so that he and/or the school administration can determine how much the students improve during that school year.

At the elementary-school level, the students sometimes answer on a copy of the test booklet which the teacher then must score by hand. At other times, the students answer on separate answer sheets which are machine-scored at the central administration office. Then the results are given to each teacher to examine and act upon. In either case, the teacher usually prepares a class profile using the results of the survey reading test.

---

[2]Oscar Krisen Buros, ed., *Reading Tests and Reviews.* (Highland Park, N.J.: The Gryphon Press, 1968).

At the secondary-school level, the guidance department usually gives all the students a survey reading test. This test often is given in the eleventh grade. The guidance department then scores the test, and places the scores in each student's cumulative folder. Each content teacher then should examine the students' reading scores in his classes so that he can provide for each student's individual reading differences as much as possible. The guidance counselor often will also interpret each student's test results to him in general terms during an individual conference.

In administering a survey reading test or the reading subtests on an achievement test (vocabulary and paragraph comprehension), you first should study the manual of the test carefully. Most survey reading tests take about 45 minutes to administer. Each student needs a pencil with an eraser, and you should have extra pencils on hand and a clock or a watch with a second hand. The room should be as quiet and free from distraction as possible. You also should establish rapport with the group of students who is going to take the test.

You should read the directions aloud, which are printed in boldface type for each subtest on the survey reading test. If you are going to use the norms provided in the test manual, you should read the directions exactly as stated in the manual and follow the time limitations carefully. If you are not going to use the norms, these considerations are not very important.

You then score the test using the key provided or have them machine-scored. You then determine a raw score for each of the subtests and record each raw score on the front cover of each student's test booklet. Usually it is then easy to convert the raw score on each subtest into a standard score, a percentile rank, stanine score, or grade equivalent by using the appropriate tables of norms in the test manual. You then record these scores on the front cover of each student's test booklet.

In interpreting the scores from any standardized survey reading test or the reading subtests on an achievement test, you should consider several things carefully. As was discussed earlier, the grade equivalent on a survey reading test tends to overestimate a student's actual instructional reading level. You also must be sure that the norms which you use were made with students who possess similar characteristics to your students in such areas as grade level, sex, and geographic location.

You also should determine the subtest scores on a survey reading test carefully to determine in which areas of reading a student seems to be weaker. If the survey reading test indicates a lower score in vocabulary, the student needs additional testing and/or corrective instruction in this reading subskill. On the other hand, if the student scored poorer in the comprehension subtest, he needs additional testing and/or corrective instruction in this reading skill. If the survey reading test does not give a total score, you may want to average the vocabulary and comprehension subtest scores on the test. You usually should average only standard scores since percentile ranks, grade equivalents, and stanines are not based on equal-interval scores.

Obviously, the administration, scoring procedures, and interpretation of scores vary from one survey reading test to another. Thus, the preceding portion of this section necessarily has been very general. In the next part of this section, you will find detailed directions for administering and scoring two survey reading tests at the elementary level and one survey reading test at the secondary level. This part of the section also should help you learn how to give and score most survey reading tests and the reading portion of most achievement tests.

Let us consider what you should do when you have given and scored a survey reading test or the reading subtests of an achievement test. As was stated earlier, you first can construct a class profile which will help you to determine the general vocabulary and comprehension ability of all of the students in a class. It also will help you to determine if the median of your class is at the level at which it should be. As an example, if a survey reading test were given in May at the fourth grade level, the median of the class profile should be 4.8. Most survey reading tests and achievement tests provide a class profile sheet with the package containing the test manual, the answer key, and the test booklet.

You also should use the class profile sheet to determine which students need additional testing and subsequent corrective reading instruction. This test can be done by using an oral reading test, a diagnostic reading test, or an Individual Reading Inventory. By the use of one or more of these devices, you can determine a student's exact word recognition or comprehension difficulties and his independent, instructional, and frustration reading levels. You can give such tests to students who scored one or more years below their potential level on the survey reading test or the reading subtests of the achievement test. The procedures for making this comparison were explained earlier in this section.

However, if a large group of your students or the entire class scored poorly on the vocabulary subtest, you should present this reading skill to the group of students or to the entire class. Depending on their grade level, there are many ways of doing this. Several ways of improving vocabulary knowledge are as follows:

    wide reading of interesting materials from different content areas
    the study of prefixes, suffixes, and word roots
    the study of word origins
    first-hand experiences
    second-hand experiences
    the use of the dictionary or glossary
    vocabulary notecards
    vocabulary notebooks
    vocabulary games

The two books *Identifying and Correcting Reading Difficulties in Children* and *Diagnosis and Correction of Reading Difficulties in Secondary School Students*[3] will give you many additional suggestions for improving vocabulary knowledge at both the elementary- and secondary-school levels. Other books which also can help you present vocabulary knowledge are found in Appendix III, page 275.

If you have determined from the survey reading test results that a group of your students or the entire class is weak in comprehension ability, you should present this

---

[3]Both of these works are written by the author of this kit and published by The Center for Applied Research in Education, Inc., New York.

reading skill to the group of students or to the entire class. There are many methods and materials which you can use for presenting comprehension skills at both the elementary- and secondary-school levels. For example, you can pose questions in a reading achievement group which call for responses at the level of comprehension which you wish to emphasize: the literal level, the interpretive level, the critical level, or the creative level. You also can construct worksheets or reading guides which emphasize the level of comprehension which you feel needs emphasis. There is a wealth of material available at both the elementary and secondary levels which is designed to improve comprehension ability. Listings of these special materials at the elementary-school level are found in the book *Identifying and Correcting Reading Difficulties in Children*.[4] A listing of these special materials at the secondary level is found in the book *Diagnosis and Correction of Reading Difficulties in Secondary School Students*.[5] Additional materials can be found in the professional books found in Appendix III.

Thus you can see how the use of a survey reading test or the subtests of an achievement test can help you point the way for more extensive diagnosis of reading difficulties by the use of other standardized tests or informal reading tests. A survey reading test should have as its ultimate purpose the improvement of corrective reading instruction at the elementary-school or secondary-school levels.

Examples of Survey Reading Tests

The last part of this section provides descriptions and guidelines for using three standardized survey reading tests. These tests are merely good examples of the many elementary- and secondary-level survey reading tests which are currently available. Many of the survey reading tests which are included in Appendix I, page 271, are equally useful.

---

[4]Miller, *op. cit.*
[5]Miller, *op. cit.*

GATES-MacGINITIE READING TESTS, PRIMARY A BATTERY

by Arthur I. Gates and Walter H. MacGinitie
Teachers College Press, Columbia University
525 West 120th Street
New York 10027

Published in 1965

Description of the Test

The Primary A Battery of the Gates-MacGinitie Reading Tests is part of a series of reading tests which is designed to evaluate reading readiness and reading in grades kindergarten through 12. This entire series of tests was developed by Arthur I. Gates and Walter H. MacGinitie of Teachers College, Columbia University. The Primary A Battery of this test evaluates vocabulary and comprehension ability in first grade. It is available in Forms I and II.

According to the manual, the vocabulary subtest evaluates a pupil's ability to recognize or analyze isolated words. This test is composed of 48 exercises, each of which contains four printed words and a picture which illustrates the common meaning of one of the four words. The child is to circle the word which is the most closely related to the picture. The comprehension subtest evaluates a pupil's ability to read and comprehend entire sentences and paragraphs. This subtest contains 34 passages of increasing difficulty and length. Each passage then is followed by four pictures. The pupil is to mark the picture which best illustrates the meaning of the passage or which answers a question in the passage.

The technical manual which accompanies all of the Gates-MacGinitie Reading Tests is very thorough and explains many aspects of these tests such as selection of items, establishment of norms, reliability, correlations between the subtest scores, conversion of scores on the 1958 Gates Reading Tests to scores on the Gates-MacGinitie Reading Tests, and averaging scores on these tests.

According to the technical manual, each item on the test was tried out by 800 pupils in the first grade and 750 pupils at adjacent grade levels. The technical manual states that only the most effective items were retained for use in the actual test. The normative testing for first grade was conducted in January, 1965. The norms were established by both fall and spring test administrations.

The test manual contains four tables on page 7 which you can use to convert the raw scores on the vocabulary and comprehension subtests into standard scores, percentile ranks, and grade equivalents. There are no different norms for boys and girls. The reliability of the test is found in Table 3 on page 8 of the technical manual. The vocabulary subtest has a reliability coefficient of .91, and the comprehension subtest has a reliability coefficient of .94. Thus, this is considered to be a reliable test. Apparently no validity data for this test is found in the technical manual.

Directions for Giving the Test

You should study the manual carefully before giving the test. According to the manual, the vocabulary subtest takes 15 minutes and the comprehension subtest takes 25 minutes to administer. It is important that you have a stopwatch or a watch or clock with a second hand to time these two subtests exactly. According to the manual, you should give the vocabulary subtest first and then give the comprehension subtest after a rest period or on another day. Each child should have at least one pencil with a good eraser, and you should have additional pencils on hand.

You then are given specific directions in the manual for distributing the test booklets. You should have the students fill in only their name on the front cover of the test booklet since you can fill in the rest of the information later. You should help the students complete the sample items on the vocabulary subtest and stop the test after exactly 15 minutes. You should later help the pupils work the sample items on the comprehension subtest and stop this test after 25 minutes. If you wish to use the provided norms, it is very important that you follow the detailed directions in the manual exactly.

Directions for Scoring the Test

Since the pupil marks his answers directly on his copy of the test booklet, you must score his test by hand. The raw score on either the vocabulary or comprehension subtest is the total number of items for which the child selected the right answer. You are provided with answer keys in the package containing the manual and the test booklets. When you have obtained the raw score for the vocabulary subtest, you can use Table I on page 7 of the manual to convert this raw score into a standard score or a percentile rank. You can use Table II to convert this raw score into a grade equivalent score. When you have obtained a raw score for the comprehension subtest, you can convert it into a standard score or a percentile rank by using Table III on page 7. Table IV on page 7 can be used to convert this raw score into a grade equivalent score.

The front page of the Gates-MacGinitie Reading Tests, Primary A, Form 1 is reprinted on page 79 so that you can see how it was completed for one first-grade pupil.

Evaluation of the Gates-MacGinitie Reading Tests, Primary A Battery

The Gates-MacGinitie Reading Tests, Primary A Battery is a revision of the Gates Primary Reading Test. However, apparently the reviews of this earlier test apply quite well to the present edition, according to the information found in *Reading Tests and Reviews.*[6] According to William Eller of the State University of New York at Buffalo, this test is easy to administer because the directions in

---

[6]Buros, *Reading Tests and Reviews,* p. 6:792.

the manual are clear and complete and because the teacher does not have to know a great deal about measurement to give it. Eller stated that this test probably will enjoy considerable popularity for years to come. Coleman Morrison of Harvard University stated that the test has certain advantages as a survey reading test and recommended it for this purpose.

This author believes that the Gates-MacGinitie Reading Tests, Primary A Battery is a very useful survey reading test for first grade. She recommends it because the directions are easy to understand and because the test is quite easy to administer. The directions for scoring the test also are fairly easy to understand and carry out.

Print your name here **Mark**

How old are you? **7-3**

When is your birthday? **February 2, 1966**

Grade **1** Date **May 3, 1973**

School **Ben Franklin** Teacher **G. Rhodes**

GATES—
MacGINITIE
READING TESTS *

A FORM 1

PRIMARY A, FORM 1

Vocabulary and Comprehension

▨☐☐☐☐☐☐☐☐☐☐

TEACHERS COLLEGE PRESS
TEACHERS COLLEGE
COLUMBIA UNIVERSITY
NEW YORK

VOCABULARY SAMPLES

A.

did   egg

(dog)   two

B.

bed   swim

milk   (fly)

To the Teacher:

BE SURE to follow the directions in the Manual (included in each test package) when giving these tests. The directions will tell you how to explain the tests and how to work the sample items with the students. Allow the exact time specified in the Manual.

VOCABULARY

Number correct **35**

Standard score **48**

Percentile score **42**

Grade score **1.9**

COMPREHENSION

Number correct **19**

Standard score **48**

Percentile score **42**

Grade score **1.7**

COMPREHENSION SAMPLES

A. Where is the baby?

B. The white box is on the shelf.

*Reprinted by permission of the publisher from the *Gates-MacGinitie Reading Tests* (New York: Teachers College Press, Copyright 1964 and 1969 by Teacher College, Columbia University).

METROPOLITAN ACHIEVEMENT TESTS–INTERMEDIATE LEVEL

by Walter N. Durost, Harold H. Bixler, J. Wayne Wrightstone, George A. Prescott, and
Irving H. Balow
Harcourt, Brace, Jovanovich, Inc.
757 Third Avenue
New York 10017

Published in 1970

Description of the Test

The Intermediate Level of the Metropolitan Achievement Tests evaluates
language, spelling, mathematics, science, and social studies in addition to reading.
You can use the word knowledge subtest and the reading subtest of the entire test
battery to evaluate reading ability. In addition, you can purchase these two
subtests in a separate test booklet if you want to evaluate only reading ability. In
either case, the Intermediate Level of this test is designed for fifth and sixth grade
and is available in Forms F, G, and H.

According to the Teacher's Directions, the word knowledge subtest contains
50 items. Each word is followed by four possible answers. The student then is to
choose the word which best completes each sentence. The reading subtest
contains eight reading selections, each of which is found by a number of
comprehension and vocabulary questions. Each selection increases in difficulty
through vocabulary, sentence length and structure, and overall length.

The student is given 15 minutes to complete the word knowledge subtest
and 25 minutes to complete the reading subtest. You also may need about 5
minutes for the preliminary portion of the test-taking. Therefore, the entire test
requires about 45 minutes to administer. Apparently the test does not evaluate
rate of reading.

The Teacher's Handbook gives detailed directions for interpreting the test
results. The scores can be expressed as standard scores, percentile ranks, stanines,
and grade equivalents. Tables 1, 2, and 3 of the Teacher's Handbook of the entire
test battery provide norms for the reading subtest. These tables help you convert
raw scores to standard scores, standard scores to grade equivalents, standard
scores to percentile ranks, and standard scores to stanines, so that you can
compare a student's performance on this test with his performance on an
intelligence test or on another reading test.

The Teacher's Handbook presents some general principles about getting the
most from test results. It further presents the use of test results in determining
class organization, selecting instructional materials, overcoming special weaknesses, and reevaluation.

Data on the reliability of the word knowledge subtest, the reading subtest,
and the total reading score are found on page 16 of the Teacher's Handbook. The

word knowledge subtest has reliability coefficients of .92 and .93, while the reading subtest has reliability coefficients of .93 and .93. The total reading score has reliability coefficients of .96 and .96. The validity of this test was defined primarily in terms of content validity.

Page 16 of the Teacher's Handbook describes the standardization of the Intermediate Level of the Metropolitan Achievement Tests. These tests were empirically standardized at two times during the 1969-70 school year. The standardization samples represented the national population in terms of geographic regions, size of city, socio-economic status, and public versus private schools. Table 4 on page 16 is devoted to the standardization samples for this test.

Directions for Giving the Test

As stated earlier, the entire test takes about 45 minutes to give. According to the Teacher's Directions, you normally can give both the word knowledge and reading subtests in one sitting. You are to have a test booklet for each student, and an answer sheet for each student if separate answer sheets are being used, an extra supply of pencils, and a watch or clock with a second hand. If you want to use the norms provided, you should read the directions exactly as they are written in the Teacher's Directions. There are various directions depending upon the different answer documents. You are not to give any help on a specific question, and you are to follow the time limits exactly.

First, you have the students fill in as much of the information on the front cover as they can. Then you can give the word knowledge subtest and the reading subtest, following the directions exactly. You should be sure to explain the samples which are illustrated in the manual.

Directions for Scoring the Test

When you have completed giving the test, it obviously must be scored. Both the entire test battery or a separate reading test can be machine scored in any number of different ways. For example, the complete battery of tests can be scored using IBM 805, IBM 1230, and Digitek-Opscan answer sheets. The Harcourt Brace Jovanovich Scoring Service can provide you with the scoring of MRC answer documents. You also can score the complete battery or the separate reading tests yourself. If the test is scored by hand, the raw score for each subtest is the number of correct answers. You then enter the number of correct answers at the end of each subtest and on the front cover of the test booklet.

Later you convert the raw score on each subtest into standard scores, stanines, grade equivalents, and percentile ranks Pages 4 and 5 of the Teacher's Handbook explain all of these scores in some detail. You are told to convert the raw scores into standard scores first by using Table 1. If you wish, you later can convert each standard score to a grade equivalent, a percentile rank, or a stanine by using Tables 2 and 3. When you have done this, you then enter these scores on the front cover of the test booklet.

On the following page, you will find the front cover of the Intermediate Level of the Metropolitan Achievement Tests, Form F completed for a fifth-grade student. Examination of this sheet can help you understand more about how this is done.

Evaluation of the Metropolitan Achievement Tests, Intermediate Level

The author has evaluated the Intermediate Level of the Metropolitan Achievement Tests quite carefully. This test has been updated considerably in content and format since 1959. The application of computer science to the scoring of the answer sheets certainly is very good. The tables found in the Teacher's Handbook are also more useful than they were in the 1959 edition of this test due to their format. The Teacher's Directions for this test are rather confusing because of the wide variety of possible answer documents provided for the test. However, perhaps this is inevitable because of the wide variety of answer documents provided.

Interpretive comprehension does not receive a great deal of attention on the reading subtest. Instead, literal comprehension is mainly emphasized. However, the test booklet has a very good format. In conclusion, the author recommends this test as a good survey reading test at the fifth- and sixth-grade grade levels.

INTERMEDIATE

METROPOLITAN ACHIEVEMENT TESTS*

FORM F

Pupil Information Box

Name *Wilson, Jack P.*

Date of Test *September 19, 1979*   [X] Boy

Date of Birth   *3*   *7*   *1962*   [ ] Girl
              Day   Month   Year

School *John Marshall*

City *Normal*   State *Illinois*

Grade *5*   Teacher *Mary Sue Johnson*

Walter N. Durost
Harold H. Bixler
J. Wayne Wrightstone
George A. Prescott
Irving H. Balow

Score Summary Box

Test	Raw Score	Standard Score	Grade Equivalent	Percentile Rank	Stanine
1 Word Knowledge	29	77	5.6	60	6
2 Reading	24	79	5.7	58	5
1 + 2 Total Reading	53	71	5.6	60	6
3 Language					
4 Spelling					
5 Mathematics Computation					
6 Mathematics Concepts					
7 Mathematics Problem Solving					
5 — 7 Total Mathematics					
8 Science					
9 Social Studies					

HARCOURT BRACE JOVANOVICH

Copyright   1970 by
Harcourt Brace Jovanovich, Inc.
All rights reserved. No part of this
publication may be reproduced or
transmitted in any form or by any
means. electronic or mechanical.
including photocopy. recording. or any
information storage and retrieval
system. without permission in writing
from the publisher. Printed in U.S.A.

*Reproduced from the Metropolitan Achievement Tests, copyright©1970 by Harcourt Brace Jovanovich, Inc. Reproduced by special permission of the publisher.

GATES-MacGINITIE READING TESTS, SURVEY F TEST

by Arthur I. Gates and Walter H. MacGinitie
Teachers College Press, Columbia University
525 West 120th Street
New York 10027

Published in 1969

Description of the Test

The Survey F Test of the Gates-MacGinitie Reading Tests is designed for grades ten through 12. It is part of a series of tests which covers kindergarten through twelfth grade. It is available in Forms 1 and 2 for scoring by hand. Survey FM Test is available in Forms 1M and 2M for machine scoring.

This test consists of the subtests of speed and accuracy, vocabulary, and comprehension. According to the manual, the speed and accuracy subtest shows how rapidly students can read with comprehension. This subtest contains 36 short paragraphs of similar difficulty which end in a question or incomplete statement. The student is to choose the word from the option of four words which best answers the question or completes the statement. The number of paragraphs read and questions answered correctly in 4 minutes indicates how rapidly a student reads with understanding.

The vocabulary subtest which contains 50 items evaluates a student's reading vocabulary. Each word is followed by five words. The student chooses the synonym from the five options. The words become more difficult in this subtest, which requires 15 minutes to administer. The comprehension subtest evaluates a student's comprehension of complete prose passages. This subtest includes 21 passages which contain 52 blank spaces. For each blank space, the student must choose the one out of five options which best completes the blank space. The items become more difficult to complete on this subtest. Since this subtest takes 25 minutes to administer, the entire test takes 44 minutes to administer in addition to the time required for completing the front page of the booklet.

The test manual briefly describes standard scores and percentile scores on page 6 of the hand-scored edition. Table I gives you the standard scores and percentile norms for the number attempted on the speed and accuracy subtest. Table II presents the standard scores and percentile norms for the number correct on the speed and accuracy subtest. Table III presents the standard scores and percentile norms for the vocabulary subtest. Table IV presents the standard scores and percentile norms for the comprehension subtest. In each case, you enter the table at one of these grade levels: 10.1, 10.5, 10.8, 11.1, 11.5, 11.8, 12.1, 12.5, and 12.8.

The test manual does contain some general information about reliability. It states that all test scores should be regarded as tentative. Apparently there is no material available in the manual regarding test validity.

Directions for Giving the Test

You should study the directions for giving the test carefully before administering it. Although you are told in the manual to follow the directions carefully, you may repeat or supplement them to be sure that the students understand them. Although the vocabulary and comprehension subtests are not considered to be timed tests, you should follow the time limits exactly. On the other hand, the manual states that accurate timing is of supreme importance in the speed and accuracy subtest. You should use a stop watch or a watch or clock with a second hand. Here are the time limits for these subtests:

speed and accuracy—4 minutes
vocabulary—15 minutes
comprehension—25 minutes

You should give the test in the proper order. You can provide a rest period between the vocabulary and comprehension subtest, or you can give the comprehension subtest on another day. Each student should have an ordinary soft lead pencil with a good eraser.

First the students should fill in the required information on the front page of the record booklet. Then you can help them work the sample items on the speed and accuracy subtest. You should stop the test after exactly 4 minutes. Next, you can help the students complete the sample items in the vocabulary subtest and stop this test after exactly 15 minutes. Last, you can help the students work the sample exercise for the comprehension subtest, and you then stop this test after exactly 25 minutes.

Directions for Scoring the Test

If you have the hand-scored edition of the test, you must score the three subtests. You are given an answer key. Two raw scores are obtained from the speed and accuracy subtest. They are the number of items attempted and the number of items answered correctly. Comparison of the second score with the first score shows how accurately the student was reading. The raw score on either the vocabulary or the comprehension subtest is the number of items which the student answers correctly. If you are using the machine-scored edition, you need not be concerned about the scoring procedure.

You can convert the raw scores into a standard score or a percentile score by using the norm tables in the manual. In the hand-scored edition of the manual, the norming tables are located on pages 8 through 11, while in the machine-scored edition of the manual, the norming tables are found on pages 12 through 15. In each case, Table I gives the standard score and percentile norms for the number attempted on the speed and accuracy subtest. Table II presents the standard scores and percentile norms for the number correct on the speed and accuracy subtest. Table III presents the standard scores and percentile norms for the vocabulary subtest, while Table IV presents the standard scores and percentile norms for the comprehension subtest.

The front page of the test booklet of the hand-scored edition of the Gates-MacGinitie Reading Tests, Survey F Battery is reprinted on the following page so that you can see how it is scored.

Evaluation of the Gates-MacGinitie Reading Tests, Survey F Battery

Several reviews of the Gates-MacGinitie Survey Reading Tests have appeared in *Reading Tests and Reviews.*[7] For example, George D. Spache of the University of Florida stated that these tests have minor limitations. However, he believed that they were profitable for use in survey testing and in evaluation of reading programs even though they are not particularly diagnostic. Morey J. Wantman of the Educational Testing Service stated that these tests are useful in determining the level of achievement of a group of pupils. However, he stated that they are not very helpful in individual diagnosis of reading difficulties.

This author recommends the Survey F Test highly for use in the secondary school. It seems to be a very good survey reading test for use at this level.

You can find a list of other standardized survey reading tests in Appendix I, page 271 of this kit.

---

[7]Buros, *op. cit.*, p. 6:793.

HAND-SCORED EDITION

Name _Felsen, John_
      (LAST)   (FIRST)

Birth date _April 2 1957_ Male __X__ Female _____
      (MONTH, DAY, YEAR)

Grade _10th_ _____ Testing date _May 5, 1973_

Teacher _Paul Adams_

School _Normal Community High School_

City _Normal_

DIRECTIONS: Read sample paragraph S 1. Under it are four words. Find the word that best answers the question.

S1. In the far north, a frozen river winds between two high mountains. It does not melt even in summer. A river like this is found only in places that are

    mild   hot   cold   sunny

The word **cold** is the best answer to the question. Draw a line under the word **cold** .

Now read paragraph S2. Find the word below the paragraph that best completes the paragraph, and draw a line under it.

S2. No one was at the airport to meet us. This worried us at first, but then we realized that we hadn't told them exactly when we would

    sail   go   stay   arrive

The word **arrive** best completes paragraph S2. You should have drawn a line under the word **arrive**.

On the next two pages are more paragraphs like these samples. When you are asked to turn the page, read each paragraph and find the word below it that best answers the question or completes the paragraph. Draw a line under the best word. Mark only *one* word for each paragraph. Do the paragraphs in the order in which they are numbered: 1, 2, 3, etc. If you can't answer a question, go on to the next one. Work as fast as you can without making errors.

**GATES—
MacGINITIE
READING TESTS** *

F FORM 2

SURVEY F, FORM 2

Speed & Accuracy

Vocabulary

Comprehension

▢▢▢▢▢▢▢▢ ▨ ▨▨

TEACHERS COLLEGE PRESS
TEACHERS COLLEGE
COLUMBIA UNIVERSITY
NEW YORK

To the Teacher:

BE SURE to follow the directions in the Manual (included in each test package) when giving these tests. The directions will tell you how to explain the tests and how to work the sample items with the students. Allow the exact time specified in the Manual.

		COMPREHENSION	VOCABULARY	SPEED & ACCURACY
COMPREHENSION	Number right	22		
VOCABULARY	Number right		27	
SPEED & ACCURACY	Number right			14
	Number attempted			17
	Raw score	22	27	17
	Standard score	43	50	46
	Percentile score	24	50	34

*Reprinted by permission of the publisher from the *Gates-MacGinitie Reading Tests* (New York: Teachers College Press, copyright 1964 and 1969 by Teachers College, Columbia University).

Standardized
Diagnostic Reading Tests

W hat type of student do you think should be given a standardized diagnostic reading test? An individual or group diagnostic reading test usually is given to a student who scores one or more years below his potential level as was explained in Section 4. An individual or a group diagnostic reading test usually is given to a disabled reader to determine his exact reading strengths and weaknesses.

This section is devoted to helping you understand the characteristics and uses of standardized diagnostic reading tests in the diagnosis of specific reading difficulties. The section opens with a description of standardized diagnostic reading tests for the diagnosis of reading difficulties. Next it presents general directions for administering both individual and group diagnostic reading tests. The section closes with a detailed description of one individual diagnostic reading test and two group diagnostic reading tests. Hopefully, this section will enable you to use standardized diagnostic reading tests more effectively in the diagnosis of a student's specific reading skill strengths and weaknesses.

Description of Standardized Diagnostic Reading Tests in the Diagnosis of Reading Difficulties

As was explained earlier, a standardized diagnostic reading test is used primarily with a student who has done poorly on a standardized survey reading test or the reading subtests of an achievement test. This a student who is reading one or more years below his potential level using the criteria described in Section 4. A standardized diagnostic reading test is an individual administered or group-administered test which attempts to determine a student's reading skill strengths in the various word recognition and comprehension skills. It also attempts to determine a student's reading levels. In the word recognition skills, a diagnostic reading test can evaluate such subskills as the following: knowledge of letter names, knowledge of consonant sounds, understanding of vowel sounds, auditory blending, understanding of base or root words, knowledge of prefixes and suffixes, whole word recognition, context clue usage, and rhyming. In the comprehension skills, a diagnostic reading test often evaluates such subskills as vocabulary, literal comprehension, and interpretive comprehension. Several group diagnostic reading tests only evaluate the word recognition skills.

You may wonder what type of student should be given a diagnostic reading test instead of an Individual Reading Inventory. In many instances, it may be better for you to give a valid Individual Reading Inventory with additional inventories in such word recognition techniques as sight word knowledge, phonetic analysis, structural analysis, context clue usage, and dictionary usage. You may mainly want to give a diagnostic reading test when you want to use a test that you are sure is more reliable and valid than is a typical Individual Reading Inventory. Therefore, you may want to give a diagnostic reading test to a severely disabled reader. You also may want to give a diagnostic reading test to a student who is not making satisfactory progress in a corrective or remedial reading program.

When should you use a group diagnostic reading test instead of an individual diagnostic reading test? Normally, you can give a group diagnostic reading test to a mildly or moderately disabled reader to whom you do not wish to take the time to give an Individual Reading Inventory. Therefore, you may want to use a group diagnostic reading test with some of the students in your classroom who are mildly or moderately disabled in reading. Since a group diagnostic reading test can be given to a number of students at one time, it does not require the administration time of either an individual diagnostic reading test or an Individual Reading Inventory.

Individual and group diagnostic reading tests only evaluate a student's reading strengths and weaknesses through the eighth-grade instructional reading level as a rule. Therefore, most of them can be used with any elementary school student. However, they normally would be given only to disabled readers at the secondary-school level. A diagnostic reading test usually cannot help you determine the causes of a student's reading difficulties. Instead, it only can pinpoint a student's exact reading strengths and weaknesses.

What do you think are the major advantages of giving either a standardized individual or group diagnostic reading test? The major advantage of using such a test over an informal reading test is that the standardized test was prepared by a reading specialist. Therefore, it normally is more reliable and valid than any informal reading test which you could formulate yourself. It is a norm referenced test. Therefore, you can compare one student or a group of students with students who possess similar characteristics such as grade level, sex, or age. Then, too, a standardized diagnostic reading test saves you considerable time over constructing such a test of your own. As you will determine from Section 7 of this kit, it takes a good deal of time and effort to construct a valid Individual Reading Inventory.

The diagnostic reading test usually does a very good job of pinpointing a student's exact reading skill strengths and weaknesses in the word recognition and comprehension skills and in establishing an instructional reading grade level for him. One of the most important characteristics of corrective or remedial reading instruction is that it should be based upon a specific or "rifle" approach instead of on a general or "shotgun" approach. This means that a student always should be presented with corrective or remedial reading instruction which stresses only those reading skills in which he has been diagnosed to be weak. Thus, you can make the analogy to firearms. The rifle blast is direct, while the shotgun blast spreads pellets all around. The use of a diagnostic reading test enables you to be specific and direct in a student's corrective or remedial reading program.

What are the disadvantages of giving any type of standardized diagnostic reading test? Usually an individual diagnostic reading test takes much time to administer and score. It often is not easy to evaluate so that its results can be used in a meaningful manner. On the other hand, the group diagnostic reading test usually takes much less time to administer, score, and interpret. Standardized diagnostic reading tests have some of the same limitations as do all standardized tests. For example, since they tend to measure experiential and cultural backgrounds, they may discriminate against socially different students.

However, notwithstanding all of their minor limitations, both individual and group diagnostic reading tests have an important place in the diagnosis of specific reading skill strengths and weaknesses. They enable the busy teacher to diagnose a student's reading difficulties with a specificity that is not possible in a survey reading test.

If you wish to see a complete listing of all of the diagnostic reading tests in print, you can consult the book *Reading Tests and Reviews.*[1] This book also contains an evaluation of most of these diagnostic reading tests, each of which was written by a reading specialist.

General Directions for Using Standardized Diagnostic Reading Tests

Since individual diagnostic reading tests vary a great deal, it is rather difficult to present general guidelines for their administration. However, in most of these tests you do not give all of the subtests to a student. The manual helps you decide which subtests to give to a particular student. It also is obvious that you must consider each student's reading skills when deciding which subtests to give him. If you found that he is weak in phonetic analysis by teacher observation or by oral reading, you will want to emphasize the subtests relating to phonetic analysis on a diagnostic reading test so that you can pinpoint this weakness specifically enough so that it can be corrected. You may then give him such subtests as letter names, letter sounds, a test on vowels, a test on initial consonants, a test on final consonants, and auditory blending.

Of course, in giving an individual diagnostic reading test, you first should establish rapport with the student. The testing should be done in a quiet room, and the child usually should sit to your left if you are right-handed. You can tell the child in general terms why he should take the test. You should time all the timed tests accurately. You do not need to follow the directions verbatim in most individual diagnostic reading tests. It is quite important that you give an individual diagnostic reading test in practice situations several times before you give it in an actual testing situation. It probably is more important for you to notice the type of errors that a student makes than to arrive

---

[1]Oscar Krisen Buros, (ed.), *Reading Tests and Reviews.* (Highland Park, N.J.: The Gryphon Press, 1968), pp. 9-12.

at a reading grade level for him. Such observation of specific types of errors does take considerable practice and experience.

A group diagnostic reading test usually only tests word recognition skills or else is a comprehensive test of reading ability, including evaluation of word recognition skills, vocabulary, and comprehension skills. Usually each student takes all of the subtests in a group diagnostic reading test. Sometimes you must give the test directions in a structured way, while you are given considerable latitude in this on other tests. You must adhere to strict time limits on some group diagnostic reading tests, while you do not have to observe time limits on other group diagnostic reading tests. Thus, you can see that there are considerable differences in the procedures for giving group diagnostic reading tests. Some of these tests are a good deal more structured than others. When you have given a group diagnostic reading test, you must, of course, then score it. In most cases, the student answers directly in the test booklet so the teacher who scores the test can examine each pupil's errors carefully. After you have scored the test, it can be interpreted in several different ways. Some group diagnostic reading tests provide norms similar to those of a standardized survey reading test. The norms can be reported in grade equivalents, stanines, or percentile ranks. In such tests, you can compare the performance of your students with the performance of students who possess similar characteristics. Such group diagnostic reading tests also have class record sheets from which you can see the reading strengths of your entire class or the group to whom you gave the test. You also can examine the reading performance of an individual student by looking at the front cover of his test booklet.

On the other hand, some group diagnostic reading tests do not have norms. Instead, the exact identification of a student's reading strengths and weaknesses is of primary importance. This is so that the teacher can design a corrective reading program which specifically will correct these reading difficulties. In such types of diagnostic reading tests, you are encouraged to complete the front page of the test booklet so that you can see the specific skill difficulties of the students.

The manuals of most diagnostic reading tests provide suggestions for a corrective or remedial reading program. In this way, they differ considerably from the test manuals of survey reading tests. However, it is obvious that these teaching suggestions should be supplemented by professional books at the appropriate level.

It is obvious that the administration, the scoring procedures, and the interpretation of scores differ in the various diagnostic reading tests. Therefore, the preceding part of this section was quite general. In the next part of this section, you will find detailed directions on how to administer and score one individual diagnostic reading test and two group diagnostic reading tests. This portion of the section also should help you learn how to give and score most individual and group diagnostic reading tests.

For the purposes of an example, let us suppose that you have found a student to be weak in auditory discrimination by the giving of either an individual or a group diagnostic reading test. What are some of the ways in which you could present this reading skill? There are a number of records available which can be used to promote auditory discrimination. Some of these are as follows on page 93:

Sounds Around Us. Scott Foresman and Company.
Listening Time Albums. Webster Publishing Company.
Auditory Training. Greystone Corporation.
Spotlight on Sound Effects. Pickwick International.

You also can have a series of objects, all but one of which begin with the same consonant. Several such objects could be a ball, a bell, a whistle, and a bat. The student then points to the object which begins with a different sound than the others. Later you can pronounce a series of words, all but one of which begin with the same consonant sound. Such a series of words could be as follows: money, mother, neighbor, matches, and man. The student then tells you which of the words begins with a sound that is different. You also can use worksheets from basal reader workbooks, or phonics workbooks, or ditto masters which can be purchased commercially. Additional suggestions for developing auditory discrimination ability are found in many of the professional books listed in Appendix III, page 275.

As another example, let us suppose that you have diagnosed a student to be weak in interpretive comprehension ability by the use of a diagnostic reading test. You can use several different methods to correct this reading skill weakness. Although interpretive comprehension can be presented to a pupil individually, often it is better to present it to a small group of students who are reading on about the same level and who are weak in this skill. Then you can have this group read a basal reader story or an assignment from a content textbook and pose questions which call for interpretive responses after they have read the material. Such questions require students to generalize, interpret, infer, draw conclusions, summarize, and read between the lines. You also can give this group of students interpretive questions to read and answer before they read a basal reader story or content assignment. Basal reader workbooks also contain pages with interpretive questions. In addition, you can purchase materials at the elementary or secondary level which are specifically designed to present interpretive comprehension. Listings of such materials may be found in many of the professional books presented in Appendix III.

Thus, you can see how the use of either an individual or a group diagnostic reading test should ascertain a student's specific reading difficulties so that you can plan a corrective or remedial reading program designed specifically for him in the light of these diagnosed reading difficulties. Then you can build on his diagnosed reading skill strengths while correcting his reading difficulties.

Examples of Individual and Group Diagnostic Reading Tests

The one individual and two group diagnostic reading tests selected for the final part of this section are useful examples of a number of diagnostic reading tests which are currently in print. The other diagnostic reading tests which are included in Appendix II, page 273, are equally useful.

DURRELL ANALYSIS OF READING DIFFICULTY, NEW EDITION

by Donald D. Durrell
Harcourt, Brace, and Jovanovich
757 Third Avenue
New York 10017

Published in 1955

Description of the Test

The Durrell Analysis of Reading Difficulty is an individual diagnostic reading test which is designed to evaluate reading skills at the first-grade through the sixth-grade reading levels. This test consists of a group of subtests in which the teacher may observe different aspects of a student's word recognition and comprehension skills in detail. It is designed to help the teacher discover a student's specific reading skill weaknesses so they can be corrected. The checklist from this test was reprinted in Section 2 of this kit. According to the manual, the checklist is one of the most important aspects of this test since the observation of individual reading errors is of more importance than are the norms which are provided for the test.

The Durrell Analysis of Reading Difficulty contains a number of different subtests. You do not give all of the subtests to any one student. Here is a very brief description of the subtests:

> *Oral Reading*—This subtest contains eight paragraphs which a student reads orally while you mark his errors. This test helps you know what other subtests to give a student.
>
> *Silent Reading*—This subtest contains eight paragraphs for silent reading. It evaluates his recall and his use of imagery.
>
> *Listening Comprehension*—This subtest contains paragraphs which you read aloud to the student. You ask him some comprehension questions about each paragraph when you have finished reading it.
>
> *Word Recognition and Word Analysis*—You use the cardboard tachistoscope in the test package for the sight word recognition of some words. If the student does not recognize a word in the flash test, you open the shutter of the tachistoscope and allow the child to study and pronounce the word.
>
> *Naming Letters—Identifying Letters Named—Matching Letters*—The non-reader or the child reading on the first-grade level should be given this test. On this test, the student is to give the letter names, or identify the letters named by the teacher, or match the letters.
>
> *Visual Memory of Words—Primary*—This is a series of identification tests for the primary-grade level in which you use the tachistoscope without the shutter. You ask the child to match a letter or a word in the tachistoscope with the same letter or word in the test booklet.

*Hearing Sounds in Words—Primary—*This test is given to a child who is reading at the third-grade level or below, but it should not be given if he does not know the names of the letters. In this subtest, the child circles words which begin with certain consonants or consonant clusters. Then he circles words that end with certain consonants or consonant clusters.

*Visual Memory of Words—Intermediate—*This subtest requires a student to write a series of words from memory which are placed in the tachistoscope without the shutter.

*Phonic Spelling of Words—*This subtest contains a number of very difficult words which the student is to spell phonetically.

*Spelling Test—*This subtest contains a primary-grade spelling list and intermediate-grade spelling list.

*Handwriting—*In this subtest you ask a first-grade child to write two or three words, while in grades two and above you give the child one of the easier paragraphs which he read orally and ask him to copy it on another sheet of paper. You give him 1 minute to do this copying.

The Durrell Analysis of Reading Difficulty takes about 30 to 90 minutes to administer. The variation in time required is due to the number of subtests which are given.

According to the manual, whenever norm tables are given in the individual record booklet, they are based on at least 1,000 students for each test. Norm tables are provided for the following subtests: oral reading, silent reading, listening comprehension, word recognition and word analysis, visual memory of words—primary, hearing sounds in words—primary, visual memory of words—intermediate, spelling, and handwriting. There apparently is no data on the validity or reliability of this test in the manual.

Directions for Giving the Test

Since the directions for giving each subtest are quite detailed, they only are briefly summarized in this kit. You should first establish rapport with the student prior to the testing. According to the manual, you can tell him that this test is designed to help you understand his reading so that you know in which areas of reading he needs help. If you are right-handed, the student should sit at your left so that you do not record the student's errors right under his eyes. Although you can give the subtests in any order, you should give the oral reading test first since you must choose the other subtests after determining the reading level obtained in this subtest. You should use a stop watch or a watch or clock with a second hand to time the oral and silent reading tests. According to the manual, you should remember that the observation of reading difficulties is the most important factor in this test.

Here are the directions for giving each subtest of the Durrell Analysis Reading Difficulty:

*Oral Reading—*Have the student read at least three selections orally while you mark his oral reading errors. If he makes two or more errors in the beginning paragraph, have him read the preceding one and have him continue down until a paragraph is read without errors. This is the basal paragraph. Then have him continue upwards until he makes seven or more errors on a paragraph or takes more than 2 minutes to read it.

Silent Reading—Have the student read paragraphs of the same difficulty as he read in the oral reading test. After he has read one paragraph, ask him to tell you everything that he can remember. Then question him specifically about what he did not remember.

Listening Comprehension—Read the paragraphs in the spiral-bound booklet aloud to the student. Then ask him comprehension questions for each paragraph. If he misses two or more questions, use a lower-level paragraph. His listening comprehension level is the level at which he missed not more than one question.

Word Recognition and Word Analysis—You first must decide what word list to use. If the child's reading level is below second grade, use lists A and B. Above the first-grade level, use lists 1 and 2. On either list, if the student makes seven or more successive errors, do not continue with the test. Put the proper list in the tachistoscope, and move the shutter up or down for about ½ second. If the student cannot recognize the letter or word, give him time to analyze the word.

Naming Letters—Identifying Letters Named—Matching Letters—The child is to give the names of the upper-case and lower-case letters in order. If he cannot name the letters, ask the child to identify them by pointing to the letters which you name. If he is unable to do this also, use the tachistoscope without the shutter and put the various letters in it. The child then matches the proper letter in the record booklet with the letter in the tachistoscope.

Visual Memory of Words—Primary—In this test, the child matches a letter or word in the tachistoscope without the shutter with a letter or word in the record booklet. The child is shown the letter or word for 2 or 3 seconds.

Hearing Sounds in Words—Primary—In this test, the child circles words which begin with consonants like the words the teacher pronounces. He then circles words that begin with the same consonant clusters as are found in some words which the teacher pronounces. Next, he circles the words which end with the same consonant as some words which are pronounced by the teacher. Last, he circles some words which end with the same consonant cluster as those pronounced by the teacher.

Visual Memory of Words—Intermediate—The student writes the words in his record booklet which are exposed on the tachistoscope. Each word is exposed for 2 or 3 seconds.

Phonic Spelling of Words—In this test the student is to spell phonetically 15 difficult words which you pronounce. Each one of them is considered to be phonetically regular.

Spelling Test—In administering this test you are to pronounce the word, read the sentence containing the word, and then repeat the word. Give List 1 for grades two or three and List 2 for grades four and above.

Handwriting—In grade one, you ask the child to write or copy two or three words. In grades two and above, give the child one of the simple paragraphs from the oral reading test and ask him to copy it on another sheet of paper. Give him 1 minute to do this.

Directions for Scoring the Test

As stated earlier, the observation of each student's specific difficulties in word recognition and comprehension is of more importance than are the norms which can be determined after scoring the various subtests. However, a number of the subtests do have scoring procedures which you can use to arrive at norms. These scoring procedures are described very briefly in this portion of this section.

Oral Reading—You first circle the figure nearest the time the student took to read the paragraph. This shows you the position in the grade at which he is located. You then place these grade levels in the paragraph-grade box. You can then determine the median score. If he answered all the questions, his comprehension is then considered to be good.

Silent Reading—You circle the figure closest to the time it took the student to read the paragraph silently. Then you place the grade levels in the paragraph-grade box and determine the median grade. If he answered all of the comprehension questions, his comprehension is good. On the other hand, if he missed two or more comprehension questions, his comprehension is poor.

Listening Comprehension—The student's listening comprehension is the level at which not more than one question was missed.

Word Recognition and Word Analysis—The norms for this test are found on page 8 of the record booklet. You can see if a student rates low, medium, or high on this test for his grade level by examining the table.

Visual Memory of Words—Primary—You count the letters or words which were identified correctly by the student. You then are able to establish a grade equivalent for this subtest of 1.5, 2.5, or 3.5.

Hearing Sounds in Words—Primary—You count the number of words which the student circles correctly. Then you can determine a grade equivalent on this subtest of 1.5, 2.5, or 3.5.

Visual Memory of Words—Intermediate—On this subtest, you can determine a student's grade equivalent by the number of correct answers which he had.

Phonic Spelling of Words—You can determine a grade equivalent according to the number of a student's right answers.

Spelling Test—You can determine grade level norms according to the number of correctly spelled words on either List 1 or List 2.

Handwriting—You can establish grade level norms by counting the letters per minute which the student wrote.

You will find the front cover of the individual record booklet of the Durrell

Analysis of Reading Difficulty reprinted on the following page. This example should help you understand how this individual diagnostic reading test can be evaluated.

Evaluation of the Durrell Analysis of Reading Difficulty, New Edition

The Durrell Analysis of Reading Difficulty has been evaluated in *Reading Tests and Reviews* by George D. Spache formerly of the University of Florida and James Maxwell of Teachers College, Columbia University.[2] According to Spache, this test battery is designed for observing the reading performance of nonreaders through the sixth-grade reading level. Spache stated that both the oral reading and silent reading tests evaluate only literal comprehension ability. For both of these subtests, Spache stated that the teacher cannot obtain an adequate sample for students who read below the third-grade level. Spache believed that the word recognition and word analysis subtests were most functional and unique. Spache further stated that no data are available on the reliability and validity of any of the subtests. According to Spache, the checklist for guiding the observation of reading behaviors was the most helpful part of the entire test battery.

Maxwell especially like the listening comprehension subtest. He also stated that all of the material was well arranged and carefully prepared. Maxwell believed that the weaknesses of this test battery were in the unsatisfactory norms for paragraph reading and the inadequacy of the word attack test.

This author believes that the Durrell Analysis of Reading Difficulty is a most useful individual diagnostic reading test. She is very impressed with the word recognition and word analysis test. On the whole, this test is not extremely difficult to administer and score as compared with one other well-known individual diagnostic reading test. However, the test could have been improved by providing data on reliability and validity. On the whole, it is still very useful for the teacher who wishes to take the time to give this type of individual reading test.

---

[2]Buros, *Reading Tests and Reviews*, p. 5:660.

Durrell Analysis of
Reading Difficulty *
NEW EDITION

**INDIVIDUAL
RECORD BOOKLET**

BY Donald D. Durrell *Professor of Education and Director of Educational Clinic, Boston University*

NAME *Mark Jones*   DATE *11-2-72*

SCHOOL *Oakwood*   EXAMINER, *Mary Jane Reid*

AGE *11-1*   GRADE *5*   REPORT TO *Frank Brown*

DATE OF BIRTH *10-1-61*   ADDRESS *Oakwood Shool*

Profile Chart

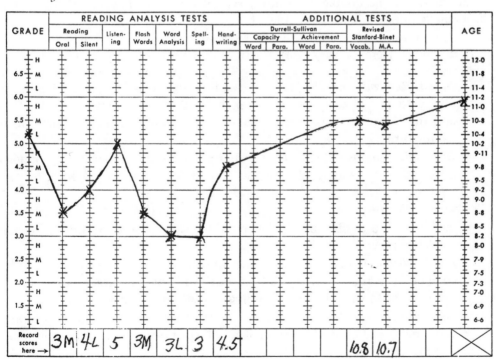

DOREN DIAGNOSTIC READING TEST OF WORD RECOGNITION SKILLS

by Margaret Doren
American Guidance Service, Inc.
Publishers' Building
Circle Pines, Minnesota 55014

Published in 1973

Description of the Test

The Doren Diagnostic Reading Test of Word Recognition Skills is a group diagnostic reading test which measures the degree of mastery which students have in the various word recognition skills. It does not evaluate comprehension ability. It is designed to be easy to administer and score. Its major purpose is to diagnose a child's specific difficulties in the word recognition skills so that these skills subsequently can be taught in a corrective or remedial reading program. This test is designed for the first-grade through the fourth-grade reading levels. Thus it can be used with some disabled secondary school students. However, it may not be particularly interesting to these older students.

This test consists of 12 subtests. Most subtests also are divided into several different parts. Here is a very brief description of the subtests in this test:

Letter Recognition—This tests the ability to recognize similar letters, the ability to recognize the same letter in the upper-case and lower-case form, and the ability to recognize the same letter in both manuscript and cursive handwriting.

Beginning Sounds—This tests the ability to match the beginning sounds in different words and to choose the correct beginning sound for a word in context.

Whole Word Recognition—This evaluates the ability to identify two matching words and to discriminate between two words which are similar in sound and appearance.

Words Within Words—This measures the ability to find the two words in a compound word, the ability to find small words within larger words, and the judgment as to when to use this skill as a method of word attack.

Speech Consonants—This tests the ability to perceive a speech consonant auditorially and the ability to recognize a word from the visual perception of a speech consonant.

Ending Sounds—This evaluates the ability to identify a word by its ending sound, the ability to choose correct endings in sentence context, and the ability to recognize plurals with irregular endings.

Blending—This evaluates the ability to apply known consonant blends in sentence context.

Rhyming—This evaluates the ability to recognize words that rhyme by auditory perception, the ability to recognize words that rhyme by visual perception, the ability to recognize that look-alike words do not always rhyme, and the ability to recognize that unlike words may rhyme.

Vowels—This subtest evaluates nine different abilities related to vowels. It tests such areas as short and long vowels, double vowels, and diphthongs.

Discriminate Guessing—This subtest measures the ability to supply missing words from clues in the context.

Spelling—This evaluates the ability to spell phonetic and non-phonetic words.

Sight Words—This measures the ability to read sight words and identify their pronunciation by their phonetic spellings.

According to the manual, the diagnosis of specific word recognition difficulties is of the utmost importance in the giving of this test. The use of norms is not considered to be as important as it is in a survey reading test. Therefore, the manual does not contain any mean scores. However, a class composite sheet which accompanies the test package can help the teacher to decide in what subskills of word recognition a group of students is weak.

Page 39 shows the correlations between this diagnostic reading test and reading achievement as measured by the Coordinated Scales of Attainment. These correlations are from .77 through .92. Table 2 on page 39 shows the correlations of the separate sections of the test with the total test score. These correlations range from .53 through .88. Apparently no information is given about the reliability of this test.

The manual presents a number of good suggestions for remedial reading activities on pages 32-38. They are in the areas of motivation, directed attention, discrimination, repetition, devices, word games, word concepts, and specific skill techniques for the areas of word recognition which are discussed in this test.

Directions for Giving the Test

According to the manual, the test may be given to as many students in a group as the teacher can supervise. Although the teacher should read the printed directions, she is not required to read them verbatim. She also can explain them further and reread them if necessary. She should complete the sample items for each subtest with the students.

Since this is not a timed test, the children should be allowed to work on each subtest until most of them have finished it. However, they should not be allowed to go ahead to another subtest. Extremely slow students can finish the subtests at a later time. The teacher herself must determine how much of the test can be given at any one sitting.

Since most of the subtests are quite easy to give, the detailed directions are not discussed in this kit. You can easily follow the directions for giving the subtests which are found on pages 12-28 of the manual.

Directions for Scoring the Test

When a group of students has completed the test, it must be scored by hand. An overlay key to facilitate scoring is available. For each subtest, you count the number of correct answers and place it on the Individual Score Sheet which is found on the back of the test booklet. You add the part scores to obtain the skill totals. You then record these total skill scores on the Individual Skill Profile on the front cover of the test booklet. Next you subtract these scores from the perfect scores to obtain the number wrong. Next you place a small x in the column below each skill on the line which corresponds to the number wrong. Then you connect the x's to complete the Individual Skill Profile. All skill totals which fall below the level of competency show the word recognition skills in which the student is weak.

You also can record all of the part scores from the Individual Score Sheet on the Class Composite sheet which accompanies the test package. This Class Composite shows you a pattern of the needs of a group if each part score with three or more errors is circled in red. Areas of group needs are indicated by a vertical column of red circles, and a student's needs are indicated in a horizontal row of red circles.

A completed front cover sheet of the test booklet is presented on the following page so that you can see how the Individual Skill Profile can be completed.

Evaluation of the Doren Diagnostic Reading Test of Word Recognition Skills

Since the second edition of this test was published in 1973, no reviews are found of it in *Reading Tests and Reviews*. However, this author believes that this is a very comprehensive test of the word recognition skills. It evaluates most aspects of the word recognition skills. However, the one subtest of words within words is of questionable value. The test undoubtedly would not be very interesting to older disabled readers because of its format. On the whole, however, the test can be recommended for a teacher who wants to give a useful group diagnostic test which only assesses ability in the various word recognition skills.

Doren Diagnostic Reading Test of Word Recognition Skills*

AGS

1973 EDITION

MARGARET DOREN, Ph.D.

NAME _Betty Marshall_ TOTAL SCORE _____

SCHOOL _Johnson_ DATE OF TESTING _1972_ _10_ _25_
Year Month Day

GRADE _Three_ DATE OF BIRTH _1964_ _9_ _3_
Year Month Day

EXAMINER _Sally Fielding_ AGE _8_ _1_ _22_
Years Months Days

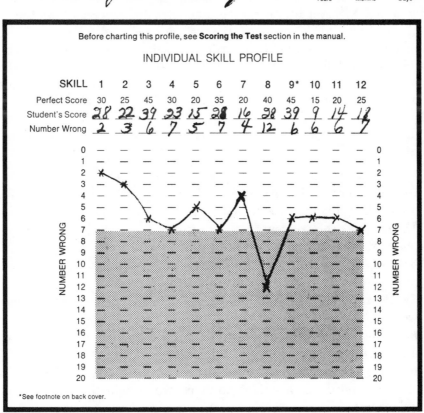

Before charting this profile, see **Scoring the Test** section in the manual.

INDIVIDUAL SKILL PROFILE

SKILL	1	2	3	4	5	6	7	8	9*	10	11	12
Perfect Score	30	25	45	30	20	35	20	40	45	15	20	25
Student's Score	28	22	39	23	15	28	16	28	39	9	14	18
Number Wrong	2	3	6	7	5	7	4	12	6	6	6	7

*See footnote on back cover.

Published by American Guidance Service, Inc., Publishers' Building, Circle Pines, Minnesota 55014

*Reproduced by permission of the American Guidance Service, Inc.

STANFORD DIAGNOSTIC READING TEST, LEVEL I AND LEVEL II

by Bjorn Carlsen, Richard Madden, and Eric F. Gardner
Harcourt, Brace, and Jovanovich
757 Third Avenue
New York 10017

Published in 1966

Description of the Test

The Stanford Diagnostic Reading Test is a group diagnostic reading test which is designed for two grade levels. Level I of the test is for the middle of second grade to the middle of fourth grade. Level II is for the middle of fourth grade through the middle of eighth grade. Each of the two levels is available in Forms W and X. Level II also can be used with disabled readers in the secondary school. According to the manuals, the tests are designed for use in the early part of the school year so that the teacher can determine in what areas of word recognition, vocabulary, comprehension, or rate of reading the entire class or a group of students is weak. This then enables the teacher to present the appropriate corrective reading instruction to the entire class or to a group of students.

Level I of the test contains seven subtests. Here is a brief description of these subtests:

Reading Comprehension—This evaluates comprehension using paragraphs from different subject matter areas. It is designed to evaluate both literal and interpretive comprehension.

Vocabulary—This presents 40 words, each of which best completes the sentence which the teacher reads.

Auditory Discrimination—This evaluates a pupil's ability to hear the similarities and differences among the sounds within words.

Syllabication—The pupil is asked to locate the first syllable in each of 20 words in this subtest.

Beginning and Ending Sounds—This tests beginning and ending sounds by using pictures of common objects.

Blending—This evaluates the ability to know the sounds of the phonetic elements and the ability to blend them into meaningful elements. It is a very unique test.

Sound Discrimination—This subtest evaluates a pupil's ability to determine the sounds and his ability to know the various spellings of phonemes within words.

Level II of the test contains six subtests. Here is a brief description of these subtests:

Reading Comprehension—This subtest evaluates literal and interpretive comprehension ability from reading paragraphs from a wide variety of subject matter areas. In this subtest literal and inferential comprehension are tested separately, and the general reading level is established from the total of these two parts.

Vocabulary—This subtest contains 40 vocabulary items from subject matter areas. The student is to mark the one of three options in each case which best completes the sentence.

Syllabication—The student is to mark the first syllable in each word. There are 24 words on this subtest.

Sound Discrimination—This subtest evaluates a student's ability to know the various sounds within words and his knowledge of the different spellings of these phonemes.

Blending—This evaluates the sounds of various phonetic elements and the student's ability to blend them into meaningful elements.

Rate of Reading—This subtest determines the rate at which a student can read a story with comprehension.

Both levels of the group diagnostic reading tests contain norms so that the teacher can compare the performance of his students with the performance of the students who were used in the norming. Tables are found which convert raw scores to grade equivalents and stanines on page 16 of the Level I manual. Similar tables are found on pages 13-15 of the Level II manual. Both of the manuals contain an additional table which enables you to convert the raw scores into percentile ranks.

Both of the manuals contain information on interpreting the test results. Each of the subtests are discussed in some detail. The manuals give a few suggestions for improving a student's performance in the reading skills which are tested. This part of each manual is quite useful. Each of the manuals also gives suggestions for remedial reading instruction. Such areas are covered as diagnosis, remedial instruction, motivation, parent involvement, vocabulary development, and word recognition skills. This part of both manuals is identical.

The reliability coefficients of Level I are found in Table 6 on page 28 of the manual. They were computed for both grades three and four. In grade three they range from .79 to .96, while in grade four they range from .73 to .96. The reliability coefficients for Level II are given in Table 6 on page 29. For this test the reliability coefficients are given for grades five, six, seven, and eight. In grade five the reliability coefficients range from .72 to .96, in grade six from .72 to .91, in grade seven from .72 to .97, and in grade eight from .72 to .97.

Validity is described in terms of content validity, construct validity, and predictive validity. Several correlations for construct validity are given in Table 9 of both levels of the test.

Each test manual contains information on the construction and standardization of the test. Both of the levels were standardized in October, 1965 with a total of about 12,000 students. At both levels, the Stanford Achievement Test: Reading and the Stanford Diagnostic Reading Test were given to all of the pupils.

Directions for Giving the Test

The manual for each level gives general directions for administering the test. Many of the suggestions are similar to those which are found in any test manual. They include such considerations as the following: an adequate supply of pencils, a quiet room, reading the directions verbatim but clarifying them when necessary, adhering strictly to the time limits, working on only one subtest at a time, and not giving the entire battery of tests on one day.

Level I should be given in four sittings. The first sitting requires about 40 minutes; the second sitting requires about 45 minutes; the third sitting requires about 37 minutes; and the fourth sitting requires about 40 minutes. Thus the test takes about 162 minutes to administer. Level II should be given in three sittings. The first sitting takes about 40 minutes; the second sitting takes about 43 minutes; and the third sitting takes about 28 minutes. Thus this test takes about 111 minutes to administer.

At each level, detailed directions are provided for giving each subtest. As was stated earlier, they are to be followed verbatim if you wish to use the norms provided for this test. In this way, this diagnostic reading test is considerably more structured than is the Doren Diagnostic Reading Test of Word Recognition Skills which was described earlier.

Directions for Scoring the Test

Since teachers wish to examine each student's responses directly from the test booklet, no separate answer sheets are used for either Level I or Level II. You can score each test booklet with a hand-scoring key which is purchased separately for each level and form of the test. The raw score for each subtest is the number of correct answers.

You then place all of the raw scores on the front cover of each student's test booklet. You can convert each of these raw scores to stanines by using Table 2 on page 16 of the Level I manual. Table 2 is used for grades 2.5 to 3.5 and 3.5 to 4.5. For Level II, you use Table 2 on pages 14-15 to convert raw scores to stanine scores for grades 4.5-5.5, 5.5-6.5, 6.5-7.5, and 7.5-8.5. With this information you can complete the front cover of either the Level I or the Level II test booklet. You then record the stanine rating for each subtest by circling it on the pupil profile on the cover of each test booklet. Then you can connect the circled stanines with straight lines to obtain a graphic picture of each student's performance.

You then can complete the Class Record and Class Analysis Chart. On the Class Record which accompanies both levels, you fill in each student's name, raw scores, and stanine scores. Next you can complete the Class Analysis for a comprehensive view of class achievement. On this chart, you determine the number of pupils at each stanine level for each of the subtests. You then can indicate the median stanine for each of these subtests. This gives you an overall view of the reading performance of the students in your class. As an example, if your class earned a median stanine of 3 on the vocabulary subtest, you will need to present this skill to most of your class. On the other hand, if the median stanine of the syllabication subtest is 8, you know that you do not have to spend much additional time on this reading skill, except with a few students who are weak in this skill.

The following page presents a completed front cover of the Level II test booklet so that you can see how this is done.

Evaluation of the Stanford Diagnostic Reading Test, Levels I and II

In the 1968 edition of *Reading Tests and Reviews* only bibliographic data can be found about Levels I and II of the Stanford Diagnostic Reading Test. Therefore, only the author's evaluation of this test is given. It appears that both levels of this test are well planned and well executed. The tables of norms and the reliability and validity of the test make it comparable to the typical survey reading test. Therefore, it is a very good test if you want a structured group diagnostic reading test. On the other hand, some teachers well may prefer a less structured diagnostic reading test.

The examples and teaching suggestions which the test manual contain can be of considerable help to classroom teachers. The test manuals are one of the strong points of this test. The division of comprehension in the Level II test into literal comprehension and inferential comprehension also is very good.

FORM W

LEVEL II

Stanford Diagnostic Reading Test®

BJORN KARLSEN • RICHARD MADDEN • ERIC F. GARDNER

NAME _Sam Fisher_
    last   first   initial

BOY ☒ GIRL ☐ GRADE _6-0_ TEACHER _Jack Foster_

SCHOOL _Eisenhower_ DATE OF TESTING _1972 9 10_
                                    year month day

CITY OR TOWN _Milwaukee_ DATE OF BIRTH _1961 5 12_
                                        year month day

STATE _Wisconsin_ AGE _11 - 4_
                      years months

T E S T	TEST 1: Reading Comprehension			TEST 2	TEST 3	TEST 4	TEST 5	TEST 6
	Literal	Inferential	Total	Vocabulary	Syllabication	Sound Discrimination	Blending	Rate of Reading
RAW SCORE	22	14	36*	31	20	31	29	16
S	9	9	9	9	9	9	9	9
T	8	8	8	8	8	8	8	8
A	7	7	7	7	7	7	7	7
N	6	6	6	6	⑥	⑥	6	6
I	⑤	5	5	⑤	5	5	⑤	5
N	4	4	④	4	4	4	4	4
E	3	③	3	3	3	3	3	③
	2	2	2	2	2	2	2	2
	1	1	1	1	1	1	1	1

*Insert Reading Comprehension Total Grade Score here.

HARCOURT, BRACE & WORLD, INC.   NEW YORK

Standardized
Listening Comprehension Tests

How can you determine a student's potential for reading improvement? Although there are several ways of doing this, one useful way is by giving him a standardized listening comprehension test. A listening comprehension test can be given alone or in combination with an equivalent reading achievement test to make the comparison between reading potential and reading achievement more definitive.

This section describes the use of a listening comprehension test for assessing a student's potential for reading improvement. Next the section presents general directions for using listening comprehension tests in determining a student's potential for reading improvement. The section closes with a detailed description of a listening comprehension-reading achievement test at the intermediate-grade level and a listening comprehension test which is designed for the junior high school level. It is hoped that this section will enable you to understand the characteristics and uses of standardized listening comprehension tests in the diagnosis of reading difficulties.

Description of Standardized Listening Comprehension Tests in the Diagnosis of Reading Difficulties

Do you think that it is important for you to determine if a student is reading up to the limits of his capacity? This is a very important consideration in providing corrective or remedial reading instruction for disabled readers in the elementary and secondary schools. If a student already is achieving up to the limits of his potential, it is unrealistic to expect him to achieve better even if he is reading below grade level. On the other hand, if he can learn to read more effectively, you must provide him with a good corrective or remedial reading program which challenges him to read up to the limits of his potential.

There are a number of ways of determining reading potential. One of these ways was described in Section 4. It involves a comparison of a student's percentile rank or stanine score on an intelligence test (preferably an individual intelligence test) and his percentile rank or stanine score on a survey reading test or the reading subtests of an achievement test. There also are several formulae which can be used to determine reading expectancy. One of these formulae was formulated by Guy Bond and Miles Tinker and is as follows:

Years in school x IQ + 1.0 = Reading Expectancy.[1]

By the use of this formula, you can see that a student with an IQ of 120 who is halfway through the seventh grade has a reading expectancy of 8.8.

6.5 x 1.20 = 7.8 + 1.0 = 8.8.

This score indicates that the student should be reading at the 8.8 grade level since he is considerably brighter than normal.

There are other formulae which can be used to determine reading expectancy or potential. Most of these are described in the book *How to Increase Reading Ability* by Albert J. Harris.[2] In this book, Harris described most of these formulae in detail and presented concrete suggestions about how to use them. Therefore, you can consult this book if you want more information about using reading expectancy formulae to determine reading capacity.

However, one of the more useful means of determining reading potential is by the use of a standardized or an informal listening comprehension test. In a listening comprehension test, you read a series of words, sentences, or paragraphs aloud to a student or to a group of students. After reading the material orally, you ask the student or group of students to respond to it in some way. Since listening and reading both are receptive language arts, they possess a number of the same characteristics. Therefore, if a student reaches the fifth-grade level on a listening comprehension test, theoretically he can attain the fifth-grade reading level if he receives the proper corrective or remedial reading instruction. There are a number of different listening comprehension tests and listening comprehension-reading achievement tests whose characteristics are discussed later in this section.

You also can formulate an informal listening comprehension test which can be used to ascertain a student's reading potential. Such a test usually is given on an individual basis. Often the graded oral reading paragraphs of an Individual Reading Inventory are used for this purpose. If a student reads these graded paragraphs aloud until he reaches his frustration reading level, there usually are a few remaining more difficult paragraphs which he has not read orally. You then can read each of these paragraphs aloud to the student. After you have finished reading each paragraph aloud, you ask the student the comprehension questions which you have formulated to accompany each paragraph. You then record his answers on your copy of the paragraphs. Usually 75 percent comprehension is considered adequate. Therefore, if the student can answer 75 percent or more of the comprehension questions which accompany the sixth-grade paragraph, theoretically he often can learn to read up to this level with proper corrective or remedial reading instruction. You will find graded reading paragraphs which can be used for a listening comprehension test in Section 7 of this kit.

---

[1] Guy Bond and Miles Tinker, *Reading Difficulties: Their Diagnosis and Correction* (New York: Appleton-Century-Crofts, 1967), pp. 91-95.

[2] Albert Harris, *How to Increase Reading Ability* (New York: David McKay Company, 1970), pp. 211-216.

You also can use several other sources to evaluate listening comprehension ability. For example, several individual diagnostic reading tests also contain listening comprehension subtests. One good example is the listening comprehension subtest of the Durrell Analysis of Reading Difficulty which is described in detail in Section 5 of this kit. As you may remember, on this subtest you read a series of paragraphs aloud to the student. After reading each paragraph aloud, you ask him a number of literal comprehension questions about it. His potential level is the point at which he can answer most of the questions correctly.

The standardized listening comprehension tests currently are of two major types. Some of them are simply listening comprehension tests in which you read a series of paragraphs aloud to a group of students. After reading each paragraph aloud, you ask a number of comprehension questions to which each student responds in his test booklet.

The other type of test combines listening comprehension and reading achievement so that you can obtain a comparison between a student's scores on these two measures. Such tests also are given to a group of students. First you ascertain a student's listening comprehension by reading a group of words, sentences, or paragraphs aloud. You then ask each student to respond to some questions in his test booklet. You then can establish a potential level for each student. Subsequently, each student takes a vocabulary subtest and a paragraph comprehension subtest to determine his reading achievement. You then can compare each student's potential level with his reading achievement level to determine if he has attained his maximum potential in reading. If a student's reading achievement level is one or more years below his potential level, he apparently can achieve better in reading with an individually prescribed reading program. Thus, in some ways the listening comprehension-reading achievement test may be more useful than the true listening comprehension test.

To what kind of student should you give either a listening comprehension test or a listening comprehension-reading achievement test? Either of these tests should be given primarily to students in the elementary and secondary school whom you suspect of being disabled in reading. These are the students whom you believe to be not reading up to their potential level. By the use of either of these tests, you can determine if such students can make reading improvement with a good corrective or remedial reading program.

When should you give a standardized listening comprehension test or a listening comprehension-reading achievement test instead of an informal listening comprehension test? Usually you should give a standardized test of this type when you want to be sure that the test which you give is valid and reliable. It is time-consuming and fairly difficult to construct a valid and reliable informal listening comprehension test as you will discover in Section 7. Even when you take great pains to construct such a test carefully, you may well discover it is not always completely valid and reliable. However, you can be quite sure that a standardized listening comprehension test or a listening comprehension-reading achievement test is both valid and reliable. Therefore, you should use such a test when you want the precision which a standardized test can provide.

You also may want to use a standardized test when you want to determine norms of potential reading ability instead of a grade level as can be obtained from an informal listening comprehension test. Since a standardized listening comprehension test or a listening comprehension-reading achievement test is norm-referenced, you have a basis for arriving at a potential reading grade equivalent by using these norms. Such norms give you a more precise estimation of a student's reading potential than is possible by the use of an informal listening comprehension test.

General Directions for Using Standardized Listening Comprehension Tests and Listening Comprehension-Reading Achievement Tests

Since standardized listening comprehension tests and listening comprehension-reading achievement tests are quite structured, they are similar in many ways to standardized survey reading tests. Usually the directions should be given verbatim but clarified if necessary. You should read the words, sentences, or paragraphs included in the test in a clear tone of voice and at a moderate rate of speed so that you can be understood by all of the students. You should practice reading this material aloud in advance. Since you are reading the material aloud, the tests are not timed. Of course, in the listening comprehension-reading achievement tests, the vocabulary and paragraph comprehension subtests which the students read are very similar to those found on a survey reading test or on the reading subtests of an achievement test. Therefore, you can refer to Section 4 if you want additional general information on administering this type of test.

· When you have given either of the two types of tests, you then must score it. Such tests usually can be hand-scored using a key, or machine-scored if you use separate answer sheets. When the tests have been scored, you can consult the appropriate table of norms. You can use these norming tables to determine potential reading grade equivalents, percentile ranks, or stanines. You then can compare the student's potential reading grade equivalent, percentile rank, or stanine score with his actual reading grade equivalent, percentile rank, or stanine score as determined from the reading subtests of a listening comprehension-reading achievement test or from a standardized survey reading test.

Since listening comprehension tests and listening comprehension-reading achievement tests vary somewhat in their administration and scoring procedures, this part necessarily has been very general. Specific directions for giving and scoring one listening comprehension-reading achievement test and one listening comprehension test are found in the final part of this section. These detailed directions also should enable you to learn how to administer and score any such type of test.

Let us consider what you should do after you have given a listening comprehension test or a listening comprehension-reading achievement test. If you have found a difference of a year or more between a student's potential reading level and his actual reading achievement level, he can be said to be disabled in reading. You then can be quite sure that the major cause of his reading disability is not inferior intellectual ability or language aptitude.

What then are the probable causes of such a student's reading disability? Since reading is a very complex process, reading disability often results from several causes operating in combination. Of course a student's reading disability can be caused by such factors as visual difficulties, minimal brain dysfunction, incompletely developed lateral dominance, chronic illnesses, or emotional maladjustment. However, one important cause of many cases of reading disability is the teacher's inability to individualize reading instruction to the point which will allow the student to achieve success in reading.

However, you can discover from a listening comprehension test or a listening comprehension-reading achievement test that a student has the potential for reading improvement no matter what the cause of his reading disability. Therefore, you can determine from such a test that the student often will make good reading improvement if you plan and execute a corrective reading program for him which is on his present level and will help him overcome his diagnosed reading difficulties. Thus, in addition to the listening comprehension test or the listening comprehension-reading achievement test, you should do additional testing to discover these exact reading difficulties. This additional testing can be done with a standardized individual or group diagnostic reading test such as those which were described in Section 5. It can also be done using an Individual Reading Inventory as is illustrated in Section 7 or inventories in the various word recognition techniques such as are described in Section 8.

Thus you can see that the listening comprehension test or the listening comprehension-reading achievement test can only indicate whether the student has the potential to profit from a good program of corrective or remedial reading instruction. You then must use some other means of testing to determine exactly what reading skills should be stressed in the program. Of course you also should consider the importance of a good teacher-student relationship in such a program. Even when the correct reading skills are presented, reading improvement may not take place unless the program operates in a good emotional environment.

Examples of Listening Comprehension and Listening Comprehension-Reading Achievement Tests

The listening comprehension and the listening comprehension-reading achievement tests selected for pages 114-121 are good examples of such tests which are currently in print.

DURRELL LISTENING-READING SERIES–INTERMEDIATE LEVEL

by Donald D. Durrell and Mary B. Brassard
Harcourt Brace Jovanovich, Inc.
757 Third Avenue
New York 10017

Published in 1969

Description of the Test

The Intermediate Level of the Durrell Listening-Reading Series is a listening comprehension-reading achievement test. It is the second test in a series of three tests called the Durrell Listening-Reading Series. The three tests are designed for use in the primary grades, the intermediate grades, and the junior high school. All of the levels of this series are designed to compare a student's listening potential and reading ability so that his reading disability can be identified with specificity. The Intermediate Level Battery is designed for grades 3.5-6. Form DE provides in one test booklet a listening test and a reading test which are designed to balance each other. Retesting of a student can be done later by the use of Form EF.

The Listening Test of this battery contains the two subtests of vocabulary listening and paragraph listening. The vocabulary listening subtest contains 96 items. This subtest is divided into eight units. Each of the units contains four columns which are headed by pictures. The teacher then reads some words, and the student classifies each word by filling in the space under the heading which best fits the word. There are 64 items in the paragraph listening subtest. The teacher then reads stories aloud which tell about people, places, or things that are alike in a number of ways but different in some other ways. After the teacher reads each story aloud, he then reads some statements about it. The student determines where each statement belongs by filling in a blank space under the right heading. As in the case of the vocabulary listening subtest, the paragraph listening subtest is composed of eight units, each one of which contains four columns.

The Reading Test also consists of two subtests—vocabulary reading and paragraph reading. The vocabulary reading subtest is composed of 96 items. It is divided into eight units, each of which contains four columns with a picture at the heading of each column. The student is to fill in the blank space in the column which contains a synonym of the vocabulary word. The paragraph reading subtest contains 64 items. It is composed of eight units, each of which contains four columns. Each unit has a passage for the student to read silently. Following each passage there are some statements which each student is to classify by filling in the answer space in one of the four columns. The entire test battery can be given to a group of students as large as the teacher can supervise.

Thus you see that the two subtests in the Listening Test correspond exactly to the two subtests in the Reading Test. This has been done so that the teacher can make a direct comparison between each student's listening comprehension ability and reading achievement.

The two vocabulary subtests take about 40 minutes to complete, while the two paragraph subtests take about 45 minutes to complete. Thus, the entire test requires about 85 minutes. However, since the teacher's rate of oral reading cannot be timed exactly, these are approximations of the time required. The test can be purchased so that it can either be hand-scored or machine-scored. The hand-scoring should be done by the use of a key folder which needs to be purchased separately.

The manual contains considerable information on validity. The comparison of listening comprehension to reading achievement is said to be very valuable in understanding the degree of a student's reading disability. Validity was established by the selection of words for the vocabulary tests and by the manner in which the passages were selected for the paragraph subtests. Validity also was established by preliminary item analyses and by the actual item analysis program.

Table 10 on page 19 of the manual gives reliability coefficients for all of the subtests in grades three, four, five, and six. The vocabulary listening subtest of the Listening Test has reliability coefficients which range between .89 and .92. The paragraph listening subtest of the Listening Test contains correlations ranging from .85 to .89. The total Listening Test has reliability coefficients which range from .92 to .95. The vocabulary reading subtest of the Reading Test contains realiability coefficients which range from .90 to .95. The paragraph reading subtest on the Reading Test has reliability coefficients which range from .87 to .91. The total Reading Test has correlations which range from .94 to .96.

The manual also contains a number of other tables. Intercorrelations were computed between part and total scores of the Listening and Reading Tests. The manual contains information on how this test was standardized. It was standardized in April, 1968 using students from 164 schools in 29 school systems. The norms then were derived from the standardization program. According to the manual, a comparison of a student's listening comprehension ability and reading achievement only can be made when the same table of grade equivalents is used for both measures. Table 1 on page 16 of the manual enables a comparison to be made between a student's potential reading grade equivalent and actual reading grade equivalent. Thus this table enables you to determine a student's probable potential for reading improvement.

The Appendix of the manual contains several other tables which can be used as supplementary norms. You can determine reading age equivalents on both the Listening and Reading Tests using Table A. You can use the tables on pages 28-31 to determine the percentile ranks and stanine scores for all of the raw scores on both the Listening Test and Reading Test.

The manual presents some suggestions for helping students who are disabled in reading. Although the suggestions presented are useful, they need to be supplemented by those found in professional books such as are listed in Appendix III.

Directions for Giving the Test

The manual of the test contains many of the same directions for administering the test as are found in the manual of any standardized test. You should give the test in a quiet room and should read the directions verbatim, although you can clarify them. You should read each passage on the Listening Test clearly and carefully but not so slowly that you lose the interest of the students. You should practice reading the material on the Listening Test orally before reading it to a group of students. Each student should have several soft lead pencils and an eraser.

You should give each vocabulary subtest and each paragraph subtest at a different sitting. However, you can give both parts of the Listening Test on the same day and both parts of the Reading Test on a subsequent day. The two vocabulary subtests take about 40 minutes to give, while the two paragraph subtests take about 45 minutes to administer. Thus, the total test requires about 85 minutes to give, in addition to the time required for completing the front cover of the test booklet. However, since the time limits are generous, this is not really a timed test.

Directions for Scoring the Test

When the students have completed the test, it must be scored. You can hand-score that edition of the test by using a six-page strip key folder which you must purchase separately. Of course, the separate answer sheets can be machine-scored at the central administration office of your school district.

When you have scored the test, you obtain a total score for each subtest. You then write the total scores on the last page of each subtest and in the score box on the front cover of each test booklet. You then complete the remainder of the score box by checking the table on page 16 of the manual. As was explained earlier, each listening raw score can be converted to a potential reading grade equivalent, while each reading raw score can be converted to an actual reading grade equivalent. If you wish to determine the percentile ranks and stanine scores of any of the raw scores on either the Listening Test or the Reading Test, you can consult the tables on pages 28-31 of the manual.

The front cover of the test booklet of the Intermediate Level of the Durrell Listening-Reading Series is reprinted on page 118 of this kit so that you can see how this test is scored.

Evaluation of the Durrell Listening-Reading Series—Intermediate Level

Only the author's evaluation of this test is included in this section. The use of parallel listening and reading tests indeed is very interesting. Since the Listening Test and Reading Test are parallel in construction and in number of items, the teacher can gain a measure of a student's reading disability by comparing the subtest scores and total scores on these two tests for one student or a group of students.

The format of the test and the test manual is unique and attractive. However, the test manual contains some rather irrelevant information under the section on validity. The table for comparing potential reading grade equivalents and actual reading grade equivalents is very useful, but one wonders why the tables of percentile ranks and stanine scores are placed in the Appendix instead of in the test manual itself. However, on the whole this is a very good test to use if you want to administer a listening comprehension-reading achievement test on the intermediate-grade level.

Durrell Listening - Reading Series*

DONALD D. DURRELL · MARY B. BRASSARD

INTERMEDIATE LEVEL   Form DE

COMBINED LISTENING AND READING TESTS – Hand-Scorable Edition

PUPIL IDENTIFICATION BOX

NAME _Baxter Betty Lou_
last   first   initial

SCHOOL _Fairhaven_

CITY _Whiteriver_ STATE _Illinois_

GRADE _5-1_ TEACHER _Jack Jensen_

DATE OF BIRTH _63_ _9_ _2_ BOY ☐ GIRL ☒ AGE _10_ _1_
yr. mo. day   yrs. mos.

SCORE BOX

Listening Test						Reading Test					
Vocabulary		Paragraphs		Total		Vocabulary		Paragraphs		Total	
1	2	3	4	5	6	7	8	9	10	11	12
Number Right	Potential Reading Grade Equiv.	Number Right	Potential Reading Grade Equiv.	Number Right	Potential Reading Grade Equiv.	Number Right	Actual Reading Grade Equiv.	Number Right	Actual Reading Grade Equiv.	Number Right	Actual Reading Grade Equiv.
53	5.3	32	4.9	85	5.1	36	3.6	22	3.3	58	3.4

Date of Testing _10/2/73_

Grade Placement _5 - 1_
yr.   mo.

Date of Testing _10/2/73_

HARCOURT, BRACE & WORLD, INC.   **NEW YORK**

---

*Reproduced from the Durrell Listening - Reading Series, copyright © 1968-1970 by Harcourt Brace Jovanovich, Inc. Reproduced by special permission of the publisher.

SEQUENTIAL TESTS OF EDUCATIONAL PROGRESS: LISTENING 3B

by The Cooperative Test Division
Educational Testing Service
Princeton, New Jersey 08540

Published in 1957

Description of the Test

The Sequential Tests of Educational Progress (STEP) evaluate a number of skills which are stressed in American elementary and secondary schools. Different tests are available in a number of different forms for the following content areas: reading, writing, listening, social studies, science, and mathematics. Of course, only the listening test is considered in this section of the kit.

The listening comprehension test is available in a number of different forms for different grade levels. Tests 1A and 1B are for college freshmen and sophomores. Tests 2A and 2B are for students in the tenth and eleventh grades. Tests 3A and 3B are for students in grades seven, eight, and nine. Tests 4A and 4B are for students in grades four, five, and six. Thus you can see that there are two forms of each listening comprehension test which is designed for a specific grade level. Each separate form of each listening comprehension test contains its own test manual. By random selection, Form 3B which can be used in grades seven, eight, and nine is analyzed for this kit. However, the analysis can apply quite well to all of the other levels and forms of the listening comprehension test.

Form 3B contains a number of different listening comprehension skills which are evaluated. This test evaluates literal comprehension. Included in literal comprehension are such subskills as finding the main idea, finding significant details, determining the sequence of ideas, and understanding denotative meanings. The test also evaluates interpretive comprehension. Interpretation includes such subskills as the implication of ideas and details, the interrelationships among ideas, and connotative meanings. The test also measures a student's evaluation and application skills. These contain the subskills of judging validity of ideas, judging sufficiency of details, criticizing organization, judging mood and effect, and recognizing intent. The material which the teacher reads aloud is of several different types. These materials were used in the formulation of the paragraphs for this test: directions, explanations, expositions, narrations, arguments, persuasions, and aesthetic materials.

After the teacher reads each selection aloud, he presents four suggested answers for each question or incomplete statement. The teacher reads each question only once, and the questions are not found in the student's test booklet. Only the suggested answers are printed in the test booklet so that the student can examine all of the options while choosing his answers. The student cannot answer directly in the test booklet. He must mark his answers on a separate answer sheet whether these answer sheets are later hand-scored or machine-scored.

Since the selections are read aloud by the teacher, this is not a timed test. Usually it takes about 90 minutes to give the entire test. Therefore, the test can be given in one 90-minute session or in two sessions of 45 minutes each. If possible, it usually is better to give the entire test at one sitting with a break between the tests.

There is a technical report which accompanies all of the STEP tests. This report contains much information on the rationale of the test, the construction and pretesting of questions, the scoring system, and the norming procedures. According to this report, content validity was established for the listening comprehension test by having well-qualified people construct and review the test. The reliability of the test was computed by using the Kuder-Richardson Formula 20. The reliability of the test was computed only for Form A. The reliabilities range from .88 to .93.

After you score the test, the manual indicates what procedures you are to follow next. You need to first convert the raw scores to a converted score. Next you convert these converted scores into a percentile band. The Teacher's Guide which accompanies all of the STEP tests presents many ways of using the test results. This guide recommends that an item-by-item analysis of the test will help your students improve their listening comprehension skills.

Directions for Giving the Test

You should first study the directions for administering and scoring Listening 3B Test. You need to have enough copies of the test booklet and separate answer sheets for all of the students who are to take the test. The students should use regular pencils if the answer sheets are to be hand-scored and special electrographic pencils if the tests are to be machine-scored. You also need to have a watch or a clock with a second hand.

You should practice reading all of the passage aloud before you actually give the test. Your rate of reading should be about that of the suggested reading time. You should pause for about 5 seconds while the students answer easy memory questions. However, you should pause about 60 seconds while the students answer questions requiring careful interpretation. All of the directions for the test, the script, the questions, and the choices which you read aloud are printed in black. All of the other directions for giving the test are printed in brown.

The students should write their name, age, class, school, and date of testing on the separate answer sheet. Then you can give the entire test in one sitting of 90 minutes or in two sittings of 45 minutes each. If possible, the test should be given in the single sitting. Students who have a severe hearing loss should not be given this test.

Directions for Scoring the Test

When the students have completed the test, it must be scored. The answer sheets can be scored by hand or by machine. If you score them by hand, you should first scan the answer sheets for items with more than one marked answer.

Of course, these items are not counted as correct. You then lay the scoring stencil on the first answer sheet so that the four dots at the bottom of the answer sheet match the hole at the bottom of the stencil. You count all of the answer marks which show through the hole in the stencil except those marked as multiple answers. You then record the raw score or total number correct on the answer sheet. If the answer sheets are machine scored, this part is done for you.

You then must change the raw scores to converted scores. On the back of the scoring stencil is a table for changing raw scores to converted scores. You then record the converted scores under the raw scores on the answer sheets. After you have obtained the converted scores, you then use the Manual for Interpreting Listening Scores. This manual explains percentile bands and norms tables. The STEP Test uses percentile bands because the test writers are convinced that a student's score on any test would vary if he took the parallel form of the same test on different days. You use the converted scores to locate the correct percentile bands.

Evaluation of the Sequential Tests of Educational Progress: Listening 3B

Emmett Betts, formerly of the University of Miami, stated that a listening comprehension test allows the teacher to note discrepancies between listening achievement and reading achievement as measured by the reading test of the STEP Series. According to Betts, the listening comprehension test may reveal causes of low achievement in reading.[3]

The author of this kit found this listening comprehension test to be well constructed. The directions for administering the test are clear. However, she found the interpretation of the test to be rather difficult, especially if a teacher wishes to use only this test in the series. The material is spread out in too many sources to make it practical. It is quite difficult to determine just where to find the different required material. The percentile band may be too wide to provide the specificity which teachers would like to have. It also is not clear why reliability coefficients only were computed for Form A of all of the listening comprehension tests. On the whole, the listening test is good since it evaluates many of the component skills of listening. However, the format for scoring the test could well be improved.

---

[3] Oscar Krisen Buros, ed., *Reading Tests and Reviews* (Highland Park, N.J.: The Gryphon Press, 1968), p. 6:810.

The Individual
Reading Inventory

Why do you think many reading specialists consider the Individual Reading Inventory to be one of the more useful of the diagnostic techniques in reading? It is mainly because this diagnostic technique offers a simple and quite accurate way of determining a student's oral reading errors and his independent, instructional, and frustration reading levels. When the graded oral reading paragraphs of an Individual Reading Inventory are used along with the inventories in the word recognition techniques which are illustrated in Section 8, a comprehensive way of determining specific reading difficulties and reading levels is provided.

This section is designed to help you understand the uses and formulation of an Individual Reading Inventory at both the elementary- and secondary-school levels. The section first describes the characteristics of an Individual Reading Inventory. Next it presents directions for administering such an inventory. The section then includes sample work lists and oral reading paragraphs for both the elementary and secondary reading levels. These word lists and graded oral reading paragraphs can be duplicated in their present form or modified in the light of your own specific needs. It is hoped that this section will enable you to use an Individual Reading Inventory effectively.

Description of an Individual Reading Inventory for the Diagnosis of Reading Difficulties

As stated above, many reading specialists feel that an Individual Reading Inventory is perhaps the most useful diagnostic tool that can be employed in determining a student's exact reading difficulties and reading levels. It can be used by an elementary classroom teacher with mildly and moderately disabled readers and by an elementary reading specialist with moderately and severely disabled readers. It also can be used by a secondary-school content teacher with mildly or moderately disabled readers and by a secondary-school remedial reading teacher with moderately and severely disabled readers. Thus, you can see that virtually every elementary and secondary school teacher should understand how to use and formulate this device.

The Individual Reading Inventory is an informal reading test. It varies somewhat in format according to different reading specialists. The Individual Reading Inventory which is outlined here is just one variation of this diagnostic technique. The following is one variation of an Individual Reading Inventory which can be given by an elementary classroom teacher, elementary reading specialist, or secondary-school reading specialist:

- Establishing rapport with the student
- Dictating a language-experience story
- Giving the Dolch Basic Sight Word Test, the Kucera-Francis Corpus, or Fry's Instant Words
- Administering the graded oral reading paragraphs
- Administering inventories in phonetic analysis, structural analysis, context clue usage, or dictionary usage

When a secondary-school content teacher gives an Individual Reading Inventory, it can consist of the following parts:

- Establishing rapport with the student
- Giving a sight word test composed of the specialized vocabulary terms from the content area
- Administering the graded oral reading paragraphs which were formulated from a series of content textbooks

You may now be wondering when you should give an Individual Reading Inventory to a student. Of course, this mainly depends upon your professional role. If you are an elementary classroom teacher, you may want to give such an inventory to a student during the first few months of the school year. Such an inventory usually would be given to a student whom you have decided is disabled in reading by the use of another diagnostic technique. Such a technique most often might be teacher observation using a structured checklist or a survey reading test. Although it would be most desirable if you could give an Individual Reading Inventory to each of your students near the beginning of the school year to determine his reading difficulties and reading levels, it is recognized that this is virtually impossible unless you have the help of a paraprofessional.

If you are an elementary- or secondary-school reading specialist, you can give an Individual Reading Inventory to each student near the beginning of a remedial reading program. An Individual Reading Inventory sometimes is given at the first meeting with a disabled reader after the teacher has established rapport with him. At other times, an Individual Reading Inventory is given later in the remedial reading program after the teacher has used a structured checklist, a survey reading test, an oral reading test, a diagnostic reading test, or a listening comprehension test. According to some reading specialists, however, a student should not be given a great number of diagnostic instruments at the beginning of a remedial reading program. To do so can overwhelm the student and contribute significantly to his dislike of reading activities. Such reading specialists believe that diagnosis and remediation always should be a continuous, interwoven process, with the initial diagnosis leading to remediation, which in turn then leads to additional diagnosis and remediation. In this case, it is advisable to give an Individual Reading Inventory shortly after the initial teacher observation and a standardized survey reading test.

A secondary school content teacher usually gives a content-oriented Individual Reading Inventory only to the moderately and severely disabled readers in his content classes. He gives such an inventory so that he can determine the level of content textbooks and supplementary reading material he should provide for such disabled readers. Such disabled readers should use textbooks which are on the instructional reading level and should use supplementary reading materials which are on the independent reading level. Sometimes a secondary-school content teacher can enlist the help of the secondary-school reading specialist in constructing and giving content-oriented Individual Reading Inventories to some of the disabled readers who are attending their content classes.

Perhaps it is useful at this point to describe in detail the characteristics of the various parts of an Individual Reading Inventory which can be used by an elementary classroom teacher, elementary reading specialist, or secondary-school reading specialist. The next portion of this section is devoted to this task.

Establishing Rapport with the Student

Any teacher who gives an Individual Reading Inventory should establish a good relationship with the student before giving him this diagnostic device. Many disabled readers have been tested many times in the past and therefore resent any type of reading test even before they begin to take it. Since this is the case, such a student may be fairly hostile and not put forth his best effort. If you take the time to help him understand the purpose of the inventory, it undoubtedly will be much more successful.

You can tell the student that he is going to take an informal reading test so that you can learn the types of material which he can read with success. You also can tell him that the inventory will help you learn in which areas of reading he is competent and in which areas of reading he needs additional help. Since most disabled readers have a negative self-concept, you should emphasize their reading strengths while correcting their reading weaknesses. You then can informally ask him questions such as these: What do you like to do after school and on Saturdays? What kind of television programs do you like to watch the best? What do you like best about reading? What is the hardest part of reading for you? Why do you think that you have trouble with reading? Why do you think that it is important for you to learn to read better? How do you think I can help you best with your reading? What subject do you like best in school? What did you enjoy doing last summer?

Dictating a Language-Experience Story

If you are giving an Individual Reading Inventory to a disabled reader in the elementary or secondary school, you may want to use a language-experience story next. A language-experience story is part of the language-experience approach to reading. This approach sometimes is very useful with moderately or severely disabled readers since such students often are able to read about their own experiences in their own language patterns much more effectively than they can read basal reader stories or textbooks. If you want to learn more about the language-experience approach, you can consult either *Identifying and Correcting Reading Difficulties in Children*[1] or *Diagnosis and Correction of Reading Difficulties in Secondary School Students.*[2]

In using the language-experience approach, you ask the student to tell you about an experience which he has had recently. Such an experience story can describe what he does on Saturday or a trip which he has taken recently. You then transcribe the story verbatim as the student dictates it to you. Later you type the story on a sheet of paper so that the student can read it aloud the next time he comes for reading help. You then can compare his ability to read his own experiences in his own language patterns with his ability to read commercially available material. If he does seem to be able to read the dictated story more effectively, you may want to emphasize this approach, especially if he is reading at the non-reader or the primary-grade reading level. Thus this approach can be used with most students in the primary grades, with moderately or severely disabled readers in the intermediate grades, or with severely disabled readers in the secondary school.

Giving a Sight Word Test

The next part of an Individual Reading Inventory can be the giving of a basic sight word test. This is a test which determines the number of words a student can recognize by sight from any one of several sight word lists. It is obvious that a student must have a good stock of sight words if he is to be an effective reader. Three of the most commonly used sight word tests are the Dolch Basic Sight Word Test, the Kucera-Francis Corpus, and Fry's Instant Words. All three of these sight word tests are discussed in detail in Section 8, and you are given directions on how to give such a test in this section. Section 8 also contains the Kucera-Francis Corpus so that you can duplicate it and administer it if you wish to do so.

Administering the Graded Oral Reading Paragraphs

The graded oral reading paragraphs can be given as the next part of an Individual Reading Inventory. The graded oral reading paragraphs in an Individual Reading Inventory are similar to those on an oral reading test as was described in Section 3 or an individual diagnostic reading test as was described in Section 5. This part of the inventory usually begins with a series of word lists which are formulated from the same basal readers as are used to formulate the graded oral reading paragraphs. From these word lists, you determine an approximate independent reading level so that you will

---

[1]Wilma H. Miller, *Identifying and Correcting Reading Difficulties in Children* (New York: The Center for Applied Research in Education, 1971), pp. 176-179.

[2]Wilma H. Miller, *Diagnosis and Correction of Reading Difficulties in Secondary School Students.* (New York: The Center for Applied Research in Education, 1973), pp. 190-192.

know what paragraphs the student should begin reading orally. Directions for constructing such word lists are given in the next part of this section, and sample word lists at various grade levels are found in the last part of this section.

The graded oral reading paragraphs are a series of passages which begin at the primer level and can continue through the twelfth-grade level. It is obvious that all students do not read all of the paragraphs. A student usually begins reading a paragraph aloud which is about two grade levels or more below his estimated independent reading level. You can make this estimation from the word lists which were mentioned earlier. The next part of this section gives you detailed directions for constructing graded oral reading paragraphs, and the last part of this section contains sample graded oral reading paragraphs from the primer level through the twelfth-grade level which you can duplicate and use if you wish to do so.

Administering Inventories in the Word Recognition Techniques

The last part of an Individual Reading Inventory can be giving informal inventories in the word recognition techniques of phonetic analysis, structural analysis, context clue usage, and dictionary usage. Section 8 of this kit gives you directions for formulating inventories in each of these word recognition techniques. This section also contains samples of each of these inventories which you can duplicate and use in their present form if they seem applicable for the students with whom you are working.

It may be useful at this point to explain briefly an Individual Reading Inventory which can be given by a secondary-school content teacher. However, more detail on this type of inventory is found in Section 9.

Establishing Rapport with the Student

The secondary-school content teacher may need to establish rapport with the student to whom he is going to give an Individual Reading Inventory only if it is given early in the school year. If this inventory is given later in the school year, the content teacher undoubtedly already has good rapport with the student. In either case, the content teacher can explain the purpose of the inventory. He can tell the student that this informal reading test will determine the kind of material the student can read with ease in that content area.

The content teacher can determine the student's attitudes toward the content area by asking questions such as the following:

- Do you think that reading about _____ (history) is easy or hard?
- Why do you think that it is hard for you?
- What kind of books do you like to read about best in _____ (history) classes?
- How do you think that reading _____ (history) textbooks could be made easier for you?
- Do you usually like _____ (history) classes?
- Why or why not?
- If you had a choice, what type of _____ (history) materials would you like to read?

Giving a Sight Word Test

The secondary-school content teacher can give a sight word test composed of a sample of the specialized vocabulary terms which are found in the content textbook used in the formulation of the graded oral reading paragraphs. Section 9 presents specific directions for formulating such a sight word test.

Administering the Graded Oral Reading Paragraphs

As the last part of a content-oriented Individual Reading Inventory, the content teacher can formulate a series of passages from a graded series of content textbooks. The content teacher can begin formulating these passages from textbooks which are two or more years below the estimated instructional reading level of the students who are to use them. Each paragraph should be accurate in content in terms of the material presented in that textbook. To establish the exact reading level of each of these content textbooks, it may be of value for the teacher to use a readability formula. The Dale-Chall Readability Formula or the Fry Readability Formula which are described in the book entitled *Teaching Reading in the Secondary School*[3] can be used for this purpose. A part of Section 9 gives detailed directions for formulating the graded oral reading paragraphs for this type of inventory.

Directions for Constructing, Administering, and Evaluating the Word Lists and Graded Oral Reading Paragraphs of an Individual Reading Inventory

The following provides detailed directions for constructing, administering, and evaluating the word lists and graded oral reading paragraphs from an ordinary Individual Reading Inventory or a content-oriented Individual Reading Inventory. To construct the word lists and graded oral reading paragraphs of a typical Individual Reading Inventory, you first must select the basal reader series or the English series which you wish to use. The elementary classroom teacher often utilizes the same basal reader series as is used in developmental reading instruction in the elementary school. The elementary school reading specialist can utilize the basal reader series which will be used as part of the remedial reading instruction. The secondary-school reading specialist can use parts of a basal reader series and graded English textbooks.

To formulate the graded word lists of a typical Individual Reading Inventory, you can turn to the vocabulary lists which are found at the end of each book. Then you make a random selection from each vocabulary list by choosing every *nth* word (fifth word, eighth word, or tenth word). Each graded word list is then composed from these words. Each word list should have at least 25 words. After choosing the words for each list, you can type them on a stencil or ditto which the student can read from. Each student should begin reading a paragraph which is at least two grade levels below his suspected instructional reading level. He continues pronouncing the words on each

---

[3]Wilma H. Miller, *Teaching Reading in the Secondary School* (Springfield, Ill.: Charles C Thomas Publishers, 1974).

word list until he reaches his frustration reading level—the point at which he has less than 90 percent accuracy in word recognition. You can use the results of the word lists to better enable you to determine which of the graded oral reading paragraphs the student should read first, and to confirm his reading grade levels as determined from the graded oral reading paragraphs.

You then can construct each of the graded oral reading paragraphs from the selected basal reader series or the English textbooks. For each paragraph, you should attempt to use only the vocabulary which is found in that book and in all the preceding books in that series. If possible, you should choose material near the middle of each reader as the basis of each paragraph since the vocabulary found near the middle of each reader usually is the most representative of that grade level. You often formulate longer paragraphs at the upper grade levels. You should try to make each paragraph as interesting as possible, although this is rather difficult at the beginning reader levels due to the limited vocabulary. You formulate several literal comprehension questions, several interpretive questions, and one question evaluating the vocabulary for each paragraph.

Then you can type each of the paragraphs on a sheet of paper so that the student can read from this copy. If possible, you should use a primary typewriter for typing the paragraphs on the primary-grade reading level. You then glue or paste each paragraph on a piece of oaktag or cardboard. Since the student's copies of the graded oral reading paragraphs then are quite durable, they can be used many times. Obviously, the student's copy of each paragraph does not contain the comprehension questions or the provision for determining the different reading levels. Figure 7-1 shows you the graded oral reading paragraphs for the third grade, second semester, typed and glued on a sheet of oaktag. (See next page.)

You also should type each of the graded oral reading paragraphs on a stencil or ditto and then duplicate it so that you can mark each student's oral reading errors on a separate copy. However, you can also use an acetate overlay. In this case, you place the overlay over a typed or duplicated copy of each oral reading paragraph and then mark each student's oral reading errors on the overlay with a marking pen. If you use an acetate overlay, you must keep a record of each student's oral reading errors and reading levels in another way.

There are sample graded oral reading paragraphs from the primer level through the twelfth-grade level in the next part of this section. Of course, you can duplicate and use them in their present form. You also can purchase several other books which contain other sample graded oral reading paragraphs. These sources are as follows: *Classroom Reading Inventory, Second Edition,*[4] *Graded Selections for Informal Reading Diagnosis: Grades One Through Three,*[5] and *Graded Selections for Informal Reading Diagnosis: Grades Four Through Six.*[6]

---

[4]Nicholas J. Silvaroli, *Classroom Reading Inventory, Second Edition* (Dubuque, Iowa: William C. Brown, Publishers, 1973).

[5]Nila Banton Smith, *Graded Selections for Informal Reading Diagnosis: Grades One Through Three* (New York: New York University Press, 1959).

[6]Nila Banton Smith, *Graded Selections for Informal Reading Diagnosis: Grades Four Through Six* (New York: New York University Press, 1963).

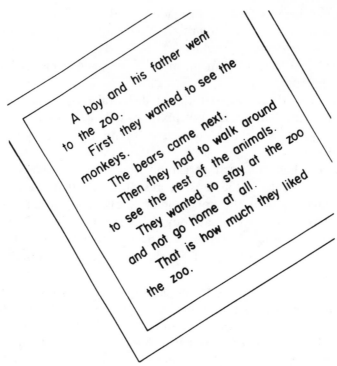

Figure 7-1

When you are ready to administer the graded oral reading paragraphs which you have selected or formulated, you request the student to begin reading a paragraph aloud, which is at least two grade levels below his estimated instructional reading grade level. You may remember how this paragraph corresponds to the basal paragraph in an oral reading test as was described in Section 2. The estimated grade level can be determined by teacher observation or the student's instructional level on the word lists which were administered earlier. It is important to have the student begin reading at a low enough level so that he will experience success with the paragraphs from the beginning and not become discouraged.

As a student reads each of the paragraphs aloud to you, you mark his oral reading errors on your copy of the paragraphs. These oral reading errors often are marked in terms of substitutions, mispronunciations, omissions, insertions, repetitions, and hesitations. You can use any marking system that you want as long as it is consistent and you are proficient in it. You can develop your own marking system or use a system such as is employed in the Gray Oral Reading Tests or the Gilmore Oral Reading Test. You also can use the following marking system for recording oral reading errors:

Omissions   Circle the entire word or letter sound (rocky)

Insertions   Insert with a caret very

Underline and write in all mispronunciations top tap

Draw a line through a substitution and write it in ~~hundreds~~ thousands

Use a wavy line to indicate a repetition **shore**

Put a check mark above a hesitation of more than 5 seconds[7] **danger**

When you first try to mark a student's oral reading errors, you undoubtedly may find this very difficult to do. Since you focus at first on the marking system, you may fall behind in the marking of oral reading errors as the student reads aloud. Therefore, it may be very beneficial for you to tape-record a student's reading of the graded oral reading paragraphs at first. You then can mark each student's errors when you later play back the tape recording. You may have to replay some of the paragraphs several times to locate all of the reading errors. Even after you are proficient in the marking system, you may want to tape-record a student's reading of the graded oral reading paragraphs. A student usually is more self-conscious about his oral reading if he sees you marking all of his errors as he reads aloud.

When should a student stop reading the paragraphs orally? You usually have him stop when he reaches his frustration reading level. The frustration reading level is similar to the ceiling level on the oral reading tests which was described in Section 2. It is the point at which the student makes many oral reading errors, has poor comprehension, appears tense and insecure, and does not want to read further.

However, when a student has reached the frustration reading level, you can use the remaining paragraphs to establish his potential or capacity level. To do this, you read each of the remaining paragraphs aloud to him and ask him the comprehension questions which accompany each paragraph. The level at which the student can answer about 75 percent of the comprehension questions correctly is called the *potential* or *capacity* level. This level corresponds to the potential reading grade level which can be determined from a listening comprehension test or a listening comprehension-reading achievement test, as was described in Section 6. It is the level to which the student may be able to learn to read with individually prescribed corrective or remedial reading instruction. In addition, you can have a student read the paragraphs silently and later orally a second time. You then notice if he makes improvement with the rereading.

One of the major purposes of using the graded oral reading paragraphs in an Individual Reading Inventory is to determine a student's reading levels. The establishment of the various reading levels is the major part of the evaluation of the graded oral reading paragraphs. There are several classification schemes which can be used to determine the reading levels. Undoubtedly the most well-known classification scheme was developed by Emmett Betts, formerly of the University of Miami.[8] Betts stated that the *independent reading level* is the point at which a student can recognize words with 99 percent accuracy and at which he has 95 percent or better comprehension. The independent reading level also can be called the basal or free reading level. A student should do recreational reading from material which interests him on the independent reading level. Betts described the *instructional reading level* as the point at which a student can identify words with 90 percent accuracy and at which he has 75 percent or better comprehension. Each student should receive reading instruction in the develop-

---

[7]See Ruth Strang, *Diagnostic Teaching of Reading* (New York: McGraw-Hill Book Company, 1969), p. 68.

[8]Emmett A. Betts, *Foundations of Reading Instruction* (New York: American Book Company, 1957).

mental, corrective, or remedial reading program at the instructional reading level. Betts stated that the *frustration reading level* is the point at which a student is less than 90 percent accurate in word recognition and is less than 50 percent accurate in comprehension. Betts also described the *potential* or *capacity* reading level as the point at which a student can answer comprehension questions with 75 percent or better accuracy from material which has been read aloud to him. This level was described earlier in this section.

George Spache, formerly of the University of Florida, recently stated that Betts' criteria for determining reading levels are too difficult for the typical student. Spache then suggested his own criteria for determining the various reading levels. According to Spache, the instructional reading level should require 75 percent accuracy in word recognition in first grade and this should increase gradually to about 94 percent accuracy in word recognition in eighth grade. He stated that the average standard should reach about 90 percent to 93 percent accuracy in word recognition by the end of third grade. Spache further stated that a student should have a 60 percent comprehension ability at the instructional reading level.[9]

Nila Banton Smith of the University of Southern California offered other criteria for determining the various reading levels. According to Smith, the instructional reading level ranges from 80 percent to 95 percent accuracy in word recognition. Smith suggested a standard of 80 percent to 90 percent accuracy in literal comprehension at the instructional reading level and 70 percent to 75 percent accuracy in interpretive comprehension at the instructional reading level.[10]

You can consider these three different types of criteria in the light of the needs of your own students. You then can choose to use the set of criteria which seems to meet your own needs the best. The word lists and graded oral reading paragraphs which are included in the next part of this section and in Section 9 use the criteria for determining reading levels of Betts. This set of criteria was chosen since it is the more widely known.

You will find detailed directions for constructing, administering, and evaluating the sight word tests and graded oral reading paragraphs of a content-oriented Individual Reading Inventory in Section 9 of this kit. You also will find sample word lists and graded oral reading paragraphs which can be used in a content-oriented Individual Reading Inventory in this section.

Sample Word Lists and Graded Oral Reading Paragraphs at the Elementary and Secondary School Levels

The last part of this section includes sample word lists and graded oral reading paragraphs which were formulated from several series of basal readers and graded English literature textbooks at the secondary level. You can duplicate and use any of these word lists and graded oral reading paragraphs, on pages 134-161, which are

---

[9]George D. Spache and Evelyn B. Spache, *Reading in the Elementary School* (Boston: Allyn and Bacon, 1973), pp. 374-377.

[10]Nila Banton Smith, *Graded Selections for Informal Reading Diagnosis,* 1959 and 1963.

appropriate for the needs of your students. You also can modify any of them that you wish. As was stated earlier, the criteria of Emmett Betts are used in this kit for determining a student's independent, instructional, and frustration reading levels in word recognition ability and comprehension ability. Instead of these criteria, you can use your own criteria or those of George D. Spache or Nila Banton Smith.

WORD RECOGNITION*

Name _____ Grade _____ Teacher _____ Date _____

Primer	First Reader	Second Reader—First Semester
1. who	blankets	golden
2. head	would	stories
3. what	porcupine	really
4. something	bears	afraid
5. how	laughed	told
6. asked	zebra	hope
7. eat	ostrich	monkey
8. boy	sat	front
9. hear	white	ending
10. house	I'll	trouble
11. does	seven	cream
12. another	before	lamb
13. girl	say	men
14. birthday	began	nothing
15. kites	picture	mail
16. gave	many	curious
17. run	race	once
18. fast	running	numbers
19. after	everything	couldn't
20. got	hurry	pop
21. fish	street	mouth
22. by	alone	air
23. sound	riding	knew
24. pulled	work	taken
25. very	use	might

Instructional level:

23 words correct   23 words correct   23 words correct

---

*The *Reading for Meaning* basal reader series published by Houghton Mifflin Company was used in the formulation of these word lists.

WORD RECOGNITION*

Name _____ Grade _____ Teacher _____ Date ____

Second Reader— Second Semester	Third Reader— First Semester	Third Reader— Second Semester
1. noodle	desk	balcony
2. wings	mountain	bite
3. pitter	ought	whiteness
4. trotted	gathered	bushes
5. I've	hang	rosy
6. wrong	certainly	declared
7. stay	ourselves	confess
8. wave	woke	kill
9. start	pies	prefix
10. feel	decide	canaries
11. pieces	acting	ma'am
12. climb	hound	crazy
13. coach	interesting	neither
14. pretty	flashed	drove
15. hurdy-gurdy	afternoon	compete
16. neat	age	impossible
17. chair	either	admitted
18. leave	copper	roar
19. bell	Dr.	flopped
20. grandfather	buried	performance
21. wife	bothered	battery
22. barn	barking	acorn
23. nose	palace	charming
24. patient	meat	human
25. rest	person	announcer

Instructional level:

23 words correct	23 words correct	23 words correct

*The *Reading for Meaning* basal reader series published by Houghton Mifflin Company was used in the formulation of these word lists.

WORD RECOGNITION*

Name _____ Grade _____ Teacher _____ Date _____

Fourth Reader	Fifth Reader	Sixth Reader
1. automobile	depending	parachuting
2. pronounce	welcome	create
3. trail	surrounded	miniature
4. stinging	proper	brows
5. metal	puppet	retorted
6. southpaw	experience	carton
7. duty	keen	obtained
8. hall	freeze	mixture
9. pell-mell	nimble	flushed
10. demanded	pint	crusade
11. socks	possess	distressing
12. seal	shirk	offense
13. remove	cloak	passenger
14. musicians	skating	infinite
15. crawling	border	structure
16. nuisance	statues	gait
17. crash	nursery	cathedral
18. iron	homestead	woodpeckers
19. frolicking	legends	hiking
20. inquisitive	ambulances	precisely
21. skimmed	quit	appreciate
22. magazine	sedan	updraft
23. terror	handcuffed	calico
24. natural	drooping	jumbled
25. delivered	madam	cluttered

Instructional level:

23 words correct   23 words correct   23 words correct

---

*The *Reading for Meaning* basal reader series published by Houghton Mifflin Company was used in the formulation of these word lists.

WORD RECOGNITION*

Name _____ Grade _____ Teacher _____ Date _____

Seventh Reader	Eighth Reader
1. abate	adjacent
2. alien	alder
3. beguile	apex
4. bigotry	astuteness
5. cadence	bewilderment
6. competent	buffet
7. dastardly	cavity
8. dehydration	conservative
9. disperse	curiosity
10. ecstasy	dishonor
11. elusive	eligible
12. feign	extravagance
13. galvanize	focus
14. homage	gully
15. immunity	inconceivable
16. jaguar	intuition
17. laden	melancholy
18. malady	obsolete
19. novice	pawn broker
20. ominous	rebuke
21. pelt	serenity
22. radius	sway
23. scruff	triumphant
24. tempest	vacancy
25. verify	wistful
26. wary	withered

Instructional level:

23 words correct   23 words correct

---

*The *Basic Curriculum Series* published by Lippincott Company was used in the formulation of these word lists. Used by permission of J.B. Lippincott Company.

WORD RECOGNITION*

Name _____ Grade _____ Teacher _____ Date _____

Ninth Reader	Tenth Reader
1. sarcastic	apprehension
2. vituperation	proprietor
3. premature	unobtrusively
4. exclamation	glimmering
5. ventilator	assaulting
6. undergraduate	replication
7. suspiciously	enterprise
8. partisans	inaudibly
9. wench	congeries
10. disobedience	organization
11. chariot	ingredients
12. fervently	fortnight
13. melee	harangue
14. ignoramus	regimental
15. haunches	nautical
16. bleating	ingenuity
17. prodigious	narrative
18. credentials	improbable
19. reconciled	transfigured
20. telegraph	remoteness
21. carbolic	apparition
22. appeased	loath
23. commuting	spectacle
24. desolation	reflective
25. myriads	platinum

Instructional level:

23 words correct   23 words correct

_____

*A graded series of English literature textbooks published by Houghton Mifflin Company were used in the formulation of these word lists.

WORD RECOGNITION*

Name _____ Grade _____ Teacher_____ Date _____

Eleventh Reader   Twelfth Reader

Eleventh Reader	Twelfth Reader
1. bulkhead	yeoman
2. contemplated	contingent
3. rancor	swound
4. innumerable	paramour
5. perambulations	enkindle
6. irreproachable	ague
7. malingers	prolific
8. rookery	heraldry
9. reverberations	pourparlers
10. downstream	cornice
11. phenomena	kampong
12. foundered	draper
13. bohemian	nauseous
14. festooned	brinded
15. immedicable	scab
16. sniveling	self-possessed
17. effrontery	sedge
18. consecrate	legioned
19. scud	caitiff
20. dispersed	soliciting
21. premeditation	purveyor
22. amethyst	cloistered
23. confidentially	symmetry
24. unreconciled	perchance
25. vociferated	emulation

Instructional level:

23 words correct   23 words correct

*A graded series of English literature textbooks published by Houghton Mifflin Company were used in the formulation of these word lists.

GRADED ORAL READING PARAGRAPH (PRIMER)

Name _____ Grade _____ Teacher _____ Date _____

THE YELLOW KITE*

Jack got a new yellow kite for his birthday. The kite had a string on it. Jack could use the string of the kite to make it fly. Jack could make his kite go up high. Janet wanted to fly the new kite. Janet liked to fly kites. Janet ran fast with the string. Janet could make the kite go up high. Then Jack made the kite go fast. Jack let the kite go up as high as it could. Then he let the kite get away.

Comprehension Questions:

1. When did Jack get the new yellow kite?
2. Who else flew the new kite?
3. What made the kite go up high?
4. Why did the kite get away?
5. Give me a sentence using the word *birthday*.

Number of words <u>87</u>

Number of words correct _____

Accuracy:

   90% <u>78</u>
   99% <u>86</u>

Comprehension:

   95% Five questions
   75% Four questions

_____

*Adapted from the following source: Paul McKee, M. Lucile Harrison, Anne McCowen, Elizabeth Lehr, and William K. Durr, *Jack and Janet* (Boston:Houghton Mifflin Company, 1966), pp. 130-136. Used by permission of the publisher.

GRADED ORAL READING PARAGRAPH (FIRST READER)

Name _____ Grade _____ Teacher _____ Date ___

THE CIRCUS COMES TO TOWN*

A circus was coming to Mary's town. Pictures of the circus were all around the town. Mary wanted to go to the circus. She wanted to see the elephants. She wanted to see the man water the elephants. Mary wanted to see the circus dog too. She wanted to see the circus dog go up a strong rope. She wanted to see the man clean the animal cages with a broom. Mary wanted to see the bears at the circus too. They had on blue caps. Mary must have money to go to the circus. Do you think that she can go?

Comprehension Questions

1. Where did Mary want to go?
2. What color caps did the bears have on?
3. Why were pictures of the circus all around Mary's town?
4. Why do you think Mary needs money to go to the circus?
5. Give me a sentence using the word *elephant.*

Number of words <u>101</u>

Number of words correct _____

Accuracy:

   90% <u>91</u>

   99% <u>100</u>

Comprehension:

   95% Five questions
   75% Four questions

---

*Adapted from the following source: Paul McKee, M. Lucile Harrison, Annie McCowen, Elizabeth Lehr, and William K. Durr, *Up and Away* (Boston: Houghton Mifflin Company, 1966), pp. 132-145. Used by permission of the publisher.

GRADED ORAL READING PARAGRAPH
SECOND READER—FIRST SEMESTER

Name _____ Grade _____ Teacher _____ Date __

OWLS ARE NIGHT-BIRDS*

Do you think that you have ever seen an owl? An owl may live in the zoo. Have you ever seen an owl in a zoo? Some people are afraid of owls because they look strange and make strange sounds. You do not have to be afraid of an owl because they are not so bad as they look and sound. Owls help farmers in their fields because they eat bugs. Owls are hard to find because they don't fly around in the daytime. They fly around at night and hide in the daytime. Owls look as if they know everything. An owl doesn't know more than other birds. It just looks as if it does.

Comprehension Questions

1. Where could you see an owl?
2. Why are some people afraid of owls?
3. Why should owls be protected?
4. Why do you think that owls fly at night instead of in the daytime?
5. Give me a sentence using the word *strange*.

Number of words <u>117</u>

Number of words correct _____

Accuracy:

   90% <u>105</u>
   99% <u>116</u>

Comprehension

   95% Five questions
   75% Four questions

---

*Adapted from the following source: Paul McKee, M. Lucile Harrison, Annie McCowen, Elizabeth Lehr, and William K. Durr, *Come Along* (Boston: Houghton Mifflin Company, 1966), p. 139. Used by permission of the publisher.

GRADED ORAL READING PARAGRAPH
(SECOND READER–SECOND SEMESTER)

Name _____ Grade _____ Teacher _____ Date ___

WHAT IS A CATBIRD?*

Have you ever heard of a catbird? A catbird is a dark bird that can make a sound just like the meow of a cat. He doesn't always make the noise of a cat. He often makes music and gives the birdcalls of another bird. The catbird is gray with a black cap. However, sometimes you can see red under his tail. Often a catbird is curious about people. Sometimes a catbird follows a man along a road just as if he likes to find out where the man is going. A catbird sometimes is curious about noises also. Often if a catbird hears a strange noise, he goes out to find out what is happening. Farmers like to have catbirds in their fields and gardens because they eat bugs that might hurt the fields and gardens. Do you think that you have ever seen a catbird?

Comprehension Questions

1. Why does a catbird have that name?
2. What color is a catbird?
3. Why do you think that catbirds should be protected?
4. How is a catbird different from other birds?
5. Give me a sentence using the word *birdcall.*

Number of words <u>147</u>

Number of words correct _____

Accuracy:

90% <u>130</u>
99% <u>143</u>

Comprehension:

95% *Five questions*
75% *Four questions*

---

*Adapted from the following source: Paul McKee, M. Lucile Harrison, Annie McCowen, Elizabeth Lehr, and William K. Durr, *On We Go* (Boston: Houghton Mifflin Company, 1966), pp. 236-237. Used by permission of the publisher.

GRADED ORAL READING PARAGRAPH
(THIRD READER–FIRST SEMESTER)

Name ⎯⎯⎯⎯⎯⎯⎯ Grade ⎯⎯⎯ Teacher ⎯⎯⎯ Date ⎯

LIGHTHOUSES*

Do you know what a lighthouse is? Long ago men began to build lighthouses to show places of great danger along the shores of oceans and lakes. Today there are hundreds of lighthouses along rocky shores and on rocky islands in all parts of the world. Most lighthouses are tall, round buildings that are wider at the bottom than at the top. Most of them are painted white so that they can be seen easily in daytime by ships. Most lighthouses have a powerful light at the top. The beam from this light shines out through a special kind of window so that it turns around and around the light. As the window turns in a lighthouse, the light appears to flash on and off. The man who lives in the lighthouse and watches the light is called the lightkeeper. When fog covers the shore of an ocean or lake, the lightkeeper uses a foghorn to warn ships of danger. By their warnings of danger, lightkeepers have saved the lives of hundreds of people.

Comprehension Questions

1. Where are lighthouses found today?
2. Why are most lighthouses painted white?
3. What makes the light in a lighthouse appear to go on and off?
4. Why is the man who takes care of the light called the lightkeeper?
5. Give me a sentence using the word *foghorn*.

Number of words 173

Number of words correct ⎯⎯⎯

Accuracy:

90% 158
99% 171

Comprehension:

95% *Five questions*
75% *Four questions*

---

*Adapted from the following source: Paul McKee, M. Lucile Harrison, Annie McCowen, Elizabeth Lehr, and William K. Durr, *Looking Ahead* (Boston: Houghton Mifflin Company, 1966), pp. 191-195. Used by permission of the publisher.

GRADED ORAL READING PARAGRAPH
(THIRD READER–SECOND SEMESTER)

Name _____ Grade _____ Teacher _____ Date __

WHAT ARE DUMB ANIMALS?*

Do you think most animals are dumb? Animals are often called dumb because they do not speak or write a language such as people do. However, many animals are smart. Animal trainers can tell you that they know how smart many animals are. Many people who have lost their sight have a seeing-eye dog which has been trained to take them wherever they want to go. Animals do understand our language very well even if they have no spoken language of their own. Many animals seem to understand everything that you say to them. An animal trainer has learned that the best way to train any animal is through kindness. When an animal does something well, he can be rewarded with something which will please him. You will find that he then is eager to do the same thing again. If an animal which you are training misbehaves, taking something away which he wants usually will teach him to behave himself.

Comprehension Questions

1. Why are animals called dumb?
2. What does a seeing-eye dog do?
3. How can an animal show you that he understands your language?
4. Why is kindness more effective than punishment in training an animal?
5. Give me a sentence using the word *misbehaves.*

Number of words <u>162</u>

Number of words correct _____

Accuracy:

   90% <u>146</u>
   99% <u>160</u>

Comprehension:

   95% *Five questions*
   75% *Four questions*

---

*Adapted from the following source: Paul McKee, M. Lucile Harrison, Annie McCowen, Elizabeth Lehr, and William K. Durr, *Climbing Higher* (Boston: Houghton Mifflin Company, 1966), pp. 274-275. Used by permission of the publisher.

GRADED ORAL READING PARAGRAPH (FOURTH READER)

Name _____ Grade _____ Teacher _____ Date __

RACCOONS*

Have you ever seen a raccoon in the forest? You will find that a raccoon is nearly as much fun to look at as a monkey and also is almost as curious about everything around him. Although a raccoon can be a household pet, he is not really a good housepet because he is so curious that he is always busy making trouble. A raccoon can use his front paws so cleverly that he can open cardboard boxes, unwrap bundles, and take the covers off jars. The name "raccoon" comes from an American Indian word which means "one who scratches with his hands." Raccoons have front paws which look like hands, and they use these paws to scratch on the ground, looking for insects that they want to eat. Raccoons eat many different foods. They are quite fond of fish and are clever at catching them with their hand-like paws. In some countries, raccoons are called "washing bears." They are called this because they usually wash their food before eating it and because they like to take baths. Sometimes a raccoon even will put a fish in the water to wash it just after he has caught it.

Comprehension Questions

1. Why is a raccoon not a good housepet?
2. What does a raccoon like to eat?
3. Why would a raccoon wash a fish which he has just caught?
4. How do you know that raccoons lived in Indian times?
5. Give me a sentence using the word *curious.*

Number of words <u>198</u>

Number of words correct _____

Accuracy:

  90% <u>178</u>
  99% <u>196</u>

Comprehension:

  95% *Five questions*
  75% *Four questions*

---

*Adapted from the following source: Paul McKee, M. Lucile Harrison, Annie, McCowen, Elizabeth Lehr, and William K. Durr, *High Roads* (Boston: Houghton Mifflin Company, 1966), pp. 158-159. Used by permission of the publisher.

GRADED ORAL READING PARAGRAPH (FIFTH READER)*

Name _____ Grade _____ Teacher _____ Date ___

WHAT IS A CUTTING HORSE CONTEST?†

Did you know that the Cutting Horse Contest is a very popular event in western rodeos? It is really a contest between highly trained horses rather than between the men who ride them. On western ranches, the cutting horse and the roping horse are very highly prized and are usually saved for special work. In the Cutting Horse Contest in a rodeo, a herd of wild range cattle are driven to one end of the arena while some mounted judges line themselves up on the other end of the arena so that they are facing the cattle. Then the cowboy contestant rides out on a cutting horse from behind the judges and picks out a steer, separates it from the herd, drives it back to the judges, and keeps it there until the time-keeper's whistle blows. The contest is judged on the smoothness and skill which the cutting horse shows. A good cutting horse should depend on his rider only for signals to show him the directions in which to drive the steer. A good cutting horse naturally needs much experience and training. A good cutting horse need not be a sleek, high-stepping horse as long as he does his job well.

Comprehension Questions

1. What is a cutting horse?
2. What can a cutting horse look like?
3. Why is a Cutting Horse Contest a contest between horses rather than men?
4. Why does a good cutting horse need quite a bit of experience?
5. Give me a sentence using the word *rodeo*.

Number of words <u>204</u>

Number of words correct _____

Accuracy:

   90% <u>184</u>
   99% <u>202</u>

Comprehension:

   95% Five questions
   75% Four questions

*See Paul McKee, Annie McCowen, M. Lucile Harrison, Elizabeth Lehr, and William K. Durr, *Sky Lines* (Boston: Houghton Mifflin Company, 1966), pp. 208-211.
†Adapted from Glenn Rounds, *Rodeo* (New York: Holiday House, Inc., 1949). Used by permission of Holiday House, Inc.

GRADED ORAL READING PARAGRAPH (SIXTH READER)*

Name _____ Grade _____ Teacher _____ Date ___

WHAT IS TREASURE-TROVE?†

Treasure-trove is any gold or silver in bars or in coins which is found hidden *in* the earth but not lying *on* the earth. Treasure-trove also can mean other valuable articles which have been hidden in the earth. Have you ever dreamed of finding a vast horde of gold or silver buried somewhere in a sandy beach or in an inland glen? Most boys and girls would like to find some treasure so that they could keep it. Many treasure-troves have been discovered in every state in the United States and in other parts of North America. You can keep the treasure-trove you find if the original owner of this treasure is unknown. The owner of the land in which the treasure was found has no claim whatsoever to any of the treasure-trove merely because he owns that property. If you find the treasure with a group of other people, each person then shares equally in it. However, each person should keep his share of the treasure for a reasonable time because the rightful owner of the treasure may appear later. Before you start looking for treasure-trove, you should realize that for each person who has found or will find buried treasure, there are a thousand unlucky searchers who never discover any treasure. You will have to decide if the treasure-trove you may discover will be worth all the time and trouble you spend.

Comprehension Questions

1. What is treasure-trove?
2. Where has treasure-trove been discovered in the United States?
3. Why should you keep your share of the treasure which you have discovered for some time after finding it?
4. Why is buried treasure quite difficult to locate?
5. Give me a sentence using the word *searcher*.

Number of words <u>235</u>

Number of words correct _____

---

*See Paul McKee, Annie McCowen, M. Lucile Harrison, Elizabeth Lehr, and William K. Durr, *Bright Peaks* (Boston: Houghton Mifflin Company, 1966), pp. 288-289.

†Adapted from Edward Rowe Snow, *True Tales of Buried Treasure* (New York: Dodd, Mead & Company, Inc., 1951). Used by permission of Dodd, Mead & Company.

Accuracy:

    90% <u>212</u>
    99% <u>233</u>

Comprehension:

    95% *Five questions*
    75% *Four questions*

GRADED ORAL READING PARAGRAPH (SEVENTH READER)

Name _____ Grade _____ Teacher ____ Date ___

ABOUT BEN FRANKLIN*

Benjamin Franklin was without a doubt a very famous man in early America and indeed one of the most famous men in western Europe as well. Franklin received many honors and made many scientific discoveries. He invented the Franklin stove, founded the *Saturday Evening Post,* invented the lightning rod, and invented a musical instrument. He even helped write the Declaration of Independence and the Constitution. Franklin was endlessly curious. When Franklin was 12 years old, he was apprenticed to his brother who was a printer in Boston. In those times, a boy learned a trade by serving an apprenticeship with a master craftsman for seven years while he learned the trade. Because he was extremely bright while his brother was not so bright, Ben often quarreled with him. Later Ben quit his apprenticeship and ran away by ship to New York. Ben later went to Philadelphia where he found a job as a printer. In Philadelphia Franklin enjoyed a freedom which he had never had before and became a man of note in Philadelphia. Franklin became quite rich early in his life and then devoted the rest of his life to serving his country and to helping mankind by scientific discoveries. Although Franklin wrote an autobiography about himself, it does not tell much about what he did during the last part of his life.

Comprehension Questions

1. What were some of Franklin's inventions?
2. What is an apprenticeship?
3. Why do you think it was difficult for Franklin to serve an apprenticeship for his older brother?
4. Why do you suppose that Franklin enjoyed Philadelphia so much?
5. Give me a sentence using the word *apprenticeship.*

Number of words <u>225</u>

Number of words correct _____

*Adapted from the following source: Glenn McCracken and Charles C. Walcutt, *Basic Reading* (Philadelphia: J.B. Lippincott Company, 1965), pp. 299-308. Used by permission of J.B. Lippincott Company.

Accuracy:

90% <u>203</u>
99% <u>223</u>

Comprehension:

95% *Five questions*
75% *Four questions*

GRADED ORAL READING PARAGRAPH (EIGHTH READER)

Name _____ Grade _____ Teacher _____ Date ___

THE STORY OF ROBINSON CRUSOE*

The adventure story of *Robinson Crusoe* was written many years ago by Daniel Defoe. This is a very famous story about a man named Robinson Crusoe who was shipwrecked during a dreadful storm at sea on a dismal island which he called "The Island of Despair." The first day Crusoe spent in accustoming himself to the dismal circumstances on the island. He thought that he might be starved to death, murdered by savages, or devoured by wild beasts. The next day he saw that his wrecked ship had floated with the high tide and was driven on shore near enough to the island so that he could get to it. He brought many goods from the ship to the island by rafts. Many months later, he surveyed the island itself. He found a brook of running water and on the banks of this brook found pleasant savannas or meadows. He also found many strong stalks of tobacco. Later he found melons and grapes on the island. During this time, he made a settlement for himself to live in which was called a hutch. He slept on a hammock-bed. Because he needed them, he made some odd, misshapen jars out of clay. However, many cracked because of the over-violent heat of the sun. Crusoe's journal contained many other stories of his life on the island, such as when he made a boat out of a cedar tree. The entire journal would be most interesting for you to read if you get the chance.

Comprehension Questions

1. Why was Crusoe shipwrecked on an island?
2. What are several things that Crusoe found to eat?
3. Why do you think that Crusoe needed jars or pots?
4. Why do you think that Crusoe tried to make a boat?
5. Give me a sentence using the word *dismal.*

Number of words 252

Number of words correct _____

---

*Adapted from the following source: Glenn McCracken and Charles C. Walcutt, *Basic Reading* (Philadelphia: J.B. Lippincott Company, 1965), pp. 49-66. Used by permission of J.B. Lippincott Company.

Accuracy:

90% <u>227</u>
99% <u>249</u>

Comprehension:

95% Five questions
75% Four questions

GRADED ORAL READING PARAGRAPH (NINTH READER)*

Name _____ Grade _____ Teacher _____ Date ___

LOCUSTS IN AFRICA†

This is a story about a farm of 3,000 acres on the ridges that rise toward the Zambesi escarpment in Africa—high, windswept country. The crop grown on this farm was maize—another name for corn. One day the farmer saw a long, low cloud advancing toward him. This rust-colored cloud contained thousands of locusts. Each farmer in the area hoped that the cloud of locusts would overlook his farm and go on to the next one. The main swarm of locusts advanced on the farm in a dense, black cloud which reached almost to the sun itself. The locusts once they landed could eat every blade and leaf of the maize in half an hour. The farmer told his daughter about how he was made bankrupt by another locust army 17 years before. As the locusts approached his farm, the air was dark with the crisscross of the insects. As the farmer brushed the locusts off himself, they looked at him with their beady eyes while they clung on with hard, serrated legs. On the farm the earth seemed to be moving, with locusts crawling everywhere. The swarms were so thick that even the boughs of the trees were weighed to the ground. Finally the army of locusts fanned their wings at dawn, and the farmer could see a faint red smear in the sky at a distance. Although the locusts were gone, the farmer was bankrupt.

Comprehension Questions

1. In what country did this story take place?
2. How often do locusts invade the same places?
3. Why are locusts so destructive?
4. Why was the farmer bankrupt after the locusts left?
5. Give me a sentence using the word *bankrupt*.

Number of words <u>239</u>

Number of words correct_____

*See Philip McFarland, Sharon Breakstone, and Morse Peckham, *Reflections in Literature* (Boston: Houghton Mifflin Company, 1972), pp. 186-191.

†Adapted from *The Habit of Loving* by Doris Lessing, Copyright © 1957 by Doris Lessing. With permission of Thomas Y. Crowell Co., Inc.

Accuracy:

90% <u>215</u>
99% <u>237</u>

Comprehension:

95% Five questions
75% Four questions

GRADED ORAL READING PARAGRAPH (TENTH READER)*

Name _____ Grade _____ Teacher _____ Date _____

WHITE'S VIEW OF THE WORLD†

This essay is about how E.B. White, a well-known writer, viewed the relationship between himself and his contemporary world. In the essay, White stated that his Selective Service order number was 10789 and his social security number was 067-01-9807. White continued to say that he was the holder of a quit-claim deed recorded in book 682, page 501 in the county in which he lived. Since White wrote his essay during the second World War, he also stated that he held Basic A Mileage Ration 108950, O.P.A. Form R-525-C. In this essay White also gave the license number of his car, the number of his left front tire, the number of his right front tire, and the numbers of his two rear tires. In this autobiographical essay, White also gave the numbers of his hair brush, and drug prescription. He even described his black dog and her license number as well as all of the ingredients in her prepared dog food. The point of view of White's essay undoubtedly was that he was forced to exist in a society which had lost its regard for the individual person. Although this essay was written in the 1940's, it obviously has implications for current American Society. In your opinion, does current American society have even less regard for the individual person than it had during the era when this essay was written?

Comprehension Questions

1. Who was E.B. White?
2. When was this essay written?
3. Why does our society think it is necessary to give each person so many different numbers?
4. What are the dangers in thinking of a person only in terms of the numbers which he has been given?

---

*Adapted from the following source: Phillip McFarland, Allen Kirschner, and Morse Peckham. *Perceptions in Literature*. (Boston:Houghton Mifflin Company, 1972), pp. 396-399.
†Summary (sans Comprehension Questions) of "About Myself" from *The Second Tree* from *The Second Tree from the Corner* by E.B. White, copyright 1945 by E.B. White. By permission of Harper & Row, Publishers, Inc.

5. Give me a sentence using the word *ingredient*.

Number of words _____239_____

Number of words correct_____

Accuracy:

    90% <u>215</u>

    99% <u>237</u>

Comprehension:

    95% *Five questions*

    75% *Four questions*

GRADED ORAL READING PARAGRAPH (ELEVENTH READER)*

Name _____ Grade _____ Teacher _____ Date ___

MARK TWAIN–CUB PILOT†

Mark Twain was a very famous author from Hannibal, Missouri, who wrote such books as *Tom Sawyer* and *Huckleberry Finn*. This story is about Mark Twain's ambition to be a steamboatman on the Mississippi River. Although he had transient ambitions of other sorts, they only were transient. His ambition to be a steamboatman always remained. He told about how once a day a cheap, gaudy packet arrived upward from St. Louis and another downward from Keokuk. He described how he saw the peaceful lapping of the wavelets of the great, majestic Mississippi against two or three wood flats at the head of the wharf. Twain wrote that he would see a film of dark smoke appearing in the sky and instantly a drayman, famous for his quick eye and prodigious voice, cried "Steamboat a-comin'!" Twain described how he fastened his eyes upon the coming boat as upon a wonder he was seeing for the first time. He described a steamboat as long and sharp and trim and pretty; as having two tall, fancy-topped chimneys; a fanciful pilothouse; a hurricane deck, and a texas deck which was fenced and ornamented with clean white railing. Twain did get to travel later on an ancient tub called the *Paul Jones.* For the sum of sixteen dollars, he said that he had the scarred and tarnished splendors of her main saloon principally to himself. He did learn how to steer this steamboat during his voyage from Cincinnati to New Orleans.

Comprehension Questions

1. What did Mark Twain always want to be when he grew up?
2. How did Mark Twain describe the appearance of a steamboat?
3. Why did Mark Twain profit from his voyage on the *Paul Jones*?
4. Why do you think that Mark Twain always wanted to be a steamboatman?
5. Give me a sentence using the word *transient*.

Number of words 248

Correct number of words _____

---

*See Philip McFarland, Allen Kirschner, Alfred Ferguson, Larry D. Benson, and Morse Peckham, *Themes in American Literature* (Boston: Houghton Mifflin Company, 1972), pp. 55-63.
†Originally paraphrased from Samuel Clemens, *Life on the Mississippi* (New York: Harper & Row, Publishers, Inc.). Used by permission of Harper & Row, Publishers, Inc.

Accuracy:

90% <u>223</u>

99% <u>246</u>

Comprehension:

95% *Five questions*

75% *Four questions*

GRADED ORAL READING PARAGRAPH (TWELFTH READER)*

Name _____ Grade _____ Teacher _____ Date ___

ABOUT SHOOTING AN ELEPHANT†

George Orwell wrote a story about a portion of his life in Burma in a story called "Shooting an Elephant." George Orwell later wrote the well-known books *Animal Farm* and *1984*. Orwell wrote that the sub-inspector at a police station in Burma said that an elephant was ravaging the bazaar. Orwell was told that the elephant was a tame one which had gone "must." He was told the elephant's mahout had set out in pursuit but had taken the wrong direction and was now a journey of 12 hours away. The elephant had devoured the stock in some fruit stalls and destroyed somebody's bamboo hut. Orwell wrote that he was not squeamish about killing animals but had never shot an elephant and never wanted to. He knew that if the elephant charged and he missed him, he would have about as much chance as a toad under a steamroller. When he finally pulled the trigger, a mysterious, terrible change came over the elephant. He looked suddenly stricken, shrunken, immensely old, as though the frightful impact of the bullet had paralyzed him. He sagged flabbily to his knees and an enormous senility settled on him. When Orwell fired a third time, that was the shot that did it for him. Orwell heard later that it took him half an hour to die. Orwell wrote that he often wondered if the Burmese people grasped that he had shot the elephant solely to avoid looking like a fool.

Comprehension Questions

1. In what country did Orwell shoot the elephant?
2. How many shots did Orwell have to fire to kill the elephant?
3. Why do you think that the tame elephant had gone "must?"
4. Can you describe how the elephant acted before he finally died?
5. Give me a sentence using the word *"must."*

Number of words <u>245</u>

Number of words correct _____

---

*See Philip McFarland, Samuel Hynes, Larry D. Benson, and Morse Peckham, *Forms in English Literature* (Boston: Houghton Mifflin Company, 1972), pp. 378-383.
†"Shooting an Elephant" is from *Shooting an Elephant and Other Essays* by George Orwell, published by Harcourt Brace Jovanovich, Inc.

Accuracy:

90% <u>221 </u>
99% <u>243 </u>

Comprehension:

95% *Five questions*
75% *Four questions*

Inventories in the
Word Recognition Techniques

I nventories in the various word recognition techniques can be given as part of an Individual Reading Inventory or in isolation to students who need such an inventory. Since it is obvious that a student cannot read efficiently without proficiency in the various word recognition techniques, it can be very useful for you to determine a student's exact strengths and weaknesses in each of the word recognition skills.

This section is devoted to helping you understand how to formulate and administer inventories in the word recognition skills of sight word knowledge, phonetic analysis, structural analysis, context clue usage, and dictionary usage. Since it is impossible to include inventories for each word recognition skill at each of the different reading levels, this section presents directions on how to construct and evaluate your own inventories in each of the word recognition techniques. In addition, it contains several sample inventories for each of the word recognition techniques which you can duplicate and give in the light of the needs of your own students. In most cases, inventories are included at the primary-grade, intermediate-grade, and secondary-school levels. Hopefully, this section will enable you to construct and use inventories in each of the word recognition techniques with success.

Description of Inventories in the Word Recognition Techniques for the Diagnosis of Reading Difficulties

As was explained in Section 7, you can give inventories in the different word recognition techniques as the last part of a traditional Individual Reading Inventory. As is explained in Sections 7 and 9 of this kit, you can give an inventory in sight word knowledge as part of a content-oriented Individual Reading Inventory. However, you also can give inventories in any of the word recognition techniques to one student or to a group of students who appear to need them. Such an inventory assesses a student's strengths and weaknesses in a word recognition technique so that you can plan a program of individually prescribed instruction for him. The last part of this section contains sample inventories in each of the word recognition techniques which can be given to an individual student or group of students.

As you may know, sight words are those words which a student should be able to recognize instantly. To be an effective reader, a student must have a good stock of sight words. Most words which a student analyzes first by another technique, such as phonetic analysis or structural analysis, eventually should become part of his stock of sight words. You may be wondering what type of student should be given a test of sight word knowledge. Such an inventory in sight word knowledge usually should be given by an elementary classroom teacher or an elementary reading specialist to a severely or moderately disabled reader—a student who is reading on the primary-grade level. Such a test also can be given by a secondary-school reading specialist to a disabled reader who is reading on the primary-grade level. Students who have been diagnosed to be deficient in sight word knowledge should master the words found on a sight word test in their individually prescribed corrective or remedial reading program.

Currently there are three basic sight word lists which are in widespread use with students who are reading at the primary-grade and intermediate-grade level. The most widely used and oldest sight word list is the Dolch Basic Sight Word List. The late Edward Dolch of the University of Illinois compiled this list in 1941 from studies done over 40 years ago. It was compiled from three then-prominent word lists. This list of 220 service words make up 70 percent of the words in first readers and 65 percent of the words in second and third readers. According to some contemporary reading specialists, this sight word list is rather old and not relevant for the present.[1] However, it still is in wide use by elementary classroom teachers and elementary and secondary reading specialists. Since permission to reprint this list could not be obtained from the publisher, you will not find it in this kit. However, you can obtain copies of the Dolch Basic Sight Word List for a nominal cost from the Garrard Press, Champaign, Illinois 61820.

The Kucera-Francis Corpus is a more recent and hence supposedly more relevant sight word list which is composed of 220 service words. Dale D. Johnson of the University of Wisconsin has discussed this list in detail. According to Johnson, Henry Kucera and W. Nelson Francis published a book entitled *Computational Analysis of Present-Day American English*. Kucera and Francis processed 1,014,232 running words by computer and then listed the most commonly used words in rank order. Eighty-two or 37 percent of the words on the Kucera-Francis Corpus are not on the Dolch Basic Sight Word List.[2] You can use the Kucera-Francis Corpus of 220 service words in place of the Dolch Basic Sight Word List. A copy of the Kucera-Francis Corpus of 220 service words is included in the last part of this section. You can duplicate this list and use it for an inventory of sight word knowledge if you wish to do so.

The third sight word list which can be used in an inventory of sight word knowledge is the Instant Words which was developed in 1957 by Edward Fry of Rutgers University. Fry has compiled several lists which total 600 words and

---

[1]Dale D. Johnson, "The Dolch List Reexamined," *The Reading Teacher*, 24 (February, 1971), pp. 449-457.
[2]*Ibid.*

encompass approximately the fourth-grade reading level. Fry's first list of 100 words is on the first-grade reading level; the second 100 words are on the second-grade reading level; the third 100 words are on the third-grade reading level; and the next 300 words are on the fourth-grade reading level.[3] Fry's Instant Words are included in the last part of this section, and you can duplicate any one of the lists you wish.

When you have discovered by the use of a sight word knowledge inventory that a student is deficient in this word recognition skill, you should attempt to correct the deficiency as soon as possible. Suggestions for doing this can be found in many sources. Two very good sources of suggestions for corrective instruction are *Identifying and Correcting Reading Difficulties in Children*[4] and *Diagnosis and Correction of Reading Difficulties in Secondary School Students.*[5] Additional suggestions are found in many of the professional books on reading which are listed in Appendix III of this kit.

Phonetic analysis can be defined as the association of phonemes (sounds) and graphemes (symbols). Since English is thought to be about 85 percent phonetically regular, it is obvious that a student must be proficient in phonetic analysis if he is to be an independent reader. Many moderately and severely disabled readers in the elementary school are deficient in phonetic analysis ability, as are most severely disabled readers in the secondary school. Therefore, it is essential that you determine a student's exact difficulties in phonetic analysis so that they can be corrected. Although you can make this determination by using teacher observation or a diagnostic reading test, you well may want to use either an individual or a group inventory in phonetic analysis to supplant or supplement either of these diagnostic devices.

An inventory in phonetic analysis can be either individually administered or group-administered. If the inventory is individually administered, it can require either an oral or a written response. On the other hand, if it is group administered, it usually requires a written response. Although more detailed directions for constructing such an inventory are given in the next part of this section, you usually use one or more basal reader manuals or workbooks or phonics workbooks as a guide in constructing such an inventory. When you have ascertained a student's specific difficulties in phonetic analysis, it is obvious that you should attempt to remedy these difficulties as quickly as possible. The two books by Miller which were mentioned earlier in this section, or any of the professional books on reading listed in the Appendix, provide suggestions for correcting difficulties in phonetic analysis.

Structural analysis is the use of word parts to obtain the pronunciation and meaning of an unknown word. Therefore, structural analysis consists of the subskills of the use of base or root words, prefixes, suffixes, syllabication, contractions, and accent. Many mildly and moderately disabled readers in the elementary and secondary school can profit from instruction in structural analysis skills which is designed specifically to overcome their diagnosed weaknesses. To diagnose difficulties in

---

[3] Edward B. Fry, *Reading Instruction for Classroom and Clinic* (New York: McGraw-Hill Book Company, 1972), pp. 58-63.

[4] Wilma H. Miller, *Identifying and Correcting Reading Difficulties in Children* (New York: The Center for Applied Research in Education, 1971), pp. 109-114.

[5] Wilma H. Miller, *Diagnosis and Correction of Reading Difficulties in Secondary School Students* (New York: The Center for Applied Research in Education, 1973), pp. 122-123.

structural analysis, you can use teacher observation or a diagnostic reading test. However, you also may want to use a structural analysis inventory.

You can use basal reader manuals or workbooks as guides in the formulation of a structural analysis inventory. Most inventories in structural analysis are individually administered or group-administered but call for written responses. Several inventories in structural analysis skills are found in the last part of this section. You can duplicate and use any of them which seem to be appropriate for the needs of your students. When you have determined a student's weaknesses in structural analysis, you can use any of the sources which were mentioned earlier in this section to help him overcome these weaknesses.

Context clue usage can be defined as obtaining the meaning, and less often the pronunciation, of an unknown word from the context in which it is located such as the surrounding sentence, paragraph, or passage. There are several different types of context clue usage, including experiential clues, comparison or contrast clues, synonym clues, summary clues, association clues, and previous contact clues. A detailed description of these different types of context clues is given in the book entitled *Teaching Reading in the Secondary School.*[6] Most reading specialists consider context clue usage to be one of the more useful of the word recognition techniques, especially if there are not too many unknown words in the material.

A context clue usage inventory usually is a written test which is either individually administered or group administered. It often is a written test which asks a student to underline the one word of several options which makes the best sense in sentence context. In constructing inventories in context clue usage, you can use basal reader manuals or workbooks as a guide. Several sample inventories in context clue usage are included in the last part of this section.

You can also give a context clue usage inventory by the use of the cloze procedure. Cloze is a diagnostic technique in which you omit every *nth* word from a written passage. For example, every *nth* word can be every fifth word, every eighth word, or every tenth word. However, you usually keep the first and last sentence of the passage intact. When you use the cloze procedure to assess a student's ability in context clue usage, you count as correct any word which makes sense in the blank space even if it is not the exact omitted word. More details about the cloze procedure and sample cloze exercises are found in Section 11 of this kit.

When you have discovered that a student is weak in context clue usage, you should, of course, correct this weakness. You can use any of the sources which were discussed earlier in this section for detailed suggestion on improving context clue usage.

Dictionary usage usually is considered a last resort in unlocking the pronunciation and meaning of the unknown terms which a student needs in his reading. Since dictionary usage consists of many subskills, it is a rather difficult word recognition technique for the typical student to master. It contains such subskills as knowledge of alphabetical sequence, understanding the use of guide words, understanding and applying phonetic analysis, and choosing the correct dictionary definition. You give an

---

[6]Wilma H. Miller, *Teaching Reading in the Secondary School* (Springfield, Illinois: Charles C Thomas Publishers, 1974).

inventory in dictionary usage to a student who is reading on the intermediate-grade level or up higher. An inventory in dictionary usage usually is individually administered or group administered but is a written test.

An inventory in dictionary usage usually should be based upon an actual dictionary on the appropriate reading level. Several sample inventories in dictionary usage are included in the last part of this section. When you have determined that a student needs instruction in dictionary usage, you can use the sources which were mentioned earlier in this section for suggestions on presenting this word recognition technique.

Directions for Constructing, Administering, and Evaluating Inventories in the Word Recognition Techniques

It is obvious that a sight word knowledge inventory is simple to administer and evaluate. For example, you can simply purchase the Dolch Basic Sight Word List from the Garrard Press in Champaign, Illinois 61820. The list contains directions for giving these sight words. To evaluate the test, you simply count the number of sight words which a student identified correctly out of the 220 words which were included on the test. You can then determine a student's approximate independent reading level on this test by using the following:

Dolch Words Known	Equivalent Reading Level
0-75	Preprimer
76-120	Primer
121-170	First reader
171-210	Second reader
About 210	Third reader or above[7]

As was stated earlier, the Kucera-Francis Corpus of 220 sight words is included in the next part of this section. You can give this sight word list on an individual basis during which the student pronounces each of the words. You also can give it on a group basis in which you use each of the 220 words as one of several options in each case. For example, the first few lines of this test could look like the following when it is given on a group basis:

1. *the*	this	had	not
2. have	they	*of*	will
3. or	*and*	a	when
4. *to*	their	up	its
5. them	him	we	*a*

You probably can use the criteria for determining reading levels which were given for the Dolch Basic Sight Word List as a fairly good estimation of a student's reading level on the Kucera-Francis Corpus.

---

[7]Miles V. Zintz, *Corrective Reading* (Dubuque, Iowa: William C. Brown Company, Publishers, 1972), p. 60.

Fry's Instant words which are included in the next part of this section also can be given on an individual basis in which a student pronounces each of the words in the appropriate lists. You can also formulate a test which can be group-administered by using each of the words in one list as one of several options in each case. For example, the first few lines of the third-grade list can look like this when it is given on a group basis:

1. *ask*	set	fat	buy
2. letter	jump	does	*small*
3. face	seven	*yellow*	same
4. *show*	fly	don't	coat
5. gave	yes	*goes*	myself

If a student can recognize about 90 percent of the words on a list correctly, that level probably is his instructional reading level. If he can recognize 99 percent of the words on the list, that grade level is probably his independent reading level.

As was stated earlier, you can duplicate any of the phonetic analysis inventories which are included in the last part of this section. However, due to space limitations, a phonetic analysis inventory for each grade level simply could not be included. You are encouraged to formulate your own phonetic analysis inventories for grade levels other than those which are included in this kit. To do so, you first can decide if you want to give an inventory which calls for oral or written responses. If it is to be an oral inventory, the student usually only needs a blank sheet of paper. If it is a written inventory, you can type it on a stencil or ditto and then duplicate it or have the student use an acetate overlay. To help you formulate the inventory, you can examine the manuals and workbooks of a basal reader series or of a phonics program at the appropriate reading grade level.

To evaluate a phonetic analysis inventory, you should determine the specific phonetic analysis skills in which a student was weak. Then these phonetic analysis skills should be presented using the appropriate materials in a corrective or remedial reading program.

Although you can duplicate any of the structural analysis inventories which are included in this section, you may want to construct some of your own since it was impossible to include inventories at all of the different reading levels. In constructing your own structural analysis inventories, you can consult the appropriate pages of the manual or the workbook of a basal reader series. You then can type the inventory on a stencil or ditto and duplicate it for each student who is to use it. However, a student also can use an acetate overlay. To evaluate a structural analysis inventory, you determine what specific subskills in structural analysis a student lacks mastery of. Then you present these structural analysis subskills using material on the appropriate level of the student.

In constructing a context clue usage inventory, you can use basal readers and basal reader workbooks at the appropriate grade level as a guide. You construct a sentence with one word omitted. You then provide several other options in addition to the correctly omitted word. These options can be similar to the correctly omitted word in configuration or structure, but should not make sense in the sentence. You can follow the models for context clue usage inventories which are found in the last part of this section. You also can duplicate any of these inventories in their present form.

In constructing a dictionary usage inventory, you usually should use an actual dictionary at the appropriate reading level. An inventory in dictionary usage is an individually administered or group-administered written test. An inventory in dictionary usage can evaluate such skills as the following: alphabetical sequence, knowledge of the pronunciation key, use of guide words, synonyms, and selection of the correct dictionary definition. In constructing a dictionary usage inventory, you can follow the models included in this section of the *kit*. You also can use any of the dictionary usage inventories which are included in this section if they seem to be appropriate. When you have determined that a student lacks mastery of dictionary usage, you should present these subskills using dictionaries on the appropriate reading level.

Sample Inventories in the Word Recognition Techniques of Sight Word Knowledge, Phonetic Analysis, Structural Analysis, Context Clue Usage, and Dictionary Usage

The last part of this section of the *kit* includes sample inventories in each of the word recognition techniques. The Kucera-Francis Corpus and Fry's Instant Words are presented. In the word recognition techniques of phonetic analysis, structural analysis, and context clue usage, one inventory at each of the following levels is presented: the primary-grade level, the intermediate-grade level, and the secondary-school level. In dictionary usage, one inventory at the intermediate-grade level and one inventory at the senior high school level are given. You can use any of the inventories as models in constructing your own inventories in the word recognition techniques.

KUCERA-FRANCIS CORPUS*

1. the	35. her	69. two
2. of	36. all	70. may
3. and	37. she	71. then
4. to	38. there	72. do
5. a	39. would	73. first
6. in	40. their	74. any
7. that	41. we	75. my
8. is	42. him	76. now
9. was	43. been	77. such
10. he	44. has	78. like
11. for	45. when	79. our
12. it	46. who	80. over
13. with	47. will	81. man
14. as	48. more	82. me
15. his	49. no	83. even
16. on	50. if	84. most
17. be	51. out	85. made
18. at	52. so	86. after
19. by	53. said	87. also
20. I	54. what	88. did
21. this	55. up	89. many
22. had	56. its	90. before
23. not	57. about	91. must
24. are	58. into	92. through
25. but	59. than	93. back
26. from	60. them	94. years
27. or	61. can	95. where
28. have	62. only	96. much
29. an	63. other	97. your
30. they	64. new	98. may
31. which	65. some	99. well
32. one	66. could	100. down
33. you	67. time	101. should
34. were	68. these	102. because

103. each	142. come	181. left
104. just	143. since	182. number
105. those	144. against	183. course
106. people	145. go	184. war
107. Mr.	146. came	185. until
108. how	147. right	186. always
109. too	148. used	187. away
110. little	149. take	188. something
111. state	150. three	189. fact
112. good	151. states	190. though
113. very	152. himself	191. water
114. make	153. few	192. less
115. would	154. house	193. public
116. still	155. use	194. put
117. own	156. during	195. thing
118. see	157. without	196. almost
119. men	158. again	197. hand
120. work	159. place	198. enough
121. long	160. American	199. far
122. get	161. around	200. took
123. here	162. however	201. head
124. between	163. home	202. yet
125. both	164. small	203. government
126. life	165. found	204. system
127. being	166. Mrs.	205. better
128. under	167. thought	206. set
129. never	168. went	207. told
130. day	169. say	208. nothing
131. same	170. part	209. night
132. another	171. once	210. end
133. know	172. general	211. why
134. while	173. high	212. called
135. last	174. upon	213. didn't
136. might	175. school	214. eyes
137. us	176. every	215. find
138. great	177. don't	216. going
139. old	178. does	217. look
140. year	179. got	218. asked
141. off	180. united	219. later
		220. knew

FRY'S INSTANT WORDS*

FIRST 100 WORDS (approximately first grade)

Group 1a	Group 1b	Group 1c	Group 1d
1. the	he	go	who
2. a	I	see	an
3. is	they	then	their
4. you	one	us	she
5. to	good	no	new
6. and	me	him	said
7. we	about	by	did
8. that	had	was	boy
9. in	if	come	three
10. not	some	get	down
11. for	up	or	work
12. at	her	two	put
13. with	do	man	were
14. it	when	little	before
15. on	so	has	just
16. can	my	them	long
17. will	very	how	here
18. are	all	like	other
19. of	would	our	old
20. this	any	what	take
21. your	been	know	cat
22. as	out	make	again
23. but	there	which	give
24. be	from	much	after
25. have	day	his	many

SECOND 100 WORDS (approximately second grade)

Group 2a	Group 2b	Group 2c	Group 2d
1. saw	big	may	ran
2. home	where	let	five
3. soon	am	use	read
4. stand	ball	these	over

*From Edward B. Fry, *Reading Instruction for Classroom and Clinic* (New York: McGraw-Hill Book Company, 1972), pp. 58-63. Reproduced by special permission of Dr. Edward B. Fry.

5. box	morning	right	such
6. upon	live	present	way
7. first	four	tell	too
8. came	last	next	shall
9. girl	color	please	own
10. house	away	leave	most
11. find	red	hand	sure
12. because	friend	more	thing
13. made	pretty	why	only
14. could	eat	better	near
15. book	want	under	than
16. look	year	while	open
17. mother	white	should	kind
18. run	got	never	must
19. school	play	each	high
20. people	found	best	far
21. night	left	another	both
22. into	men	seem	end
23. say	bring	tree	also
24. think	wish	name	until
25. back	black	dear	call

THIRD 100 WORDS (approximately third grade)

Group 3a	Group 3b	Group 3c	Group 3d
1. ask	hat	off	fire
2. small	car	sister	ten
3. yellow	write	happy	order
4. show	try	once	part
5. goes	myself	didn't	early
6. clean	longer	set	fat
7. buy	those	round	third
8. thank	hold	dress	same
9. sleep	full	fall	love
10. letter	carry	wash	hear
11. jump	eight	start	yesterday
12. help	sing	always	eyes
13. fly	warm	anything	door
14. don't	sit	around	clothes
15. fast	dog	close	though

16. cold	ride	walk	o'clock
17. today	hot	money	second
18. does	grow	turn	water
19. face	cut	might	town
20. green	seven	hard	took
21. every	woman	along	pair
22. brown	funny	bed	now
23. coat	yes	fine	keep
24. six	ate	sat	head
25. gave	stop	hope	food

FOURTH 100 WORDS (approximately fourth grade)

Group 4a	*Group 4b*	*Group 4c*	*Group 4d*
1. told	time	word	wear
2. Miss	yet	almost	Mr.
3. father	true	thought	side
4. children	above	send	poor
5. land	still	receive	lost
6. interest	meet	pay	outside
7. government	since	nothing	wind
8. feet	number	need	Mrs.
9. garden	state	mean	learn
10. done	matter	late	held
11. country	line	half	front
12. different	remember	fight	built
13. bad	large	enough	family
14. across	few	feel	began
15. yard	hit	during	air
16. winter	cover	gone	young
17. table	window	hundred	ago
18. story	even	week	world
19. sometimes	city	between	airplane
20. I'm	together	change	without
21. tried	sun	being	kill
22. horse	life	care	ready
23. something	street	answer	stay
24. brought	party	course	won't
25. shoes	suit	against	paper

FIFTH 100 WORDS (approximately fourth grade)

Group 4e	Group 4f	Group 4g	Group 4h
1. hour	grade	egg	spell
2. glad	brother	ground	beautiful
3. follow	remain	afternoon	sick
4. company	milk	feed	became
5. believe	several	boat	cry
6. begin	war	plan	finish
7. mind	able	question	catch
8. pass	charge	fish	floor
9. reach	either	return	stick
10. month	less	sir	great
11. point	train	fell	guess
12. rest	cost	hill	bridge
13. sent	evening	wood	church
14. talk	note	add	lady
15. went	past	ice	tomorrow
16. bank	room	chair	snow
17. ship	flew	watch	whom
18. business	office	alone	women
19. whole	cow	low	among
20. short	visit	arm	road
21. certain	wait	dinner	farm
22. fair	teacher	hair	cousin
23. reason	spring	service	bread
24. summer	picture	class	wrong
25. fill	bird	quite	age

SIXTH 100 WORDS (approximately fourth grade)

Group 4i	Group 4j	Group 4k	Group 4l
1. become	herself	demand	aunt
2. body	idea	however	system
3. chance	drop	figure	lie
4. act	river	case	cause
5. die	smile	increase	marry
6. real	son	enjoy	possible
7. speak	bat	rather	supply
8. already	fact	sound	thousand

9. doctor	sort	eleven	pen
10. step	king	music	condition
11. itself	dark	human	perhaps
12. nine	themselves	court	produce
13. baby	whose	force	twelve
14. minute	study	plant	rode
15. ring	fear	suppose	uncle
16. wrote	move	law	labor
17. happen	stood	husband	public
18. appear	himself	moment	consider
19. heart	strong	person	thus
20. swim	knew	result	least
21. felt	often	continue	power
22. fourth	toward	price	mark
23. I'll	wonder	serve	president
24. kept	twenty	national	voice
25. well	important	wife	whether

Name _____ Grade _____ Teacher _____ Date _____

ORAL PHONETIC ANALYSIS INVENTORY (First-grade level)

Tell me the letter that these words start with:

boy	neighbor	kite	rock
fish	lamb	wind	yellow
saw	made	gate	mother
rain	join	doll	puppy
very	city	happy	talk

Tell me the letter that these words end with:

fox	sleep	another	goat
father	mittens	houses	dog
rabbit	look	red	him
leg	fly	ball	penny
hen	box	jump	ran

Tell me the two letters that these words start with:

black	place	stay	break
brown	crack	train	flag
friend	green	snow	smile
cry	clown	smoke	glad
free	dry	sky	twinkle

Name _____ Grade _____ Teacher _____ Date ___

WRITTEN PHONETIC ANALYSIS INVENTORY (Fourth-grade level)

Mark the vowel long — , short ∪ , or silent ȩ in these words:

eager	ledge	climb	tailor
husband	polite	example	insistent
greatest	scrape	sailboat	helicopter
cruise	tiger	child	coast

Mark the double o's long — or short ∪ in these words:

brook	moose	cookie	balloon
wood	toothless	spook	hook

Underline the consonant cluster (consonant blend or consonant digraph) which are found in these words:

smart	scramble	creature	shield
whinny	clothes	telephone	choice
touch	clang	thimble	bank
breathless	splashing	wrinkle	dreadful

Underline the diphthong found in each of these words:

ground	royal	mountain	plow
employ	powder	broil	bounce

Mark ⩗ all of the silent letters in these words:

wrap	gnat	whose	ghost
bell	cheese	wringer	knight
fright	maybe	goldmine	wagonload
handle	quite	kindle	squeak

Mark Ә the schwa sound in each of these words:

pupil	label	comma	button
animal	elephant	pencil	microscope
circus	minus	bacon	hippopotamus

Name ——————— Grade ———— Teacher ——— Date ——

WRITTEN PHONETIC ANALYSIS INVENTORY (Secondary-school level)

Mark the vowels long — , short ∪ , or silent ℰ , in the following words:

relieve	strange	chestnut	swift
straight	gratify	rubbish	increase
estimating	exceeding	prevail	inspire
indicate	statement	eligible	inhabitants

Mark ϑℏ all of the silent letters in these words:

bough	slaughter	though	khaki
hour	doubt	bright	wrench
bless	limb	slight	gnarled

Mark ϑ the schwa sound in each of these words:

buffalo	container	diamond	fiction
negative	consent	sanction	armament
accommodate	entertain	comedy	mixture

Underline the diphthong in each of these words:

schoolboy	proud	ground	they
bough	shower	moisten	couch
frown	broiling	powder	house

Rewrite each of these words in its conventional spelling to show that you know how to read them in phonetic spelling:

kar ϑ t	karb ϑ n	plaz ϑ	shure
pleazhure	pich	shugar·	moshon
teknik	egzample	boks	antik

Name _____ Grade _____ Teacher _____ Date ___

STRUCTURAL ANALYSIS INVENTORY (Second-grade level)

Underline the base or root word in each word:

sliding	dropping	running	hopped
babies	cries	happier	dried
funniest	happiest	hopping	trapped

Underline the prefix in each word:

untie	below	enjoy	before
unhappy	already	belong	across
also	asleep	became	along

Underline the suffix in each word:

waiting	cats	swinging	horns
sleepy	squealed	squirrels	wished
folded	washes	teaches	trucks

Underline the base or root word in each word:

pointed	sniffs	dresses	nearer
glasses	waiting	watched	stretched
burned	fires	cakes	brothers

Divide each of these compound words by drawing a / between each of the two small words:

fireman	playground	snowman	cowgirl
sunshine	without	gumdrop	cowboy
scarecrow	playmate	policeman	airport

Optional oral test

Pronounce each of the following contractions:

don't	I'm	o'clock	doesn't
can't	I've	they've	isn't
aren't	we'll	it's	didn't

Name _____ Grade _____ Teacher _____ Date ____

STRUCTURAL ANALYSIS INVENTORY (Fifth-grade level)

Underline the base or root word in each word:

blossoms	immediately	wreckage	nodded
commenced	newness	inspecting	trapper
reappear	buzzers	commonly	benefited

Underline the prefix in each word:

disappoint	recover	microphone	unusual
dissolve	misspell	although	displease
misplace	encircle	defrost	midsummer

Underline the suffix in each word:

nothingness	solemnly	tiniest	tomatoes
hesitated	carefully	tasty	cunning
pleasantly	thankful	achievement	graceful

Divide these compound words into syllables by placing a / between each small word:

earthworm	honeycomb	overjoy	undersecretary
overcome	honeybee	waterfall	fireworks
earthquake	railroad	backbreaking	deerskin

Divide these words into syllables by placing a / between each syllable:

committee	applause	sandal	creature
silent	advantage	regardless	civil
custom	exclaim	moment	valley
people	planning	hunter	invention
lightning	bottom	mouthful	remember
stallion	astride	picket	motionless
straggler	igloo	cucumber	gelatin

Why did you divide *silent* as you did?

Why did you divide *committee* as you did?

Why did you divide *sandal* as you did?

Why did you divide *picket* as you did?

Mark the accented syllable in this way about'   for each word:

number	again	forward	handkerchief
belong	around	something	message
snappy	runner	suddenly	beside
enlarge	content	indeed	button

Name ————————— Grade ———— Teacher ———— Date ——

STRUCTURAL ANALYSIS INVENTORY (Secondary-school level)

Underline the base or root word in each word:

scornfully	distraught	hydroplane	disdainful
unfamiliar	loneliness	offhandedly	formality
attachment	companions	immediately	disappearance

Underline the prefix in each word:

submarine	deport	dismantle	enfold
translate	tricycle	nonsense	abnormal
binocular	deport	improbable	promote

Underline the suffix in each word:

disturbance	gracious	pleasantly	credible
baggage	vicinity	egotism	instinctively
proximity	acquaintance	occurrences	curiosity

Divide these compound words by placing a / between each of the two syllables:

chairman	foreman	bricklayer	moonlight
highlight	parlormaid	nineteen	overshoe
overlook	thundershower	clergyman	grandchildren

Divide each of these words into syllables by placing a / between each syllable:

superintendent	describe	doctor	remedial
obstinate	impulse	desolation	convenience
distraught	insolent	grossly	ardent
remnant	safety	currency	certainty
translation	distance	reflection	admission
parchment	application	experiment	phantom
leafy	tempest	impending	azure

Why did you divide *impulse* as you did?

Why did you divide *application* as you did?

Why did you divide *phantom* as you did?

Why did you divide *azure* as you did?

Mark **around´** the accented syllable in each word:

abate	perplexing	action	abound
solution	connection	basement	bemoan
terminate	obese	tedious	cannon
perform	primrose	beautiful	fantastic

Name _____ Grade _____ Teacher _____ Date _____

INVENTORY IN CONTEXT CLUE USAGE (Third-grade level)

Underline the word which makes the best sense in each sentence:

1. John put the _____ ice cream into a dish and handed it to Ann.
   melting
   making
   matching

2. Soon she had all the _____ and birds back in their cages.
   another
   animals
   ahead

3. You might as well settle down and stop your _____ and struggling.
   squealing
   strong
   stepping

4. The cry came from a _____ little girl.
   followed
   fastened
   frightened

5. Mrs. Jackson made thick sandwiches of bread and raspberry _____.
   joined
   jam
   jump

6. There is no doubt that children are _____ .
   night
   noise
   noisy

7. Someone had left a bunch of violets on his way home from the _____ park.
   amusement
   amazement
   amuse

8. The freight _____ made a round trip.
   trap
   train
   trim

9. There once was a _____ who had lived to a ripe old age.

> farming
>
> farm
>
> farmer

10. The leaves became thick on every branch and _____ .

> twin
>
> twine
>
> twig

Name _____ Grade _____ Teacher _____ Date _____

INVENTORY IN CONTEXT CLUE USAGE (Sixth-grade level)

Underline the word which makes the best sense in each sentence:

1. Sally watched the red _____ of flame lick around the oak logs in the
   fireplace.   tables

                         tongues

                         tongs

2. After two tries he _____ to hop up on the oven door.

                         managed

                         managing

                         manager

3. The subject of bird _____ , or journeys, has fascinated men for
   centuries.   migrate

                        machines

                        migrations

4. Fred thought that this _____ boy was going to laugh at his rather
   ungainly horse.   unknown

                            umbrella

                            unharnessing

5. The hotel should have chairs and beds so that foreign guests could be

   _____ .

   contained

   comfortable

   compartment

6. The shrill whistle of the engine _____ through the valley long before
   Mary could see the train   edged
   coming around the bend.   echoed

                                   easiest

7. _____ systems will have to be perfected so that the present water
           can be used over and over again.

   Filtration

   Filters

   Funnels

8. There are many studies taking place at present to prove or _____ this
   theory.   dismay
                                                            disprove
                                                            distance

9. We are glad that out Italian friends introduced us to _____ .
                                                  pizza
                                                  pretty
                                                  pitch

10. You will have to find an occupation that is less _____ .
                                              dangerous
                                              displaying
                                              destroyed

Name _____ Grade _____ Teacher _____ Date ____

INVENTORY IN CONTEXT CLUE USAGE (Secondary-school level)

Underline the word which makes the best sense in the sentence:

1. Mrs. Short shouted triumphantly after him as she watched his figure with _____ as it disappeared into the hall.
container
contempt
courageous

2. She was no more than the servant, but a very _____ old lady wearing her spectacles on the end of her nose.
independent
impunity
irrelevant

3. Dr. Peterson came out of the corridor looking distraught and _____ .
haranguing
haggard
hypocrisy

4. The swing of his nature took him from extreme _____ to devouring energy.
languid
languor
labyrinth

5. The _____ sand slope allowed no escape from a spot which I had visited most involuntarily.
terminate
transgress
treacherous

6. We had reached the same crowded _____ in which we had found ourselves in the morning.
thoroughness
thoroughfare
thoroughly

7. I know that you share my love of all that is _____ and outside the conventions and humdrum routine of every-day life.
bizarre
billion
bigot

8. The little house was hidden among the dense _____ on the island.

    faint

    foliage

    foundation

9. It was a region of _____ , emptiness, truth, and dignity.

    loneliness

    lonelier

    lonesome

10. He never said that he would be glad to listen to an _____ .

    hypochondriac

    hysteria

    hydrogen

Name _____ Grade _____ Teacher _____ Date ___

INVENTORY IN DICTIONARY USAGE* (Intermediate-grade level)

1. On what page are the two guide words *mounted* and *movement* located?
2. Look up the word *gopher.* What are the two guide words on this page?
3. What does the word *defensive* mean?
4. On what page are the two guide words *postpone* and *pottery*?
5. According to this dictionary, what is the sound of the *e* in the word *lead,* which means to guide or to conduct?
6. According to the pronunciation key of this dictionary, how is the long *o* sound such as in the word *flow* marked?
7. On what page are the two guide words *nationalism* and *nature* located?
8. According to this dictionary, what is the meaning of the word *plateau*?
9. What are the two guide words on the page upon which the word *situation* is located?
10. According to this dictionary, what word is a synonym of the word *skillful*?

Webster's New Practical School Dictionary. (New York: American Book Company, 1964).

Name _____ Grade _____ Teacher _____ Date ___

INVENTORY IN DICTIONARY USAGE* (Senior high school level)

1. Look up the word *jeopardy*. What are the two guide words on this page?
2. What does the word *precarious* mean?
3. On what page are the two guide words *transcript* and *translate* located?
4. What is the meaning of the word *hemoglobin*?
5. On what page are the two guide words *dependency* and *depute* located?
6. According to this dictionary, how is the short *e* as in the word *less* written?
7. What is the meaning of the word *epidermis*?
8. On what page are the two guide words *incognizant* and *inconveniently* located?
9. According to this dictionary, what are the synonyms of the word *moral*?
10. What are the two guide words on the page on which the word *reprieve* is located?

**Webster's Seventh New Collegiate Dictionary* (Springfield, Mass.: G. & C. Merriam Company, 1963).

Adapting the
Individual Reading Inventory
to Content Areas

Do you think that many students in the intermediate grades and in secondary school find it difficult to read content textbooks in social studies and science? Unfortunately, it is true that many social studies and science textbooks have a readability level which is two or more years above the grade level in which they were designed to be used. Students simply cannot experience success in these content areas unless they are provided with reading materials which they can read successfully.

This section is designed to help you individualize reading instructions in social studies and science in the intermediate grades and in secondary school. It will do this by describing how to use a content-oriented Individual Reading Inventory to determine a student's independent, instructional, and frustration reading levels. The section first describes the characteristics of an Individual Reading Inventory when it is used in social studies and science. Next, the section presents directions for constructing, administering and evaluating an Individual Reading Inventory in social studies and science. Last, the section presents one sight word test and one graded oral reading paragraph from social studies at the intermediate-grade level and one sample sight word test and graded oral reading paragraph from social studies at the secondary-school level. Also presented in this section are one sample sight word test and one graded oral reading paragraph in science at the intermediate-grade and at the secondary-school level.

Description of an Individual Reading Inventory in Social Studies and Science for the Diagnosis of Reading Difficulties

Although the characteristics of a content-oriented Individual Reading Inventory were described briefly in Section 7, they are described in greater detail in this section. A content-oriented Individual Reading Inventory can be given by an intermediate-grade teacher or a secondary-school content teacher to those disabled readers in a class who simply cannot cope with the required content textbook. Therefore, you would give such an inventory only to the moderately and severely disabled readers in a class. You can give the sight word tests and graded oral reading paragraphs of an Individual Reading Inventory so that you can determine what content textbooks and supplementary reading materials should be given to a disabled reader.

As was stated briefly in Section 7, the following is one outline of a content-oriented Individual Reading Inventory:

- Establishing rapport with the student
- Presenting a sight word test composed of some of the specialized vocabulary terms from the content area
- Administering the graded oral reading paragraphs which were constructed from a series of content textbooks

It is useful to describe at this time each of these various parts of a content-oriented Individual Reading Inventory in detail.

Establishing Rapport with the Student

Obviously, you should establish a positive relationship with the student before giving him a content-oriented Individual Reading Inventory. Although this may present the greatest amount of difficulty at the beginning of a semester, it is important to explain the purpose of the inventory to the student even if you know him quite well. You can explain the purpose of a content-oriented Individual Reading Inventory to a student in the following way: "I would like you to take this informal inventory which I have made for you so that I can learn what textbooks and library books you can read successfully in this content area. After you have taken this inventory, I will know what kind of textbooks, library books, magazines, and newspapers you will enjoy reading and can read successfully in this area."

You also can gain insights into how a student feels about social studies or science and how he feels about reading materials in these two areas by asking him questions like these:

Do you like to read (social studies, science) textbooks?
Do you enjoy learning about _____?
What do you think is the most interesting thing you have learned in _____?
What do you think is the easiest for you about learning _____?
What do you think is the hardest for you about learning _____?
Do you sometimes have difficulty in reading and studying the required textbook in _____?
What kinds of material do you like to read for pleasure in _____?

Giving a Sight Word Test

The second part of a content-oriented Individual Reading Inventory often is a sight word test which you formulate from some of the specialized vocabulary terms which are found in the content textbooks which you used to formulate the graded oral reading paragraphs. This sight word test composed of specialized vocabulary terms corresponds to the Dolch Basic Sight Word Test, the Kucera-Francis Corpus, or Fry's Instant Words, which can be given in the traditional Individual Reading Inventory as was described in Section 7. The use of a sight word test can help you to determine a student's independent, instructional, and frustration reading levels in the content area.

Administering the Graded Oral Reading Paragraphs

The last part of a content-oriented Individual Reading Inventory is the giving of the graded oral reading paragraphs which were constructed from a series of content textbooks. These graded oral reading paragraphs should begin at least two grade levels below the suspected instructional reading level of a student who is to use them. They should continue at least one grade level above the independent reading level of the student who is to use them. Each paragraph also should be correct in terms of the content material which is presented in that textbook. As was explained in Section 7, you may want to check the readability level of each of the textbooks which you use to formulate the graded oral reading paragraphs by using the Dale-Chall Readability Formula or the Fry Readability Formula.

The student then can read each of the paragraphs orally while you mark his oral reading errors in terms of omissions, insertions, mispronunciations, substitutions, repetitions, and hesitations. You then are able to establish his independent, instructional, and frustration reading levels in terms of the criteria described in Section 7.

Directions for Constructing, Administering, and Evaluating the Word Lists and Graded Oral Reading Paragraphs of a Content-Oriented Individual Reading Inventory

This part of the section discusses in detail how to construct, administer, and evaluate the sight word tests and graded oral reading paragraphs in a content-oriented Individual Reading Inventory. To prepare the sight word tests, you first must choose a graded series of social studies or science textbooks at the intermediate-grade or secondary-school level. This usually should be the series of social studies or science textbooks which are used in your elementary or secondary school. You then randomly select some of the specialized vocabulary terms which are found in the glossary of each of the textbooks to construct a sight word test. You can choose every nth specialized vocabulary term to formulate the sight word test. Each sight word test should consist of at least 25 terms. You then can type each sight word test on a sheet of paper and glue it to a sheet of cardboard or oaktag so that it can be used many times by the students. Next, you can type each sight word test on a stencil or ditto and duplicate it so that you can mark the words which a student fails to pronounce correctly. You then determine each student's independent, instructional, and frustration reading levels in that content area by using the criteria which were described in detail in Section 7 and are reviewed briefly later in this section.

You use the same graded series of social studies or science textbooks to formulate the graded oral reading paragraphs of the content-oriented Individual Reading Inventory. You can turn toward the middle of each content textbook and formulate a coherent passage from the material which is found in that chapter. The passage should be approximately 100-200 words long and should contain about as much specialized vocabulary as is typically found in that section of the textbook. It is important that each of the passages be accurate in terms of the content which is presented in that textbook. You then type each passage on a sheet of paper so the students can read it aloud. You can make each passage durable by pasting it to a piece of cardboard or oaktag or by covering it with a sheet of acetate. You then type each of the passages, the comprehension questions which accompany it, and the formulae for determining the various reading levels on a stencil or ditto. Then you can duplicate these passages so that you can mark each student's oral reading errors and record his answers to the comprehension questions.

You then have the student begin reading the content-oriented graded oral reading paragraphs aloud while you mark his oral reading errors. You may want to tape-record his oral reading so that you can mark his errors later when you play back the tape. Here is a copy of the marking system which has been suggested in this kit.

Omissions	Circle the entire word or letter sound (vegetables)
Insertions	Insert with a caret very ^
Underline and write in all mispronunciations	citrus citrūse
Draw a line through a substitution and write it in	~~hurt~~ harm
Use a wavy line to indicate a repetition	religious
Put a check mark above a hesitation of more than 5 seconds	cuľture

You later can use the criteria of Betts, Spache, or Smith which were described in detail in Section 7, or your own criteria, to determine each student's independent, instructional, and frustration reading levels in that content area. You will recall that the criteria of Betts are used in determining reading levels for this kit.

Each student should read tradebooks and other supplementary materials in social studies and science on his independent reading level. He should read and study social studies and science textbooks which are on his instructional reading level. Usually he should not be required to read materials in social studies and science which are on his frustration reading level.

Sample Sight Word Tests and Graded Oral Reading Paragraphs in Social Studies and Science at the Intermediate-Grade and Secondary-School Levels

Following are several sample sight word tests and graded oral reading paragraphs at the intermediate-grade and secondary-school levels which were formulated from social studies and science textbooks. You can duplicate and use any of these sight word tests or graded oral reading paragraphs which are appropriate for your students. You also can modify them or use them as models if you wish to do so. As was stated earlier, the criteria of Emmett Betts are used in this kit for determining reading levels. Instead of these criteria, you can use your own criteria or those of George D. Spache or Nila Banton Smith.

SIGHT WORD TEST IN SOCIAL STUDIES* (Fifth-grade level)

Name _____ Grade _____ Teacher _____ Date _____

1. abolitionist
2. astronomy
3. Bay Area Rapid Transit
4. capital
5. Chinatown
6. climate
7. conquistadores
8. cultural pluralism
9. economy
10. fertilizer
11. Great Plains
12. income tax
13. labor union
14. longhouse
15. metropolitan area
16. mountain basin
17. nuclear energy
18. pollution
19. race prejudice
20. reservoir
21. selva
22. social security
23. strike
24. technology
25. urban decay

Instructional level:

23 words correct

*Bass, Herbert J., *Man and Society* (Morristown, N.J.: Silver Burdett Company. © 1972 General Learning Corporation). Used by permission.

GRADED ORAL READING PARAGRAPH
IN SOCIAL STUDIES (Fifth-grade level)*

MEXICAN-AMERICANS IN TEXAS†

Name _____ Grade _____ Teacher _____ Date _____

There are a number of Mexican-Americans who live in Hidalgo County, Texas. These Mexican-Americans raise cotton, vegetables, corn, and citrus fruits. Most of these Mexican-Americans continue to speak Spanish even though they were born in the United States. Mexican-Americans call their section of the town el pueblo mexicano, which means "the Mexican town." Mexican-Americans do not want to hurt their families or bring sadness to them. The shoppers in the Mexican section of town are quite relaxed and gay. Most Mexican-Americans in Hidalgo County believe that Anglos value making money too much. Most Mexican-Americans also are very religious. The Mexican-Americans in Hidalgo County continue to keep their culture alive.

Comprehension questions:

1. What do the Mexican-Americans in Hidalgo County raise?
2. What language is spoken by Mexican-Americans?
3. Why do you think that most Mexican-Americans think that Anglos value making money too much?
4. Why do the Mexican-Americans in Hidalgo County want to continue their own culture?
5. Give me a sentence using the word *religious.*

Number of words <u>108</u>

Number of words correct _____

Accuracy:

90% <u>97</u>
99% <u>107</u>

Comprehension:

95% *Five Questions*
75% *Four Questions*

---

*Adapted from the following source: Herbert J. Bass, *Man and Society* (Morristown, N.J.: Silver Burdett Company, 1972, pp. 109-110. © 1972 General Learning Corporation). Used by permission.
†See Marion R. Daugherty and Carl H. Madden, *The Economic Process* (Glenview, Ill.: Scott, Foresman and Company, 1969).

SIGHT WORD TEST IN SOCIAL STUDIES* (Secondary-school level)

Name _____ Grade _____ Teacher _____ Date ___

1. absolute advantage
2. capital
3. collective bargaining
4. competition
5. demand curve
6. derived demand
7. economic growth
8. equation of exchange
9. goods and services
10. indirect tax
11. interfactor substitution
12. land
13. macroeconomics
14. mixed economy
15. national income
16. opportunity cost
17. price index
18. productive resources
19. real capital
20. scarcity
21. specialization
22. law of supply and demand
23. technology
24. velocity of circulation
25. workable competition

Instructional level:

23 words correct

_____

*See Marion R. Daugherty and Carl H. Madden, *The Economic Process* (Glenview, Ill.: Scott, Foresman and Company, 1969).

GRADED ORAL READING PARAGRAPH IN SOCIAL STUDIES
(Secondary-school level)

THE CONSUMER IN THE ECONOMY*

Name _____ Grade _____ Teacher _____ Date ____

A man's income is a valuable indicator of his tastes, political views, education, and even his age. The income of a family determines its role as a consumer—the amount of goods and services it receives, and thus its degree of economic health. Consumers set the guidelines for production by their dollar choices in markets. These choices are called consumer patterns of expenditures. To measure the incomes of families, officials consider living units. They look at the characteristics of a living unit—the number of people in it, whether it is urban or rural, and the specific needs of the unit. Location can be a factor in income differences. It is true that American families do not receive equal incomes in each of the 50 states. Although it is also true that each American belongs to some minority, the economic impact of minority status, class consciousness, and inequality of opportunities falls the heaviest on blacks, working women, and the elderly. The black unemployment rate is higher than the white race in every occupational group. The median income of employed females are only half those of employed males. When an older worker tries to find a new job, it is much harder for him than for a younger man to locate new employment. The onus of practicing discrimination does not fall on any one group alone. Unions, industry, government, and the general public all have participated.

Comprehension questions:

1. What are the characteristics of a living unit?
2. What types of people are discriminated against in jobs?
3. Why do American families not receive equal income in all of the 50 states?
4. Why do you think that blacks do not receive as much income as whites?
5. Give me a sentence using the word *inequality*.

Number of words <u>235</u>

Number of words correct _____

Accuracy:

90% <u>212</u>

99% <u>233</u>

Comprehension:

95% *Five Questions*

75% *Four Questions*

SIGHT WORD TEST IN SCIENCE* (Sixth-grade level)

Name _____ Grade _____ Teacher _____ Date _____

1. action
2. atom
3. block and tackle
4. chemical change
5. comet
6. control
7. diffusion
8. egg cell
9. energy
10. fixed pulley
11. fulcrum
12. graft
13. hydra
14. instinct
15. lever
16. microphone
17. mutant
18. nerve impulse
19. orbit
20. pistil
21. potential energy
22. radioactive
23. reservoir
24. sensory neuron
25. telescope

Instructional level:

23 words correct

---

*See Paul F. Brandwein, Elizabeth K. Cooper, Paul E. Blackwood, Elizabeth B. Hone, and Thomas P. Fraser, *Concepts in Science,* Level Six (New York: Harcourt Brace Jovanovich, Inc., 1972).

GRADED ORAL READING PARAGRAPH IN SCIENCE (Sixth-grade level)

YOUR BODY'S DEFENSES*

Name_____ Grade _____ Teacher _____ Date _____

Did you know that your body is always on the defense against bacteria? Your body wins most of its battles against bacteria. When you have a cold, your body is being attacked by a *virus*. It often takes your body only a short time to overcome the viruses which cause a cold. However, overcoming attacks by other viruses or organisms may take a longer time. Your skin is your first line of defense against viruses. In the inside of your body you also will find cells that are a line of defense against bacteria. Covering cells line inside cavities of the body which can be easily reached by infectious bacteria. Sneezing and coughing are reflexes that help get rid of bacteria. When you breathe, bacteria and other harmful substances are caught in the mucus of the nose and throat. They are removed from the body by sneezing and coughing. When you scrape or cut yourself and break the skin, harmful bacteria may fall on the open wound and begin to feed. This growth of harmful bacteria is called infection.

Comprehension questions:

1. What is a virus?
2. How can sneezing and coughing help your body to get rid of bacteria?
3. Why does your body win most of its battles against bacteria?
4. Why should you put an antiseptic on an open wound?
5. Give me a sentence using the word *bacteria*.

Number of words <u>179</u>

Number of words correct _____

Accuracy:

   90% <u>161</u>
   99% <u>177</u>

Comprehension:

   95% Five Questions
   75% Four Questions

SIGHT WORD TEST IN SCIENCE* (Secondary-school level)

Name _____ Grade _____ Teacher _____ Date ____

1. absolute zero
2. alternates
3. aromatic compounds
4. beta particle
5. chain reaction
6. covalent bond
7. diode
8. electric effect
9. energetic particle
10. fossil fuels
11. galvanometer
12. halogens
13. inert
14. isotopes
15. liquid
16. molecules
17. north-seeking pole
18. pentane
19. plasma
20. prism
21. ray
22. scientific notation
23. spectrum
24. temperature
25. transverse wave

Instructional level:

23 words correct

---

*George A. Williams, Max C. Bolen, and Ray B. Doerhoff, *Physical Science* (New York: Webster Division, McGraw-Hill Book Company, 1973).

GRADED ORAL READING PARAGRAPH IN SCIENCE (Secondary-school level)

WHAT IS "HOT"?*

Name _____ Grade _____ Teacher _____ Date ___

You know that kinetic energy is the energy of motion and that everything that moves has kinetic energy. All matter is composed of very tiny particles, and these particles are in constant movement. The kinetic energy of movement inside things is called internal kinetic energy. The total internal kinetic energy of a body is called heat. The temperature of a body is a measure of the average internal kinetic energy of all the tiny particles within it. A thermometer is one of the many instruments which is used to measure temperature. Most thermometers are glass tubes which contain mercury which rises and falls. The temperature is read from a scale which is placed on or near the thermometer. The marks on the thermometer are called its scale, and its divisions are called degrees. A thermometer can have a Celsius temperature scale or a Fahrenheit scale. It can also have the Kelvin or absolute scale. The zero point on the Kelvin scale is called absolute zero. Much work has been done in the field of low-temperature study, which is called cryogenics.

Comprehension questions:

1. What is all matter composed of?
2. What is the temperature of a body?
3. How are all thermometers alike?
4. How are thermometers different?
5. Give me a sentence using the word *kinetic.*

Number of words 179

Number of words correct _____

Accuracy:

   90% 161

   99% 177

_____

*Adapted from the following source: George A. Williams, Max C. Bolen, and Ray B. Doerhoff, *Physical Science* (New York: Webster Division, McGraw-Hill Book Company, 1973), pp. 117-124.

Comprehension:

95% Five Questions
75% Four Questions

The Group
Reading Inventory

Do you think that most students in the intermediate grades and in the secondary school possess the special skills and abilities which are needed for effective comprehension of social studies and science textbooks? It is an unfortunate fact that a number of students just do not have the skills which they need to read and study social studies and science textbooks with success. However, if you determine what special skills and abilities a group of students lacks, you can provide the appropriate corrective reading instruction in an intermediate-grade classroom or a secondary-school classroom.

This section can help you provide corrective reading instructions in social studies and science classes for those groups of students who need it. The section first describes the characteristics of several different types of group reading inventories which you can use in social studies and science classes. Next the section presents directions for constructing, administering, and evaluating these several kinds of group inventories. The section closes with three examples of group reading inventories. You are given a sample of one group informal reading text on using the aids in a social studies textbook at the intermediate-grade level. An example of a group reading inventory which can determine if a student can read the required textbook is taken from a secondary school social studies textbook. Also included is a group informal reading test which was formulated from a chapter in a secondary-school science textbook. You can duplicate and use any of these informal reading tests or use them as models for tests which you can construct from you own social studies and science textbooks.

Description of Group Reading Inventories in Social Studies and Science for the Diagnosis of Reading Difficulties

As was stated earlier, a number of students in the intermediate grades and the secondary school simply are not able to read and study the required social studies and science textbooks with success. Although lower-level textbooks usually should be provided for the moderately and severely disabled readers in these classes, many of the average and mildly disabled readers need to be taught the special skills and abilities which are required for effective study of the chosen social studies or science textbooks. However, you must determine which of these reading skills and abilities a group of students does not possess so that you can present them. It obviously is a waste of time to present reading skills which a group of students already possesses. A group reading inventory can help you determine what special reading skills and abilities you should present in social studies and science classes.

There are three major types of group informal reading tests which are described in this section. One group informal reading test can help you determine if your students can use the aids which are found in their social studies and science textbooks effectively. This informal reading test usually is given at the beginning of a course or semester. You may be surprised how many students in the intermediate grades and in the secondary school cannot use textbook aids such as the table of contents, the index, the glossary, italicized words, maps, graphs, diagrams, tables, and pictures. This is an open-book test in which each student shows his competency in using these different textbook aids.

The next type of informal reading test can be called an informal reading inventory. It is designed to see if your students can read and study the required social studies or science textbook with success. In this test, students are to read a passage of 1,000-2,000 words from the middle of the required social studies or science textbook. When the students have finished reading this passage, they are to respond to it in writing in a free response. They also answer a number of objective questions about this passage. These questions can evaluate a student's ability in such reading skills as the following: understanding a directly stated and implied main idea, noting important details, literal comprehension, interpretive comprehension, and critical reading.

The third type of group informal reading test is a test which is based on a specific chapter located near the middle of the required social studies or science textbook. This is an open-book test which should be given near the beginning of the course or semester. It is designed to determine if your students possess the special reading skills which are required to comprehend the chosen social studies or science textbook with success. It can include a matching vocabulary exercise composed of specialized vocabulary terms included in the chapter. It also can contain some literal, interpretive, critical, and creative comprehension questions from the chapter. It can contain objective questions about the main ideas and important details which are found in that specific chapter.

Directions for Constructing, Administering, and Evaluating Group Reading Inventories in Social Studies and Science

As was stated before, one group informal reading test can help you determine if your students can use the textbook aids which are found in the required social studies and science textbooks. To construct this type of informal reading test, you simply use your required social studies or science textbook. You then formulate about 15 questions on the use of the various textbook aids such as the table of contents, the index, the glossary, the italicized words, the maps, the graphs, the diagrams, the tables, and the pictures. These questions should require the students to use the various textbook aids effectively. In giving this type of informal reading test, you simply ask the students to use their textbook to locate the answers to the questions. You can give them all the time which they need to complete this test. In evaluating this informal reading test, you simply make a tally of which of the textbook aids your students are not able to use effectively. Then you present the use of these various textbook aids to your entire class or to small groups in your class. These presentations should use your students' own social studies and science textbooks as much as possible. It does little good to present this type of informal reading test if you do not follow up on the results of the test. You will find one example of this type of test which was constructed from an intermediate-grade social studies textbook in the next part of this section.

In constructing the group informal reading inventory, you first choose a passage of about 1,000-2,000 words from near the middle of the required social studies or science textbook. You then have the students read this passage from their textbook silently. You can time them if you wish to do so. They then respond to the copy of the group reading inventory which you have typed and duplicated. The first part of this inventory can contain several open-ended questions which each student is to respond to in writing. Several such open-ended questions can be as follows: What was this passage about? What did the author say about _____? When you examine each student's free responses in detail, you can determine quite a bit about his ability to organize his thoughts, react to the selection, and spell correctly. Then the student can answer the objective questions which you have prepared on this passage. These objective questions can be multiple-choice questions, true-false questions, or short-answer questions. In social studies, the following special reading skills and abilities can be evaluated: understanding the implied main ideas, noting significant details, understanding time sequence, understanding cause-effect relationships, interpretive comprehension ability, and critical reading ability. In science, the following reading skills can be evaluated: understanding a directly stated main idea, recognizing significant details, reading to follow directions, and literal comprehension ability.

In evaluating a group reading inventory, you obviously determine in which of the special reading skills and abilities your students are weak. You then can present these special reading skills to the entire class or to a group of students in the class. Obviously, you always should follow up on the results of this type of informal reading test.

The third type of informal reading test is the test on a specific chapter from a social studies or science textbook. In this type of test, you ask the students to read a specific chapter which is located near the middle of their required social studies or science textbook. They can take all the time which they need to read this chapter carefully. They then can respond to an informal reading test which you have typed and duplicated for them. They usually can refer back to the chapter while they are taking the test. The first part of this test often includes a matching vocabulary exercise composed of some of the specialized vocabulary terms which are found in that chapter. It also often includes some literal, interpretive, critical, and creative comprehension questions which are based upon that specific chapter. It also can contain several objective questions about the main ideas and important details which are found in the chapter.

In evaluating this type of informal reading test, you determine which special reading skills and abilities will need to be taught to a group of students or to your entire class. You may need to present the specialized vocabulary terms found in a social studies or science chapter before your students read that chapter. You also may need to stress interpretive comprehension, critical reading, or creative reading.

Sample Group Reading Inventories in Social Studies and Science

The last part of this section includes one group informal reading test on using textbook aids which was constructed from an intermediate-grade social studies textbook. Also included is an example of a group reading inventory from a secondary-school social studies textbook, and an informal reading test on a specific chapter which was formulated from a secondary-school science textbook. You can duplicate and use any of these informal reading tests or use them as models for tests which you can construct from your own social studies and science textbooks.

INFORMAL READING TEST ON USING TEXTBOOK AIDS*

Name ——————————— Grade ——————— Teacher ——————— Date ————————

1. On what page does Chapter 4 begin?

2. According to the index of this book, on what two pages is Henry Ford mentioned?

3. What is the title of the map on page 152?

4. What are the subheadings in Chapter 21 of this textbook?

5. According to page 51, what does the italicized word *colonies* mean?

6. According to the picture on page 328, who invented the cotton gin?

7. According to the graph on page 210, what is the black population of Chicago?

8. According to the glossary of this textbook, what is the definition of the word *barter*?

9. How many chapters are there in this textbook?

10. On what page does the glossary of this textbook begin?

11. According to the picture on page 269, in what city is Sugar Loaf Mountain located?

---

*Bass, Herbert J., *Man and Society* (Morristown, N.J.: Silver Burdett Company. © 1972 General Learning Corporation). Used by permission.

12. According to the glossary of this textbook, what is the definition of the word *mestizo*?

13. According to the index, on what pages are the Great Plains mentioned?

14. According to the map on page 336, what states contain petroleum deposits?

15. According to the table of contents, how many Units does this textbook contain?

GROUP READING INVENTORY*

Name _____ Grade _____ Teacher _____ Date ___

Source of Reading Selection

   Leo J. Alilunas and J. Woodrow Sayre, *Youth Faces American Citizen-
   ship.* (Philadelphia: J.B. Lippincott Company, 1965), pp. 227-231.

Length of Reading Selection

   About 1,900 words

Subject Area

   Problems of Democracy

Grade Level

   Senior high school

Brief Summary

   This selection discusses the definition of minority groups and discusses
   the attitudes held by many American citizens toward various minority
   group people.

Part One

What did the author say about how minority group members are discriminated against?

_____

*Used by permission of J.B. Lippincott Company.

Part Two

A. It is important to select the important details in what you read. Here are statements of details in the selection you have read. If the statement is true, put a "T" on the line before the statement. If the statement is false, put an "F" on the line before the statement.

—— 1. Minorities are discriminated against because of their appearance, religion, language, and social and economic status.

—— 2. The Swedish people are discriminated against.

—— 3. Minorities do not have good opportunities for medical care.

—— 4. The first Chinese exclusion law was passed in 1940.

—— 5. Dr. Ralph J. Bunche is a black man.

B. It is important to get the main ideas from your reading. Check the statements below that are the main ideas in this passage.

——1. Various racial, ethnic, and religious groups are often called minority groups.

——2. Problems of minorities are not limited to countries ruled by dictators.

——3. Mexican-Americans have been listed as undesirables.

——4. James Reston is a correspondent for the *New York Times.*

——5. Some colleges restrict educational opportunities for minorities through their use of a quota system of admission.

C. It is important for you to draw generalizations and conclusions from what you have read. Which of the following generalizations or conclusions can be correctly drawn from this passage?

——1. Minority group members have not always had equal opportunities in the United States.

——2. The 1954 Supreme Court decision ruled racial segregation unconstitutional in public schools.

——3. A democratic society should not practice discrimination against minority group members.

——4. Many groups have been discriminated against at various times in our history.

___5. Americans of British stock are at the top of the social-distance scale in the United States.

D. It is important to know the exact meaning of words you read. Below are sentences with a word underlined in each. Under each sentence are four choices. Put a check in front of the best meaning for the underlined word as it is used in this passage.

___1. "The right of minorities to decent housing was limited by the practice of restrictive *covenants.*"
  A. contracts
  B. letters
  C. ideas
  D. designs

___2. "Such clauses have been declared *unconstitutional* by the Supreme Court."
  A. disgusting
  B. illegal
  C. unfair
  D. unenforcable

___3. "Negroes, the Irish, Italians, Jews, Poles, Scandinavians, and Asiatics were given the most common character *stereotypes.*"
  A. names
  B. images
  C. lacking individuality
  D. occupations

___4. "The ADL report urges that minority groups be interpreted not as out-groups but as valuable, *dynamic,* and contributing elements in our culture."
  A. powerful
  B. useful
  C. happy
  D. working

___5. "Problems of minorities are not limited to countries ruled by *dictators.*"
  A. presidents
  B. kings
  C. governors
  D. autocratic rulers

Tell how you went about reading this material. What did you do to get the main ideas? What did you do to get the details? What did you do when you didn't know a word?

INFORMAL READING TEST ON A SPECIFIC CHAPTER*

Name _____Grade _____ Teacher _____Date_____

A. *Matching Vocabulary Exercise*

____1. labrum
____2. abdomen
____3. Malpighian tubules
____4. spiracles
____5. nymph
____6. metamorphosis
____7. pupa
____8. instars
____9. mandible
____10. maxilla

a. stages from molt to molt
b. the changes through which an insect passes in his life
c. a single tongue-like structure
d. numerous small tubes at the union of the stomach
e. the outside of each mandible
f. rough-edged jaws
g. this is composed of eleven segments
h. the inactive stage of an insect
i. the young stage of a grasshopper
j. the upper lip of an insect
k. this is attached to the prothorax
l. these are small openings on each of the first eight segments of the abdomen

B. Put a check in front of the following statements which are true.

____1. The first appendages on an insect are a pair of antennae.

____2. There are three kinds of muscle tissue in a grasshopper.

____3. The digestive tract of an insect is large with a crop preceding the stomach.

C. Put a check in front of the following generalizations which are true.

____1. All insects have all of the characteristics of arthropods.

____2. All insects have a complete metamorphosis.

____3. If we understand the metamorphosis of an insect, we can control it more effectively.

D. Why do you think it is important to study about insects and their behavior?

E. How can you apply what you have learned in this chapter to Rachel Carson's book *Silent Spring*?

---

*Source: David F. Miller and B.B. Vance, *Science of Biology* (Philadelphia: J.B. Lippincott Company, 1965), pp. 289-294. Used by permission of J.B. Lippincott Company.

The Cloze
Procedure

Do you know how the cloze procedure can be used in elementary and secondary schools? Since this is a relatively new technique, a number of elementary and secondary school teachers are not aware of the potential of this technique for determining reading levels and ability in context clue usage. In fact, the cloze procedure is one of the most versatile and useful of the diagnostic devices.

This section is designed to help you understand the construction and uses of the cloze procedure at the elementary- and secondary-school levels. The section first briefly describes the characteristics of a cloze exercise. Next, it tells you in detail how to formulate, administer, and evaluate a cloze exercise. The section closes with a sample cloze exercise at the primary-grade reading level, at the intermediate-grade reading level, and at the secondary-school level. This section then should enable you to use this very important diagnostic device with success.

Description of Using the Cloze Technique in the Diagnosis of Reading Difficulties

The cloze procedure was developed by Wilson Taylor in 1953 and is based upon the psychological theory of closure.[1] This theory states that a person wants to complete any pattern which is not complete. In the case of the cloze procedure, the pattern is a passage from which every nth word was omitted. Since 1953 the cloze procedure has been studied by a number of researchers such as John Bormuth of the University of Chicago, Marion Jenkinson of the University of Alberta, and Earl Rankin of the University of Kentucky. Such researchers have discovered that the cloze procedure can be used as an alternative way of determining reading levels.[2] You can see that the cloze procedure then can be used in place of the graded oral reading paragraphs of an Individual Reading Inventory as was described in Section 7 of this kit.

You can construct a cloze exercise from a basal reader, tradebook, or

---

[1] Wilson L. Taylor, "Cloze Procedure: A New Tool for Measuring Readability," *Journalism Quarterly,* 30 (Fall, 1953), pp. 415-433.

[2] Eugene R. Jongsma, "The Cloze Procedure: A Survey of the Research," *ED 050 893* (Bloomington, Indiana: Indiana University, August, 1971).

content textbook at either the elementary or secondary-school level. In constructing a cloze exercise, you omit every nth word from a passage of about 250 words in length while keeping the first and last sentence intact. You then have the students complete each of the blanks. If you are using a cloze exercise to determine reading levels, you count only those completed blanks as correct which are identical to the original passage. On the other hand, if you are using a cloze exercise to improve ability in context clue usage, you count synonyms of each deleted word as correct. Detailed directions for using the cloze procedure for both of these purposes are found in the next part of this section.

You will find a cloze exercise easy to construct. Your students usually will very much enjoy completing a cloze exercise. The cloze procedure also is quite easy to evaluate. Therefore, you may very well wish to use it in place of the graded oral reading paragraphs of an Individual Reading Inventory with average or above average readers to determine their various reading levels or to improve their ability in context clue usage. You also may wish to use the cloze procedure as a supplement to the graded oral reading paragraphs of an Individual Reading Inventory with disabled readers as a check on their independent, instructional, and frustration reading levels.

Directions for Formulating, Administering, and Evaluating the Cloze Procedure in the Diagnosis of Reading Difficulties

Following are detailed directions on how to formulate, give, and evaluate a cloze exercise at the primary-grade, intermediate-grade, or secondary-school level. In using a cloze exercise, you first should choose the material which is to be evaluated. This should be a passage which a student needs to be able to read with understanding. As was stated earlier, this passage can be from a basal reader story, a tradebook, or a content area textbook. You then select a passage of at least 250 words from the chosen material. You should next type a passage on a stencil or ditto and duplicate it so that each student who is to complete the exercise has a copy of his own. You type the first and last sentence of the passage intact. In the remainder of the passage, every nth word should be omitted and a blank about 15 spaces long should be inserted in place of each omitted word. As an example, the nth word can be the fifth, eighth, or tenth word. Usually you do not omit proper nouns. You will find sample cloze exercises at various reading levels in the last part of this section. You can duplicate and use any of these cloze exercises in their present form or use them as models of cloze exercises which you can construct from the appropriate basal readers, tradebooks, or content textbooks.

A cloze exercise usually is given to a group of students. However, it also can be given to an individual student. Each student should be encouraged to complete the exact deleted word in each case. You can give him all the time which he needs to complete the cloze exercise. In determining a student's independent, instructional, and frustration reading level, he must fill in the exact word if he is to receive credit for it.

In evaluating a cloze exercise, you first count the number of blanks in the passage. Next you count the number of blanks which were completed with the exact omitted word. As you will see later, if a student has completed about 45% to 50% of the blanks with the exact omitted word, the material probably is on his instructional reading level. If a student has completed 60% or more of the blanks correctly, the material probably is on his independent reading level. However, if you want to determine exactly how the cloze procedure corresponds to the various reading levels established by the graded oral reading paragraphs on an Individual Reading Inventory, the following procedure can be followed:

1. Divide the number of words exactly replaced by the total number of blanks.
2. Multiply this figure by 1.67 to determine the average comprehension.

These two examples may help to clarify the process:

Example 1
22 exact replacements
50 blank spaces

$22 \div 50 = 44\%$ correct replacement
$44 \times 1.67 = 73.48\%$ comprehension

Example 2
29 exact replacements
50 blank spaces

$29 \div 50 = 58\%$ correct replacement
$58 \times 1.67 = 96.86\%$ comprehension

You then can relate these comprehension scores to the reading levels which were described in Section 7. As you may remember, the most widely used criteria for determining reading levels were developed by Emmett Betts. According to Betts, the independent reading level requires 95% or better comprehension, while the instructional reading level requires 75% or better comprehension. The frustration reading level is the point at which a student is less than 50% accurate in comprehension ability.[3] However, you also can use the criteria of Spache or Smith or formulate your own criteria as was explained in Section 7.

Let us now consider how to use the results of a cloze exercise in improving instruction in reading. Let us suppose that you wish to determine the ability of your sixth-grade students to read a particular social studies textbook. Before they attempt to use the textbook, you can formulate a cloze exercise from a passage of about 250 words in this textbook. The students then can complete this cloze exercise during class. You will find that most of them enjoy doing so. You then can determine each student's ability to comprehend the textbook by using the formula in this section. If you have determined that the book was on the independent reading level for several students, you may want to select a more difficult social studies textbook for such students. On the other hand, if you have determined that the textbook is too difficult for some of your students, you will need to choose an easier textbook for them. Such

---

[3]Emmett A. Betts, *Foundation of Reading Instruction* (New York:American Book Company, 1957).

students also later could be given an Individual Reading Inventory in social studies as was explained in Section 9 to verify your findings from the cloze exercise. Therefore, it is obvious that you should use the results of a cloze exercise to help individualize reading instruction.

A slightly different procedure is followed when cloze is used for improving ability in context clue usage. In a recent journal article, Robert Bortnick and Genevieve Lopardo have presented a useful sequence which you can follow with your students. They recommend the following steps:

1. Each student should read the entire cloze passage silently.
2. Each student then should reread the cloze passage, writing in the words which seem to fit in the blanks.
3. Later in a class discussion, each student is encouraged to offer his reasons for choosing the words he used to fill in the blanks. His teacher then can praise him for any completed words which make sense in the sentence.
4. Each student then can compare his responses with the original passage.
5. In a class discussion, the students can compare both passages, and the discussion can focus on whether the meaning was changed by certain responses.[4]

Thus, the cloze procedure can give your students the opportunity to apply context clue usage meaningfully. You should praise your students who have completed a cloze passage with acceptable words even if these words were synonyms of the actual deleted words. As an example, if a student substituted the word *large* for *huge,* he has made good use of context clues. However, if he has substituted the word *fat* for *fast,* he has not used context clues effectively. If you find that a student is weak in context clue usage, you should provide corrective or remedial reading instruction in this word recognition skill. The two books *Identifying and Correcting Reading Difficulties in Children*[5] and *Diagnosis and Correction of Reading Difficulties in Secondary School Students*[6] will provide you with many concrete suggestions about how to improve context clue usage at both the elementary- and secondary-school levels. The professional books on reading which are listed in the Appendix also will provide you with additional help in this area.

You will find the cloze procedure to be an extremely helpful screening device which can be used with elementary and secondary school students to determine the various reading levels. It also can be used to improve ability in context clue usage. It is so useful because it is easy to formulate, administer, and evaluate. Most students also find the cloze procedure a very interesting diagnostic device to complete.

---

[4]Robert Bortnick and Genevieve S. Lopardo, "An Instructional Application of the Cloze Procedure," *Journal of Reading,* 16 (January, 1973), 296-300.

[5]Wilma H. Miller, *Identifying and Correcting Reading Difficulties in Children* (New York: The Center for Applied Research in Education, 1971), pp. 126-129.

[6]Wilma H. Miller, *Diagnosis and Correction of Reading Difficulties in Secondary School Students.* (New York: The Center for Applied Research in Education, 1973), pp. 148-149, 149-152.

Sample Cloze Exercises at the Primary-Grade, Intermediate-Grade, and Secondary-School Levels

The last part of this section includes one sample cloze exercise at each of the following levels: the primary-grade level, the intermediate-grade level, and the secondary-school level. You can duplicate and use any one of these cloze exercises in its present form. However, you also can use each of the cloze exercises as a model in constructing your own cloze exercise from the appropriate basal reader, tradebook, or content textbook.

CLOZE PROCEDURE (THIRD-GRADE LEVEL)

"Johnny Maple-Leaf"*

Have you ever wondered how a leaf begins and ends its life? Let's pretend we are looking up into _____ branches of a maple tree. There, on _____ bottom branch, is Johnny Maple-Leaf, just beginning _____ appear.

One sleepy spring afternoon Johnny Maple-Leaf _____ out of his tight brown bud. He _____ a deep breath and slowly stretched out.

_____ were branches all around him with hundreds _____ little leaves popping out just like himself.

_____ on the ground there were little Quaker _____ and Jack-in-the-pulpits bowing to one another in _____ wind.

Rabbits played leapfrog over an old _____ stump. A field mouse scampered about looking _____ things to eat. Two squirrels gathered sticks _____ build a nest in the top of the tree. _____ orioles and robins flew about in the _____.

And a big old owl sat in _____ hole in the tree and said whrooooooo.

_____ the sun went down it grew cooler. _____ Maple-Leaf curled up just a little.

He _____ this was the best place in the _____ world for him to be, and he _____ to sleep.

Each day Johnny Maple-Leaf grew _____, and turned dark green. The sun was _____. But down below, it was cool and _____ and mossy. And there was always something _____ beneath the tree. Many flowers bloomed. There _____ pink lady slippers and wild ginger, violets _____ May blossoms. A dog came crashing through _____ a fox while a chipmunk scolded from _____ safe branch.

Birds came and built their nests in the branches all about Johnny Maple-Leaf.

*From Paul A. Witty and Alma Moore Freeland, "Johnny Maple-Leaf," *Meadow Green* (Boston: D.C. Heath and Company, 1968), pp. 65-67. © 1968 by D.C. Heath and Company. Reprinted by permission of the publisher.

"Johnny Maple-Leaf"
Answer Key

the
the
to
broke
took
There
of
Down
ladies
the
tree
for
to
Bright
sunlight
a
As
Johnny
decided
whole
went
larger
hot
damp
happening
were
and
chasing
a

CLOZE PROCEDURE (FIFTH-GRADE LEVEL)

"Helen Keller"*

Even after my illness I remembered one of the words I had learned in these early months. It was the word "_____," and I continued to _____ some sound for that _____ after all other speech _____ lost. I ceased making _____ sound "wah-wah" only when _____ learned to spell the _____.

My hands felt every _____ and observed every motion, _____ in this way I _____ to know many things. _____ I felt the need _____ some communication with others _____ began to make crude _____. A shake of the _____ meant "No" and a _____, "Yes," a pull meant "_____" and a push, "Go." _____ it bread that I _____? Then I would imitate _____ acts of cutting the _____ and buttering them. If _____ wanted my mother to _____ ice cream for dinner _____ made the sign for _____ the freezer and shivered, _____ cold. My mother, moreover, _____ in making me understand _____ good deal. I always _____ when she wished me _____ bring her something, and _____ would run upstairs or _____ else she indicated. Indeed _____ owe to her loving _____ all that was bright _____ good in my long _____.

I understood a good _____ of what was going _____ about me. At five _____ learned to fold and _____ away the clean clothes _____ they were brought in _____ the laundry, and I _____ my own from the _____. I knew by the _____ my mother and aunt _____ when they were going _____, and I invariably begged _____ go with them.

I was always sent for when there was company, and when the guests took their leave, I waved my hand to them, I think with vague remembrance of the meaning of the gesture.

_____

*From Eldonna L. Evertts and Byron H. VanRoekel, "Helen Keller," *Crossroads.* (New York: Harper and Row, 1966), pp. 195-196.

"Helen Keller"
Answer Key

water
make
word
was
the
I
word
object
and
learned
Soon
of
and
signs
head
nod
come
Was
wanted
the
slices
I
make
I
working
indicating
succeeded
a
knew
to
I
anywhere
I
wisdom
and
night
deal
on
I
put
when

from
distinguished
rest
way
dressed
out
to

CLOZE PROCEDURE (EIGHTH-GRADE LEVEL)*

"Rip Van Winkle"†

Whoever has made a voyage of the Hudson must remember the Catskill mountains. They are a dismembered _____ of the great Appalachian _____, and are seen away _____ the west of the _____, swelling up to a _____ height, and lording it _____ the surrounding country. Every _____ of season, every change _____ weather, indeed, every hour _____ the day, produces some _____ in the magical hues _____ shapes of these mountains, _____ they are regarded by _____ the good wives, far _____ near, as perfect barometers. _____ the weather is fair _____ settled, they are clothed _____ blue and purple, and _____ their bold outlines on _____ clear evening sky; but _____, when the rest of _____ landscape is cloudless, they _____ gather a hood of _____ vapors about their summits, _____, in the last rays _____ the setting sun, will _____ and light up like _____ crown of glory.

At _____ foot of these fairy _____, the voyager may have _____ the light smoke curling _____ from a village, whose _____ roofs gleam among the _____, just where the blue _____ of the upland melt _____ into the fresh green _____ the nearer landscape. It _____ a little village, of _____ antiquity, having been founded _____ some of the Dutch _____ in the early times _____ the province, just about _____ beginning of the government _____ the good Peter Stuyvesant (_____ he rest in peace!), _____ there were some of _____ houses of the original _____ standing within a few _____, built of small yellow _____ brought from Holland, having _____ windows and gable fronts, _____ with weathercocks.

In that same village, and in one of these very houses (which, to tell the precise truth, was sadly timeworn and weather-beaten), there lived, many years since, while the country was yet a province of Great Britain, a simple, good-natured fellow, of the name of Rip Van Winkle.

*See Glenn McCracken and Charles C. Walcutt, "Rip Van Winkle," *Basic Reading–8* (Philadelphia: J.B. Lippincott Company, 1965), pp. 220-221.
†Reprinted by permission of Hart Publishing Company, New York.

"Rip Van Winkle"
Answer Key

branch
family
to
river
noble
over
change
of
of
change
and
and
all
and
When
and
in
print
the
sometimes
the
will
gray
which
of
glow
a
the
mountains
described
up
shingle
trees
tints
away
of
is
great
by
colonists
of

the
of
may
and
the
settlers
years
bricks
latticed
surmounted

The Interest
Inventory

Why do you think that you should give a student an interest inventory? It is especially important to ascertain the interest of reluctant readers and disabled readers so that these can be used in motivating them to read for pleasure. It is certainly true that interest often evokes effort.

This section is designed to help you identify the general interests and reading interests of average and above average readers, reluctant readers, and disabled readers so that these interests can be used in reading improvement. The section first describes the relation between interests and reading improvement and presents the general characteristics of an interest inventory. Next it gives you directions for constructing, administering, and evaluating an interest inventory. The section closes with sample interest inventories at the primary-grade level, the intermediate-grade level, and the secondary-school level. These interest inventories can be duplicated in their present form or modified as you wish. It is hoped that this section will enable you to use the interests of your students for reading improvement.

Description of Using an Interest Inventory in the Diagnosis of Reading Difficulties

It may be useful at the outset to discuss briefly the role interest can play in reading improvement. To illustrate this point, consider an area in which you have little interest. As an example, if you have never been to a hockey game or seen one on television, it is doubtful that you would have much interest in reading a hockey rule book. On the other hand, if you are vitally interested in antiques, you obviously would read a book describing the antiques of a certain period with a great deal of interest.

You can apply this analogy to elementary and secondary school students. For example, a ninth-grade boy may have little motivation to read for pleasure since he is a reluctant reader. However, he may be very interested in learning how to customize a car since he admires the customized cars of some older boys whom he knows. If you are aware of his special interest in customizing cars, it probably would be quite easy to motivate him to read books and magazines on this topic. An interest inventory can help you discover this interest quite easily.

You might like to know that students' interests have been somewhat researched in the past. For example, the most well-known of this type of study was conducted by George Norvell over a period of 25 years and was reported in 1950. Norvell discovered that sex differences were the most significant factor in determining a student's reading interests. This finding indicated that boys and girls have reading interests which differ significantly. According to Norvell, the age and intelligence did not make great differences in their reading interests. It is also interesting to note that Norvell found that girls sometimes liked books for boys, but boys disliked books for girls at all times. Norvell discovered that boys like adventure stories, animal stories, mystery stories, sport stories, and humorous stories. On the other hand, he found that girls liked romance stories, family life stories, school stories, patriotic stories, humerous stories, and some adventure stories.[1]

Mary L. Smith and Isabel V. Eno reported quite similar findings in 1961.[2] Arthur V. Olson and Carl L. Rosen recently discovered that black students in secondary school wanted to read stories about teen-age problems, social relations, various occupations, and romance. However, in this study, sex differences were more important than were race differences.[3]

There are a number of ways in which you can determine the interests of your students so that these can be capitalized on when you are recommending books for them to read for pleasure. Obviously, the best way to determine a student's general interests and reading interests is to talk with him informally. You may have opportunities to do this before or after school, during recess, during independent activities time, or during sports activities which you coach. However, you may find that the time to do this is rather limited, especially if you are working with a large group of students. Therefore, you may wish to use an interest inventory to supplement such informal teacher-student discussions.

An interest inventory is a diagnostic device which enables you to determine the interests of a student. It can be given on an individual or a group basis. Since a child in the early primary grades usually cannot complete an interest inventory himself, you usually must give him this device individually. This also may be the case for a disabled reader in the intermediate grades and for a severely disabled reader in the secondary school. However, most students in the intermediate grades and the secondary school can complete an interest inventory in a group situation. It is obvious that you then should use the results of an interest inventory in recommending books for a student to read independently for pleasure.

---

[1] George Norvell, *The Reading Interests of Young People* (Boston: D.C. Heath, 1950).

[2] Mary L. Smith and Isabel V. Eno, "What Do They Really Want to Read?" *The English Journal,* 50 (May, 1961), pp. 343-345.

[3] Arthur V. Olson and Carl L. Rosen, "A Comparison of Reading Interests of Two Populations of Ninth-Grade Students," in Arthur V. Olson and Wilbur S. Ames (Editors), *Teaching Reading Skills in Secondary Schools: Readings* (Scranton, Penn.: International Textbook Company, 1970), pp. 365-369.

Directions for Constructing, Administering, and Evaluating an Interest Inventory for the Diagnosis of Reading Difficulties

You normally do not have to formulate your own interest inventory. In most cases, you can duplicate and use any of the interest inventories which are found in the next part of this section. Since an interest inventory is not specific to a particular classroom or school system in the way that an Individual Reading Inventory may be, you undoubtedly will find one of the interest inventories which are included in this kit to be suitable for your use.

However, if you do wish to construct your own interest inventory, you need to determine a student's interests in several areas. You should ascertain such areas of interest as the following: hobbies, favorite after-school activities, favorite television programs, favorite types of books, use of the public library, and types of books and magazines which are available in the home.

When you administer an interest inventory, you can tell the student or group of students that you want to find out more about their favorite activities and books so that you can help them select reading materials which they will find interesting and appealing. As was stated earlier, you may have to give an interest inventory orally and transcribe the answers on a copy of the inventory if the student is unable to complete it independently. Otherwise, a student can complete an interest inventory independently. You can give him all the time which he needs to complete the interest inventory.

Obviously, you evaluate each interest inventory informally. You can examine each interest inventory carefully, trying to determine a student's specific interests, so that these interests can be capitalized on in choosing various kinds of reading materials. You should try to determine a student's interests in such areas as the following: his hobbies, his other unique interests, his favorite kind of reading material, his favorite television programs, and his favorite after-school activities.

You then may want to complete an index card for each student on which you briefly list all of his special interests. You can file all of these index cards in a small file box for easy future reference. Such a card could look like the following:

See Interest Inventory Card on next page →

Name _____ Grade _____ Teacher _____ Date _____

RESULTS OF THE INTEREST INVENTORY

Independent reading level_____

Favorite kind of books_____

_____

Hobbies and special interests_____

_____

_____

Favorite after-school activities _____

_____

_____

Favorite television programs_____

_____

Other important interests_____

_____

_____

Let us suppose that a third-grade student has completed an interest inventory. From this interest inventory, you have determined that this boy is very interested in collecting insects. The next step is to help him locate a number of books on insects which he can read with success. Although most of these books should be on his independent reading level, it is acceptable to let him choose a more difficult book occasionally since he has a real motivation to read books about insects. You can encourage him to use the results of his reading by preparing something concrete such as a display of insects for a bulletin board. The student also can give an oral report on insects to a small group or to the rest of the class as another way of following up his reading.

As another example, if you find that a sixth-grade girl is enthralled with the television program "The Waltons," you may be able to interest her in the era of the Depression. Although much of this reading should be done from tradebooks which are on her independent reading level, she may want to obtain factual information about this historical period by reading parts of several social studies textbooks which are on her instructional or independent reading level. Later, this student can give an informal oral presentation during which she relates some facts and anecdotes about the era of the Depression.

From these two examples you can gain an idea of how to use the results of an interest inventory in individualizing reading instruction. Of course, sometimes you may need to help reluctant readers develop new interests. However, even in this case an interest inventory can help you make a good start in using a student's interests for reading improvement.

Sample Interest Inventories at the Primary-Grade, Intermediate-Grade, and Secondary-School Levels

This part of the section includes one sample interest inventory at each of the following levels: the primary-grade level, the intermediate-grade level, and the secondary-school level. You can duplicate and use any of these interest inventories in the light of the needs of your own students. You also can modify any of these interest inventories if you wish to do so. If a student cannot complete an interest inventory independently, you may wish to give it orally and transcribe the student's answers.

Name _____ Grade _____ Teacher _____ Date ___

INTEREST INVENTORY (Primary-grade level)

Oral or written form

1. What is the name of your favorite book which someone has read aloud to you?

2. What is the name of your favorite book or story which you have read for yourself?

3. What kind of stories and books do you like to hear read aloud to you?

4. Have you ever been to the library with your mother or father or your brother or sister?

5. What are the names of some of the books which you have at home?

6. What are the names of your two favorite television programs?

7. Do you read the funny paper at home?

8. What is the name of your favorite comic book?

9. What do you really like to do after school?

10. What do you really like to do on a Saturday?

11. What kind of games do you like to play?

12. Do you collect anything? If you do, what kind of things do you like to collect?

13. Do you enjoy reading for fun?

14. Where does your family like to go for a summer vacation?

15. What do you like to do best with your mother? (father)

Name _____ Grade _____ Teacher _____ Date ___

INTEREST INVENTORY (Intermediate-grade level)

Written form

1. How much do you like to read?

   very much_____

   quite a lot_____

   not very much_____

   not at all_____

2. What are the titles of several books which you really enjoyed?

3. What are the titles of some of the books in your home?

4. Do you have a library card?

5. How many books have you checked out from the library during the last month?

6. What part of the newspaper do you like to read the best?
   comic section_____

   sport section_____

   news section_____

   society section_____

   editorials_____

   letters to the editor_____

7. What magazines do you read regularly?

8. What type of comic books do you enjoy reading?

9. What are the names of your three favorite television programs?

10. What sports do you like to watch on television?

11. What do you usually do after school?

12. Of all the things which you do after school, what one thing do you like to do the best?

13. What do you often do on Saturday?

14. Of all of the things you do on Saturday, what one thing do you like to do the best?

15. What kind of hobbies do you have?

16. Do you have any collections? If you do, what do you collect?

17. What do you want to be when you grow up?

18. Where do you usually go on vacation with your family?

19. Have you ever gone to camp in the summer? If you have, what did you enjoy the most about camp?

20. What other states have you visited?

Name _____ Grade _____ Teacher _____ Date ___

INTEREST INVENTORY (Secondary-school level)

Written form

1. What is the title of the book which you have read recently that you liked the best?

2. What is the title of the best book which you ever have read?

3. How much do you like to read for pleasure during your spare time?

   very much_____

   somewhat_____

   not very much_____

   not at all_____

4. If there are books in your home, what are the titles of several of them?

5. Do you read the newspaper every day?

6. What part of the newspaper appeals the most to you?

   news stories_____

   editorial page_____

   society page_____

   teen-age page_____

   sports section_____

   comic section_____

   agriculture section_____

7. What type of comic books do you enjoy reading?

8. How many books have you borrowed from the library during the last month?

9. What magazines do you read regularly?

10. What kind of things do you usually do after school?

11. What type of things do you usually do on a weekend?

12. What subjects do you like best in school?

13. What hobbies or collections do you have?

14. What clubs or groups do you belong to?

15. What sports do you enjoy watching?

16. What are the titles of the last few movies which you have seen?

17. What living person do you admire the most?

18. What person from history do you admire the most?

19. What do you like to do during summer vacation?

20. Of the following kinds of books, which ones would you like to read for pleasure?

football_____

baseball_____

basketball_____

adventure stories_____

animal stories_____

historical novels_____

problems of teen-agers_____

biographies and autobiographies of famous people_____

mystery stories_____

career stories_____

science-fiction_____

nature stories_____

scientific experiments_____

The Incomplete
Sentences Test

Have you ever used a projective technique? A projective technique is a device which can help you determine how a student feels about himself and his reading problems without his being aware of exactly what you are doing. There are a number of different projective techniques which can be used as diagnostic devices. While some of these can be administered and evaluated only by a psycholgist, psychiatrist, or guidance counselor, there are a number of projective techniques which you can construct, administer, and evaluate yourself. One of these projective techniques is the Incomplete Sentences Test which is described in this section. A number of other useful projective techniques are described in Section 14.

This section is designed to help you use the Incomplete Sentences Test in the discovery of reading difficulties. The section first describes the characteristics of all projective techniques and of the Incomplete Sentences Test. The section next describes how to formulate, give, and evaluate an Incomplete Sentences Test. Several sample Incomplete Sentences Tests which you can duplicate and use are found in this section. You also can modify any of these tests if you wish to do so. Hopefully, this section will enable you to use an Incomplete Sentences Test effectively to determine causes for reading difficulties so that they subsequently can be corrected in an individually prescribed corrective or remedial reading program.

Description of Using an Incomplete Sentences Test to Determine the Causes of Reading Difficulties

It may be valuable at the beginning of this section to discuss the characteristics of projective techniques briefly. As was stated earlier, a projective device can help you determine how a student views himself and his reading difficulties without his knowing exactly what you are trying to find out. This can enable you to obtain a more accurate view of a student and the probable causes for his reading difficulties than you otherwise might be able to do. Since most disabled readers are very concerned about their lack of reading progress, they often are just not able to discuss their view of themselves and their reading difficulties truthfully with their teacher. It is not always that they wish to hide their true feelings from the teacher. More often, they probably are not able to view themselves and their reading problems realistically.

Most of the sophisticated projective techniques must be given and evaluated by either a school psychologist, a psychiatrist, or a guidance counselor. This type of projective technique often would be given only to a student who is thought to be quite severely emotionally maladjusted. This type of projective technique is designed to determine the probable causes for a student's emotional maladjustment and therefore for his subsequent reading difficulties. Some of these sophisticated projective techniques are the Rorschach Inkblot Test, the Children's Apperception Test, the Thematic Apperception Test, the Bender Visual-Motor Gestalt Test, and the Goodenough-Harris Draw-a-Man Test.

However, there are a number of projective techniques which you as a reading teacher can formulate, administer, and evaluate quite easily yourself. You would give most of these projective techniques to the mildly or moderately disabled readers with whom you are working. However, you also can give any of them to average and above average readers if you want to learn more about how such students view themselves and their reading ability. Most students enjoy completing such projective devices very much.

Since the Incomplete Sentences Test is one of the more useful projective devices, it is placed in a section by itself in this kit. Other projective devices are found in Section 14. In an Incomplete Sentences Test, a student is to respond orally or in writing to a number of incomplete sentences. If the beginning part of each sentence is structured properly, you often can gain much insight into how a student views himself and his reading difficulties. The Incomplete Sentences Test usually has to be given orally on an individual basis to a student in the early primary grades or to an older severely disabled reader. You then must record this student's answers yourself on a duplicated copy of this projective device. Otherwise, an Incomplete Sentences Test can be given in a group situation to a number of students who each completes his copy of this projective device independently. You will find that an Incomplete Sentences Test is quite easy to construct and administer. Although it may be slightly more difficult to evaluate, you soon will become adept at gaining insight into a student and his reading ability, as a result of using this device.

Directions for Constructing, Administering, and Evaluating an Incomplete Sentences Test in Determining the Causes of Reading Difficulties

Normally you do not have to construct an Incomplete Sentences Test to use with your students. In most instances one of the Incomplete Sentences Tests which are included in the next part of this section will be suitable for your use. Since an Incomplete Sentences Test usually does not have to be specific to a particular classroom or school situation, you often can use one of the samples included in this kit at the appropriate grade level. You can duplicate and use any of the Incomplete Sentences Tests which are included in the next part of this section.

However, you can construct your own Incomplete Sentences Test if you wish to do so. The tests found in this kit should be valuable models for you to use in this area. In formulating an Incomplete Sentences Test, you can assess such areas about a student and his view of reading as the following: his attitude toward reading, his attitude toward school, his attitude toward his home and family, and his emotional adjustment.

An Incomplete Sentences Test is quite easy to administer. As was stated earlier, you usually must give this projective device individually to a student who cannot read and write sufficiently well enough to complete this device without your help. You then must transcribe his answers on a copy of the Incomplete Sentences Test. In all other instances, you can give this projective device in a group situation with each student completing his copy of the test independently. You simply can tell the students that you would like them to complete some sentences which have been designed to help you understand their attitudes a little better. You also can tell them that you will use the results of this test to help you teach them reading skills more effectively. You then can give them all the time which they need to complete this projective device. If they cannot complete several of the sentences, you can tell them that these sentences can be left blank. However, the students should be encouraged to complete as many of the sentences as possible. Most students will enjoy completing this projective device.

Obviously, the evaluation of an Incomplete Sentences Test requires considerable thought although it is done informally. First you should look at all of the responses of a student to gain a general overall view of his attitudes. You then can categorize the responses into such areas as these: attitude toward reading, attitude toward school, attitude toward home and family, and emotional adjustment. Perhaps the evaluation of an Incomplete Sentences Test will be made more clear by examination of several sample sentences under each of these general areas.

Attitude Toward Reading

1. I think that the hardest thing about reading is *everything.*
2. I think that reading books is *very hard.*
3. I think that reading comic books is *kind of fun.*
4. I would like to be able to *read better.*

From these four responses, you can infer that this intermediate-grade student probably is a disabled reader who may be reading material which is mainly on his frustration reading level. He probably rarely experiences success with reading activities.

Attitude Toward School

1. School is *a very boring place.*
2. Studying in school is *a real drag.*
3. Doing homework is *stupid.*
4. Going to college is *not for me.*

From these four responses, you can determine that this junior high school student dislikes school and school activities. Perhaps this was due to an unsatisfactory teacher-student relationship or to a lack of reading ability. Either of these assumptions can be confirmed or rejected by examining other parts of the Incomplete Sentences Test.

Attitude Toward Home and Family

1. I think that my father is *kind of mean.*
2. I think that my mother is *always picking on me.*
3. I think that my sister is *my mother's pet.*
4. I think that my home is *too noisy.*

From these four responses of a third-grade boy, you can infer that he has a rather unfavorable attitude toward his home and family. His home environment may cause him to be emotionally maladjusted, which in turn may cause his reading problem. However, this assumption should be verified or rejected by tactful conversation with the student, his parents, or by the use of other projective devices as are explained in Section 14.

Emotional Adjustment

1. It makes me happy when *my father is nice to me.*
2. It makes me sad when *I get yelled at at home.*
3. I sometimes am afraid of *lots of different things.*
4. I sometimes worry about *almost everything.*

You should look at the emotional adjustment of this intermediate-grade student very carefully. Although it appears from these four responses that she is emotionally maladjusted, you should consider this assumption very carefully. It should be verified or rejected by careful teacher observation perhaps supplemented by visits to the school psychologist or the elementary guidance counselor. It often is easy to infer too much from this part of an Incomplete Sentences Test. Therefore, assumptions about a student's emotional adjustment should be acted upon with great care.

How do you act upon the results of an Incomplete Sentences Test? It is obvious that this varies according to your findings. If you have discovered that a student has a negative attitude toward reading activities, you must help him change this attitude toward a more positive one. You can help him do this by giving him reading tasks which he can complete with success and which give him personal satisfaction. You also can help him overcome his reading disability by providing him with the appropriate corrective or remedial reading instruction. It also is important that you develop a positive relationship with him.

If you have determined from the test that a student dislikes school, you will need to work on building more positive attitudes toward school and school activities. The teacher-student relationship is the most important factor in this area. You must show the student that you genuinely accept him with his strengths and weaknesses and will help him to overcome his academic weaknesses. You must give him school tasks with which he usually can succeed. You also should try to make school relevant and meaningful for him.

You may not be able to change a student's attitudes toward his home and family to any great degree. An interview with the mother and father can give you insights into a student's home environment which may be useful in helping you develop your own positive relationship with the student at school. However, you must conduct such an interview with great tact and caution if you are not to alienate the parents. A number of the professional books on reading listed in Appendix III of this kit present specific suggestions on how to conduct parent-teacher interviews.[1]

You may be able to influence a student's emotional adjustment to a degree in school. Of course, you can do this by developing a positive teacher-student relationship with him. This relationship should be based on mutual respect, admiration, and acceptance. You also can help to improve a student's emotional adjustment by providing him with interesting reading tasks which he can complete with success. It is obviously true that nothing succeeds like observed success. However, you also must know when to refer an emotionally maladjusted student for professional counseling from a school psychologist, a psychiatrist, or a guidance counselor. It probably is better to over-refer students for professional counseling than not to refer one student who really may need such counseling. You probably should enlist the help of one of these professionals whenever you believe a student is truly emotionally maladjusted.

Sample Incomplete Sentences Tests at the Primary-Grade, Intermediate-Grade, and Secondary-School Levels

This part of Section 13 contains one sample Incomplete Sentences Test at each of the following levels: the primary-grade level, the intermediate-grade level, and the secondary-school level. You can duplicate and use any of these incomplete sentences tests according to the needs of your students. You also can modify any of these tests if you want to do so. If a student cannot complete an Incomplete Sentences Test independently, you may want to give it orally and transcribe the student's responses.

---

[1] See, for example, W.H. Miller, *Identifying and Correcting Reading Difficulties in Children,* pp. 202-203, and W.H. Miller, *Diagnosis and Correction of Reading Difficulties in Secondary School Students,* pp. 250-251.

Name _____ Grade _____ Teacher _____ Date _____

INCOMPLETE SENTENCES TEST (Primary-grade level)

Oral or written form

1. I think that learning to read is_____

2. I think that my mother is_____

3. I think that my teacher is_____

4. I wish that I could_____

5. I think that my home is_____

6. The thing that scares me the most is_____

7. Sounding out words is_____

8. I think that school is_____

9. I like to read stories about_____

10. The thing that makes me the happiest is_____

11. My teacher thinks that I_____

12. I am really proud of myself when_____

13. I think that my father is_____

14. The thing that I like best about school is_____

15. The thing that makes me the maddest is_____

16. My father thinks that reading is_____

17. I think that my brother is_____

18. One thing that I don't like about school is_____

19. If I had all the money in the world, I would_____

20. I think that my sister is_____

21. My mother thinks that reading is_____

22. The thing that makes me the saddest is_____

23. I think that watching television is_____

24. The thing that I like best about learning to read is_____

25. The thing that is the hardest about learning to read is_____

Name _____ Grade _____ Teacher _____ Date _____

INCOMPLETE SENTENCES TEST (Intermediate-grade level)

Written form

1. It is hard for me to_____

2. It makes me sad when_____

3. I never want to_____

4. I wish that my father_____

5. The thing that I like best about reading is_____

6. I think that my family is_____

7. When I grow up, I would like to_____

8. It is easy for me to_____

9. I think that my teacher is_____

10. I always have had trouble with_____

11. I wish that my mother_____

12. I think that reading books is_____

13. I think that my brother is_____

14. The thing that I like best about being at home is_____

15. I think that school is_____

16. I sometimes worry about_____

17. Sometimes the words in reading_____

18. I think that my favorite person is_____

19. I sometimes am afraid of_____

20. My favorite day of the week is_____

21. I wish that I_____

22. It makes me angry when_____

23. I would like to be able to_____

24. I get ashamed when_____

25. I think that the hardest thing about reading is_____

26. I really like it when my father_____

27. The thing that I like best about school is_____

28. I think that reading comic books is_____

29. I think that my sister is_____

30. I think that most teachers are_____

31. I like to read books about_____

32. It makes me happy when_____

33. One thing that I don't like about school is_____

34. I really like it when my mother_____

35. I feel proud of myself when_____

Name _____ Grade _____ Teacher _____ Date _____

INCOMPLETE SENTENCES TEST (Secondary-school level)

Written form

1. My favorite subject in school is_____

2. I think that reading comic books is_____

3. I sometimes am afraid of_____

4. I never want to_____

5. Most of my teachers are_____

6. Going to college is_____

7. I hope that I can_____

8. I think that my life is_____

9. I like it when my father_____

10. My favorite person is_____

11. I get kind of depressed when_____

12. Doing homework is_____

13. I think that my brother is_____

14. Most of all I would like to get_____

15. My home usually is_____

16. I get angry when_____

17. I am unhappy when_____

18. Grandparents are_____

19. My mother thinks that reading is_____

20. I hope that my future is_____

21. I wonder if_____

22. The most important person I know is_____

23. My parents feel that my report card is_____

24. I like to read books about_____

25. I think that school is_____

26. I think reading the newspaper is_____

27. I hope that I will never have to_____

28. The hardest thing about reading is_____

29. I wish I_____

30. I sometimes get nervous when_____

31. I always have thought that reading was_____

32. The easiest thing about reading is_____

33. I am happy when_____

34. I hope that special help in reading_____

35. I don't like it when my mother_____

36. Studying in school is_____

37. I think that my sister is_____

38. I like it when my mother_____

39. The thing I like best about reading is_____

40. I would really like to_____

41. One thing I don't like about reading is_____

42. When I get out of school, I hope to_____

43. I sometimes worry about_____

44. I think that reading science books is_____

45. If I could be anything in the world, I would want to be_____

46. I don't like it when my father_____

47. In an English class, I usually like to read most about_____

48. I think that reading social studies books is_____

49. My father thinks that reading is_____

50. I think that reading math word problems is_____

Other Projective Techniques
Which Can Be Used by the Teacher

Do you know some useful projective techniques in addition to the Incomplete Sentences Test which was described in Section 13 of ths kit? There are a number of other simple-to-use projective techniques which can help you gain insights into how a student views himself and his reading difficulties. Some of these simple projective techniques are open-ended stories, reading autobiographies, sociometric techniques, story assignments, and the Wish Test.

This section is designed to help you learn how to formulate and use these simple projective techniques to help you understand better how a student views himself and his reading problems. The section first briefly reviews the characteristics of all projective techniques and describes the characteristics of several simple projective techniques in detail. Next, it presents directions for constructing, administering, and evaluating these simple projective techniques. The section next presents one open-ended story which can be used at the intermediate-grade level. You are given directions for using a sociogram at the elementary-school level. The section also presents some story topics which can be used at the intermediate-grade level. A sample Wish Test which you can give at the primary-grade level also is included in this section. You can use any of the projective techniques which are included in this section in their present form or modify them in the light of the needs of your own students.

Description of Using Simple Projective Techniques in Determining the Causes of Reading Difficulties

As was described in detail in Section 13, a projective technique can help you discover how a student views himself and his reading difficulties without his knowing exactly what you are trying to determine. This then can help you to obtain a more accurate view of a student and the probable causes of his reading difficulties than you otherwise could do. It is difficult for most disabled readers to verbalize their feelings about themselves and their reading

257

difficulties in a realistic way. As was explained in Section 13, The Incomplete Sentences Test is one of the most useful of these simple projective techniques.

However, there also are a number of other projective techniques which you can use at the elementary or secondary school levels to determine how a student views himself and his reading problems. These projective techniques are quite easy to construct and give. However, they must be evaluated carefully to obtain accurate insights into a student and his reading difficulties. You can, however, learn to evaluate these simple projective techniques after a little thought and practice. The characteristics of the following simple projective techniques are discussed in this section: open-ended stories, reading autobiographies, sociometric techniques, story assignments, and the Wish Test.

The open-ended story is similar in some ways to the Incomplete Sentences Test. It often can be used to determine a student's attitudes toward school and learning activities. The open-ended story can be given on an individual or a group basis. You can either read the story aloud and ask the student to respond to it orally, or have the student read the story silently and respond to it in writing. It presents a situation to the student which requires judgment on his part as to an appropriate course of action. It often evaluates his attitudes in such areas as honesty, truthfulness, or responsibility. The sample open-ended story included later in this section should provide you with a good model of this type of projective technique.

A reading autobiography can be called a retrospective report as well as a projective technique. It is designed to help you understand a student's reading history so that you can determine some probable causes for his present reading difficulties. It is designed to discover his success in reading and his attitude toward reading from the time when he first learned to read through the present. A reading autobiography can be either structured or open-ended. If it is structured, a student responds to a group of questions in a *yes* or *no* manner. If it is open-ended, you direct the student to write about his reading history. Examples of a structured reading autobiography and an open-ended reading biography are found in the last part of this section. You can duplicate and use either of these reading autobiographies in their present form or modify them according to the needs of your own students.

You can use a sociometric technique to gain information about the social structure of a class which you are teaching. You can learn from such a technique which students are well accepted and desired by their classmates. You also can learn which students in a class are not accepted by the rest of their classmates. You often may be surprised by the results of a sociometric device. Since it is impossible to separate a student's learning of reading skills from the climate in which it takes place, you should use the social structure of a class to provide activities that will maximize each student's feelings of acceptance and belonging. One sociometric technique is presented in this section. Directions for constructing a sociogram from the results of this sociometric technique are given in the next part of this section.

You can use story or theme assignments to discover how a student views himself, his attitudes toward school, his attitudes toward reading, his attitudes toward his home and family, and his general emotional adjustment. This projective device can be used in the upper primary grades, in the intermediate grades, and in the secondary school. Since you only give the students a story or theme topic, it is a very simple projective device to use. The student writes creatively on this topic. You then can read the story or theme later trying to infer as much as possible from it. However, you should not force a student to let you read a story if he does not want you to do so. A student should only allow you to read a story if he chooses to do so. The last part of this section contains a number of theme and story topics.

The Wish Test is an adaptation of the Incomplete Sentences Test which was discussed in Section 13. This test contains a number of incomplete sentences which all begin with the words "I wish." These incomplete sentences are designed to discover a child's desires and wishes. They often can indicate quite a bit about his attitudes and emotional adjustment. This test probably is the most useful at the primary-grade or the early intermediate-grade levels. A sample Wish Test which you can duplicate and use is found in the last part of this section.

Directions for Constructing, Administering, and Evaluating Simple Projective Devices in Determining the Causes of Reading Difficulties

In most instances, you can duplicate and use the various projective devices which are found in the last part of this section. Since they are not specific to a particular school situation, you usually will not have to formulate your own version of any of these projective devices.

However, if you wish to determine a student's attitudes about a particular situation, you can structure your own open-ended story. The student then can read this story silently and write his own conclusions to the story. However, you will have to read the story aloud to a child in the early primary grades or to a disabled reader. Such a student then can give his reactions to the open-ended story orally. An open-ended story can assess a student's attitudes in such areas as the following: honesty, home and family, or various school situations.

You should not infer too much from a student's responses to an open-ended story. Instead, you must consider his response in connection with his other behavior to form a total behavior pattern.

Undoubtedly you will want to use the structured reading autobiography which is included in the last part of this section. However, if you wish to construct your own structured reading autobiography, you should assess such areas of a student's reading history as the following: home prereading experiences, success in primary-grade reading, success in intermediate-grade reading, reading interests of the family, previous reading difficulties, and present reading interests. You can use the open-ended reading autobiography which is included in this section as a good model for constructing this type of reading autobiography.

In administering a structured reading autobiography, you simply ask the students to read each question silently and check *yes* or *no*. If you wish to give this type of reading autobiography to a severely disabled reader, you may have to read each question aloud to the student. Most disabled readers can read the directions for an open-ended reading autobiography themselves.

In evaluating a structured reading autobiography, you can determine when a student began to have difficulty with reading instruction. You also may be able to determine what parts of reading, such as phonetic analysis or comprehension, cause a student the greatest amount of difficulty. Of course, you also can determine the student's present attitudes toward reading.

The evaluation of an open-ended reading autobiography may be somewhat more difficult. You can examine the student's sentence structure and spelling to notice his achievement in these language arts. You also can notice the grade level at which he began having difficulty with reading, his earlier attitudes toward reading, and his present attitudes toward reading.

Chooser \ Chosen	Mary	Bob	Sally	Frank	Martha	Jack
Mary			1		2	3
Bob			1		3	2
Sally	2	3			1	
Frank		2			3	1
Martha	2		1			3
Jack		1	2		3	
Totals	2	3	4	0	5	4

Figure 14-1

To formulate a sociogram, you simply ask a student to write down the names of two or three students that he chooses to sit near, to be with on the playground, or to walk to school with. You then tabulate each student's choice on a sheet of paper so that you can see the total number of times that each child has been chosen. You then list the names of all the children in your class both vertically and horizontally, and the totals at the bottom of the columns containing each child's name become the data for constructing the sociogram. You then plot the sociogram. Figure 14-1 lists the names of six students whose data are used in making the sociogram for this kit. Figure 14-2 then shows you the sociogram which was formulated for these six students.

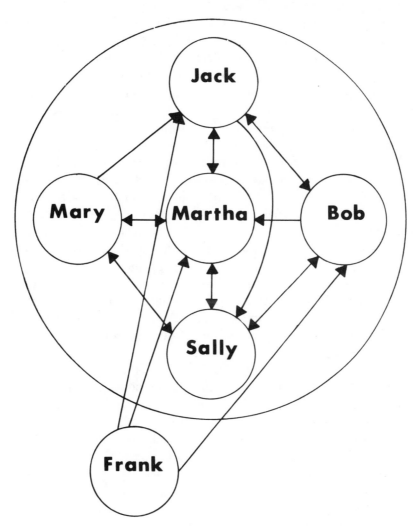

Figure 14-2

When you give a student a story or theme assignment, you often should give him the choice of several story assignments instead of giving him just one topic on which he can write. The student then can be encouraged to write as much as he wishes, expressing his true feelings on the topic which he has chosen. As was stated earlier, you should not require him to let you read the story which he has written unless he is willing to have you do so. If he is, you can examine his story, trying to discover insights into such areas of the student as the following: emotional adjustment, desires, attitudes toward his home and family, and attitudes toward school and reading activities.

However, you should be careful not to infer too much about a student from only one of his stories. You can learn more by noticing patterns which you find in several stories and by observing his behavior over a period of time. Although many insights can be gained about a student by examining his creative writing, teachers sometimes have been guilty of inferring too much from one story.

In most cases, you can use the Wish Test which is included in the last part of this section in its present form. However, you can also modify it if you wish to do so. As was stated earlier, the Wish Test can be given orally to a student in the early primary grades or to an older disabled reader who cannot read or write sufficiently well enough to be able to complete it independently. In all other cases, you can complete it independently. You need only give a direction such as the following for the completion of the Wish Test: "This sheet of paper contains some sentences which you are to finish. In them you can write about some things that you wish for and would like to have." A student should not be required to complete any sentences which he feels that he cannot. However, you should encourage him to finish as many sentences as possible.

The evaluation of a Wish Test requires some thought as does the evaluation of most of the projective techniques which are discussed in this section. From careful examination of a student's response to this projective device, you can gain insights into his desires and wishes. These desires are in such areas as the following: wish for a more satisfactory parent-child relationship or home environment, desire for material things, desire to achieve better in school-related activities such as reading, or the desire to achieve a specific goal such as in sports. You should be careful not to infer too much from this projective device. Assumptions made from this projective technique should be verified or rejected by the use of other means such as careful teacher observation or another projective technique.

The use you make of the findings from a Wish Test vary, of course, according to the areas in which they are found. You can help a student attain his wish to achieve better in a school-related activity such as reading by providing him with the corrective or remedial reading instruction he needs to attain this desire. The positive relationship which you build with him also can help him to attain this desire. It often may be more difficult for you to help him attain his wishes in other areas.

Sample Simple Projective Devices at the Primary-Grade, Intermediate-Grade, and Secondary-School Levels

This part of the section contains sample projective techniques at the primary-grade, intermediate-grade, and secondary-school levels. Included are one open-ended story, a structured autobiography, an open-ended reading autobiography, a sociogram, some story topics, and a Wish Test. You can use any of the projective techniques in their present form or modify them if you wish to do so.

Name _____ Grade _____ Teacher _____ Date ___

OPEN-ENDED STORY (Intermediate-grade level)

What Should Jimmy Do?

Since Jimmy has four brothers and sisters, he often is not able to get all of the toys that he would like to have. His father and mother just cannot afford to buy a lot of toys for Jimmy and his brothers and sisters.

For a long time, Jimmy has very much wanted to buy a special model of a drag racer. He has seen a model like the one he wants at Brown's Department Store. It costs about $4.50. Although he asked his father and mother to buy it for him, they just can't figure out a way to earn that $4.50 either.

One day on the way home from school, Jimmy saw something green caught in a bush. When he stopped to look at it more closely, he saw that it was money. It was a five dollar bill! How Jimmy wanted to keep that money so that he could buy his model drag racer. After all, he had heard the saying "Finders, Keepers." Should he keep the money and buy his model drag racer? Should he take the five dollar bill to the police station in his neighborhood and tell the police that he found it? What should Jimmy do?

Name _____ Grade _____ Teacher _____ Date ___

STRUCTURED READING AUTOBIOGRAPHY
(Secondary-school level)

	yes	no
1. When you were small, did anyone in your family read aloud to you?	—	—
2. When you were small, were there books in your home for you to look at and read?	—	—
3. When you were in first grade, did you enjoy learning to read?	—	—
4. Did you have trouble with reading when you were in the primary grades?	—	—
5. When you were in the primary grades, did you enjoy reading for pleasure?	—	—
6. Were you a good reader when you were in the intermediate grades?	—	—
7. When you were in the intermediate grades, did you enjoy reading comic books?	—	—
8. Did you enjoy going to elementary school?	—	—
9. Have you ever had trouble sounding out words?	—	—
10. Have you ever had trouble understanding what you read?	—	—
11. Do you now enjoy reading for fun?	—	—
12. Do you now have a library card?	—	—
13. Have you been to the library within the last month?	—	—
14. Does your mother enjoy reading for pleasure?	—	—
15. Does your father enjoy reading for pleasure?	—	—
16. Do you enjoy reading in bed?	—	—
17. Would you rather watch television than read?	—	—
18. Do you think that you are a good reader now?	—	—
19. Do you read aloud to younger children?	—	—
20. Are there books and magazines in your home for you to read?	—	—
21. Do you enjoy reading paperback books?	—	—
22. Do you read the newspaper regularly?	—	—
23. Do you have difficulty with reading today?	—	—
24. Do you use the dictionary to look up the pronunciation and meaning of words which you do not know?	—	—
25. Do you enjoy reading social studies textbooks?	—	—

Name _____ Grade _____ Teacher _____ Date _____

OPEN-ENDED READING AUTOBIOGRAPHY
(Intermediate-grade level)

You can write at this time about how you learned to read and how you feel about reading now. Do you remember how you were taught to read in first grade? How did you do in reading in first grade? At that time what part of reading was the hardest for you? How did you do in reading in second and third grade? Have you ever had trouble sounding out words? Have you ever had trouble understanding what you read? Today what do you enjoy the most about reading? Today what is the hardest about reading for you? Why do you think you have trouble with this part of reading?

Name _____ Grade _____ Teacher _____ Date _____

SOCIOMETRIC DATA (Elementary-school level)

What person would you like to sit near?

    1st choice_____

    2nd choice_____

    3rd choice_____

What persons are the best players to be with on the playground?

    1st choice_____

    2nd choice_____

    3rd choice_____

What person would you like to walk to school with?

    1st choice_____

    2nd choice_____

    3rd choice_____

STORY AND THEME TOPICS (Intermediate-grade level)

What I Want to Be When I Grow Up

The Person That I Like the Best

Some Things That Make Me Happy

One Thing That I Was Punished For

What I Would Do if I Had $10,000

Some Things I Like Best About My Home

My Most Important Problem

One Thing That Is Very Hard for Me to Do

Some Things That Make Me Unhappy

What I Wish for Most

The Person That I Like the Least

What I Think That Other People Feel About Me

Some Things I Like Best About My Family

One Thing That I Would Really Like to Do

Some Things That People Don't Understand About Me

Some Things That Make Me Angry

Some Things That I Would Like to Change About My Home and Family

One Thing That I Like Best About Other People

Name _____ Grade _____ Teacher_____ Date _____

WISH TEST (Primary-grade level)

Oral or written form

1. I wish I were_____

2. I wish that I could have_____

3. I wish that my mother_____

4. I wish that my teacher_____

5. I wish that I would not have to_____

6. I wish that my father_____

7. I wish that my friends_____

8. I wish that my brothers and sisters_____

9. I wish that I were not_____

10. I wish that school_____

11. I wish that my home_____

12. I wish more than anything else that_____

13. I wish that reading_____

14. I wish that I were able to_____

15. I wish that my family_____

APPENDICES

APPENDIX I

Survey Reading Tests

Elementary school level

American School Achievement Tests. Available from the Bobbs-Merrill Company. There are four batteries which can be used in grades one through nine. The various batteries test word recognition, word meaning, sentence meaning, and paragraph meaning.

California Reading Tests. Available from the California Test Bureau. There are three batteries in this test for use in grades one through six. Each battery tests vocabulary and comprehension.

Gates-MacGinitie Reading Tests. Available from Teachers College Press, Columbia University. These tests can be used in grades one through six. They evaluate vocabulary and comprehension and are available in three different forms.

Iowa Silent Reading Tests: New Edition. Available from Harcourt Brace Jovanovich. This test contains an elementary battery for grades four through eight. It tests silent reading in the areas of sentence meaning, paragraph meaning, vocabulary, rate, and comprehension.

Lee-Clark Reading Tests: 1963 Revision. Available from the California Test Bureau. These test batteries can be used in kindergarten through grade two. They evaluate reading readiness and reading achievement.

Metropolitan Reading Tests. Available from Harcourt Brace Jovanovich. These tests can be used from the end of first grade through eighth grade. They measure word knowledge, word discrimination, and paragraph comprehension. They are available in Forms A and B.

Sequential Tests of Educational Progress: Reading. Available from the Educational Testing Service. This test contains two levels for the elementary-school level. It evaluates the ability to recall ideas, make inferences, sense the author's mood, analyze presentation, and criticize.

Stanford Reading Tests. Available from Harcourt Brace Jovanovich. These test batteries evaluate word-study skills, word reading, word meaning, and paragraph meaning. They are available in three forms.

Secondary school level

American School Achievement Test. Available from the Bobbs-Merrill Company. This test measures vocabulary and paragraph meaning. The Advanced Reading Test is designed for grades seven through nine.

California Phonics Survey. Available from the California Test Bureau. This test has eight subtests about different aspects of the knowledge of phonetic analysis. It is designed for use in grades seven through college.

California Reading Tests. Available from the California Test Bureau. The junior high level of these tests is for grades seven through nine, and the advanced level is for grades nine through college. Each level evaluates vocabulary and comprehension ability.

Cooperative English Tests: Reading Comprehension. Available from the Educational Testing Service. One battery of this test can be used in grades nine through 12 and one battery can be used in grades 12 through 14. Each battery measures vocabulary, comprehension, and rate of comprehension.

Diagnostic Reading Tests. Available from the Committee on Diagnostic Reading Tests. This test can be used in grades one through college. It evaluates vocabulary, comprehension, and rate of reading.

Gates-MacGinitie Reading Tests. Available from Teachers College Press, Columbia University. Survey E is designed for grades seven through nine and Survey F is designed for grades ten through 12. Each form measures vocabulary, comprehension, and speed and accuracy.

Metropolitan Reading Test. Available from Harcourt Brace Jovanovich. The advanced level is for grades seven and eight and measures vocabulary and paragraph comprehension.

Nelson-Denny Reading Test, Revised Edition. Available from Houghton Mifflin Company. This test is designed for grades nine through 12 and is available in two forms. It measures vocabulary, comprehension, and rate of reading.

Sequential Tests of Educational Progress: Reading. Available from the Educational Testing Service. Level 3 is for grades seven through nine, Level 2 is for grades ten to 12, and Level 1 is for college. Each level evaluates the ability to recall ideas, make inferences, criticize, and sense mood and purpose.

Stanford Reading Test. Available from Harcourt Brace Jovanovich The Advanced test is for grades 7-9.9 and is available in three forms. It tests word meaning and paragraph meaning.

Diagnostic Reading Tests

Botel Reading Inventory. Available from Follett Educational Corporation. This is a group-administered diagnostic reading test which is designed for grades one through 12. It has tests of phonetic analysis, word recognition, and word opposites.

Developmental Reading Tests. Available from Lyons & Carnahan. This group-administered test is available in an Intermediate-level form which is designed for grades four through six. It measures vocabulary, literal comprehension, reading for interpretation, reading for information, reading for relationships, and reading for appreciation.

Diagnostic Reading Tests. Available from the Committee on Diagnostic Reading Tests. The diagnostic tests in this series range from grades one through college. The various forms measure such aspects of reading as oral word attack (individually administered), silent word attack, vocabulary, silent comprehension, auditory comprehension, rate of reading, rate in social studies, and rate in science.

Doren Diagnostic Reading Test. Available from the American Guidance Service. This group diagnostic test is designed for reading level two through eight. It measures beginning sounds, sight words, discriminate guessing, speech consonants, vowels, ending sounds, and blending.

Durrell Analysis of Reading Difficulty: New Edition. Available from Harcourt Brace Jovanovich. This is an individual diagnostic reading test which contains subtests of oral reading, silent reading, listening comprehension, word analysis, phonetic analysis, writing, and spelling.

Gates-McKillop Reading Diagnostic Test. Available from Teachers College Press, Columbia University. This is an individual diagnostic reading test for severely disabled readers. It contains paragraphs for oral reading and subtests of word perception, phrase perception, syllabication, letter names and sounds, visual blending, auditory blending, and spelling. It is available in two forms.

McCullough Word Analysis Test. Available from Ginn and Company. This is a group test designed for grades four through eight. It evaluates initial consonant clusters, comparing vowel sounds, matching symbols with vowel sounds, identifying phonetic respellings, finding a root word, dividing between syllables, and using a pronunciation key.

273

Roswell-Chall Diagnostic Reading Test. Available from the Essay Press. This is a group test for analyzing phonetic analysis knowledge.

Spache Diagnostic Reading Scales. Available from the California Test Bureau. This is an individual test for grades one through eight. It contains 22 graded reading passages, three word lists, and six supplementary phonics tests.

Stanford Diagnostic Reading Test. Available from Harcourt Brace Jovanovich. Level I is designed for use in grades 2.5-4.5 and Level II is designed for use in grades 4.5-8.5. Each is a group test with subtests of comprehension, vocabulary, syllabication, auditory skills, phonetic analysis, and rate of reading.

APPENDIX III

List of Professional Books on Reading*

Barbe, Walter B. *Educator's Guide to Personalized Reading Instruction.* Englewood Cliffs, New Jersey: Prentice-Hall, 1961.

Bond, Guy L. and Miles A. Tinker. *Reading Difficulties: Their Diagnosis and Correction.* New York: Appleton-Century-Crofts, 1967.

Carter, Homer L.J. and Dorothy J. McGinnis. *Diagnosis and Treatment of the Disabled Reader.* New York: The Macmillan Company, 1970.

Cushenbery, Donald C. *Reading Improvement in the Elementary School.* West Nyack, New York: Parker Publishing Company, 1969.

Dechant, Emerald V. *Diagnosis and Remediation of Reading Disability.* West Nyack, New York: Parker Publishing Company, 1968.

Dechant, Emerald V. *Improving the Teaching of Reading, Second Edition.* Englewood Cliffs, New Jersey: Prentice-Hall, 1970.

Farr, Roger. *Measurement and Evaluation of Reading.* New York: Harcourt Brace Jovanovich, 1970.

Fry, Edward. *Reading Instruction for Classroom and Clinic.* New York: McGraw-Hill Book Company, 1972.

Gillingham, Anna and Bessie E. Stillman. *Remedial Training for Children with Specific Disability in Reading, Spelling, and Penmanship.* Cambridge: Educators Publishing Service, 1960.

Harris, Albert J. *How to Increase Reading Ability.* New York: David McKay Company, 1970.

---

*These professional books on reading are only representative of the area. Many other books could equally well have been included.

275

Heilman, Arthur W. *Principles and Practices of Teaching Reading.* Columbus, Ohio: Charles E. Merrill Books, 1967.

Kennedy, Eddie C. *Classroom Approaches to Remedial Reading.* Itasca, Illinois: F.E. Peacock Publishers, 1971.

LaPray, Margaret. *Teaching Children to Become Independent Readers.* New York: The Center for Applied Research in Education, 1972.

Miller, Wilma H. *Diagnosis and Correction of Reading Difficulties in Secondary School Students.* New York: The Center for Applied Research in Education, 1973.

Miller, Wilma H. *Elementary Reading Today: Selected Articles.* New York: Holt, Rinehart and Winston, 1972.

Miller, Wilma H. *Identifying and Correcting Reading Difficulties in Children.* New York: The Center for Applied Research in Education, 1971.

Miller, Wilma H. *Teaching Reading in the Secondary School.* Springfield, Illinois: Charles C Thomas Publisher, 1974.

Miller, Wilma H. *The First R: Elementary Reading Today.* New York: Holt, Rinehart and Winston, 1972.

Roswell, Florence and Gladys Natchez. *Reading Disability: Diagnosis and Treatment.* New York: Basic Books, 1964.

Spache, George D. *Good Reading for Poor Readers.* Champaign, Illinois: Garrard Press, 1972.

Spache, George D. and Evelyn B. Spache. *Reading in the Elementary School.* Boston: Allyn and Bacon, 1973.

Strang, Ruth. *Diagnostic Teaching of Reading.* New York: McGraw-Hill Book Company, 1969.

Strang, Ruth. *Understanding and Helping the Retarded Reader.* Tucson: University of Arizona Press, 1965.

Wilson, Robert M. *Diagnostic and Remedial Reading for Classroom and Clinic.* Columbus, Ohio: Charles E. Merrill Books, 1972.

Woolf, Maurice D. and Jeanne A. Woolf. *Remedial Reading: Teaching and Treatment.* New York: McGraw-Hill Book Company, 1957.

Zintz, Miles V. *Corrective Reading.* Dubuque, Iowa: William C. Brown Company Publishers, 1972.

APPENDIX IV

List of Book Publishers

American Book-Van Nostrand Company, 450 West 33rd Street, New York 10001

Barnell Loft, Ltd., 111 South Centre Avenue, Rockville Center, New York 11570

Basic Books, Inc., Publishers, 10 East 53rd Street, New York 10022

Benefic Press, 10300 West Roosevelt Road, Westchester, Illinois 60153

The Bobbs-Merrill Co., Inc., 4300 West 62nd Street, Indianapolis, Indiana 46268

Burgess Publishing Company, 7108 Olms Lane, Minneapolis, Minnesota 55435

The Center for Applied Research in Education, Inc., 521 Fifth Avenue, New York 10017

Continental Press, Inc., Elizabethtown, Pennsylvania 17022

Coward, McCann & Geoghegan, Inc., 200 Madison Avenue, New York 10016

Dell Publishing Company, 1 Dag Hammarskjold Plaza, 245 East 47 Street, New York 10017

Dodd, Mead & Company, 79 Madison Avenue, New York 10016

Doubleday & Company, Inc., 277 Park Avenue, New York 10017

Educators Publishing Service, Inc., 75 Moulton Street, Cambridge, Massachusetts 02138

Garrard Publishing Company, 1607 North Market Street, Champaign, Illinois 61820

Ginn and Company, 191 Spring Street, Lexington, Massachusetts 02173

Grosset & Dunlap, Inc., 51 Madison Avenue, New York 10010

Harcourt Brace Jovanovich, Inc., 757 Third Avenue, New York 10017

Harper & Row, Publishers, 10 East 53rd Street, New York 10022

Holt, Rinehart and Winston, Inc., 383 Madison Avenue, New York 10017

Houghton Mifflin Company, 2 Park Street, Boston, Massachusetts 02107

International Reading Association, 6 Tyre Avenue, Newark, Delaware 19711

J.B. Lippincott Company, East Washington Square, Philadelphia, Pennsylvania 19105

The John Day Company, Inc., 257 Park Avenue South, New York 10010

McGraw-Hill Book Company, 1221 Avenue of the Americas, New York 10020

David McKay Co., Inc., 750 Third Avenue, New York 10017

Macmillan, Inc., 866 Third Avenue, New York 10022
Meredith Corporation, 750 Third Avenue, New York 10017
Charles E. Merrill Publishing Company, 1300 Alum Creek Drive, Columbus, Ohio 43216
Parker Publishing Company, Inc., West Nyack, New York 10994
Prentice-Hall, Inc., Englewood Cliffs, New Jersey 07632
The Ronald Press Company, 79 Madison Avenue, New York 10016
Scott, Foresman and Company, 1900 East Lake Avenue, Glenview, Illinois 60025
Albert Whitman & Company, 560 West Lake Street, Chicago, Illinois 60606

APPENDIX V

List of Test Publishers

American Guidance Service, Circle Pines, Minnesota 55014

The Bobbs-Merrill Co., Inc., 4300 West 62nd Street, Indianapolis, Indiana 46268

Bureau of Educational Research and Service, University of Iowa, Iowa City, Iowa 52240

California Test Bureau, Del Monte Research Park, Monterey, California 93940

Committee on Diagnostic Tests, Inc., Mountain Home, North Carolina 28758

Consulting Psychologists Press, 577 College Avenue, Palo Alto, California 94306

Educational Test Bureau, 120 Washington Avenue Southeast, Minneapolis, Minnesota 55414

Educational Testing Service, Princeton, New Jersey 08540

Ginn and Company, 191 Spring Street, Lexington, Massachusetts 02173

Guidance Testing Associates, 6516 Shirley Avenue, Austin, Texas 78751

Harcourt Brace Jovanovich, Inc., 757 Third Avenue, New York 10017

Houghton Mifflin Company, 110 Tremont Street, Boston, Massachusetts 02107

Language Research Associates, 950 East 59th Street, Chicago, Illinois 60630

Lyons & Carnahan, 407 East 25th Street, Chicago, Illinois 60616

The Mills Center, 1512 East Broward Boulevard, Fort Lauderdale, Florida 33301

The Psychological Corporation, 304 East 45th Street, New York 10017

Scholastic Service, 480 Meyer Road, Bensenville, Illinois 60611

Science Research Associates, Inc., 259 East Erie Street, Chicago, Illinois 60611

Teachers College Press, Teachers College, Columbia University, 525 W. 120th Street, New York 10027

Western Psychological Services, 12035 Wilshire Boulevard, Los Angeles, California 90025

Winter Haven Lions Research Foundation, Box 112, Winter Haven, Florida 33880